SAGE was founded in 1965 by Sara Miller McCune to support the dissemination of usable knowledge by publishing innovative and high-quality research and teaching content. Today, we publish over 900 journals, including those of more than 400 learned societies, more than 800 new books per year, and a growing range of library products including archives, data, case studies, reports, and video. SAGE remains majority-owned by our founder, and after Sara's lifetime will become owned by a charitable trust that secures our continued independence.

Los Angeles | London | New Delhi | Singapore | Washington DC | Melbourne

DISASTER RELIEF AND THE RSS

DISASTER RELIEF AND THE RSS

Resurrecting 'Religion' through Humanitarianism

MALINI BHATTACHARJEE

Los Angeles | London | New Delhi
Singapore | Washington DC | Melbourne

First published in 2019 by

 SAGE Publications India Pvt Ltd
B1/I-1 Mohan Cooperative Industrial Area
Mathura Road, New Delhi 110 044, India
www.sagepub.in

SAGE Publications Inc
2455 Teller Road
Thousand Oaks, California 91320, USA

SAGE Publications Ltd
1 Oliver's Yard, 55 City Road
London EC1Y 1SP, United Kingdom

SAGE Publications Asia-Pacific Pte Ltd
18 Cross Street #10-10/11/12
China Square Central
Singapore 048423

Published by Vivek Mehra for SAGE Publications India Pvt Ltd. Typeset in 10/12.5 pt Stone Serif by Zaza Eunice, Hosur, Tamil Nadu, India.

Library of Congress Cataloging-in-Publication Data Available

ISBN: 978-93-532-8551-7 (HB)

SAGE Team: Rajesh Dey, Safia Hassan and Rajinder Kaur

For Ma, Baba and Sub
My Home in the World

Thank you for choosing a SAGE product!
If you have any comment, observation or feedback,
I would like to personally hear from you.

Please write to me at **contactceo@sagepub.in**

Vivek Mehra, Managing Director and CEO, SAGE India.

Bulk Sales

SAGE India offers special discounts
for purchase of books in bulk.
We also make available special imprints
and excerpts from our books on demand.

For orders and enquiries, write to us at

Marketing Department
SAGE Publications India Pvt Ltd
B1/I-1, Mohan Cooperative Industrial Area
Mathura Road, Post Bag 7
New Delhi 110044, India

E-mail us at **marketing@sagepub.in**

Subscribe to our mailing list
Write to **marketing@sagepub.in**

This book is also available as an e-book.

Contents

List of Illustrations

Figures

Tables

List of Abbreviations

ABVP	Akhil Bharatiya Vidyarthi Parishad
ARI	Asia Research Institute
BJD	Biju Janata Dal
BJP	Bharatiya Janata Party
BJS	Bharatiya Jana Sangh
BMS	Bharatiya Mazdoor Sangh
BSF	Border Security Force
HFA	Hyogo Framework for Action
HSS	Hindu Swayamsevak Sangh
HUDCO	Housing and Urban Development Corporation
IDRF	India Development and Relief Fund
KVT	Kutch Vikas Trust
NDMA	National Disaster Management Act
NGOs	non-governmental organizations
NMO	National Medicos Organisation
OSDMA	Odisha State Disaster Mitigation Authority
RSB	Rashtriya Sewa Bharti
RSS	Rashtriya Swayamsevak Sangh
UBSS	Utkal Bipanna Sahayata Samiti
UNISDR	United Nations International Strategy for Disaster Reduction
VHP	Vishwa Hindu Parishad
VKA	Vanavasi Kalyan Ashram

Glossary of Terms

Ahir: An ethnic group in Kutch which falls under the category of Other Backward Class (OBC).

Bal swayamsevak: Members of the RSS who are under the age of eighteen.

Bhoomi pujan: A Hindu ritual conducted before initiating new construction projects to seek the blessings of Goddess Earth, to ward off possible obstacles and to increase positive vibrations which would enable a successful outcome.

Dalit: Literally means 'broken or grounded'; refers to persons who are excluded from the fourfold Hindu *varna* system and formerly considered 'untouchables'.

Dana: Gifts or the act of giving.

Hindu rashtra: Hindu nation.

Kar seva: Literally means 'offering service for a religious cause'. The term was popularized by the Sangh Parivar during the Ram Janmabhoomi movement; those who participated in the demolition of the Babri mosque were referred to as kar sevaks by the Parivar.

Langar: Community kitchen, common in Sikh tradition.

Nishkam karma: Desireless action.

Prabhat gram: An ideal village.

Pracharak: A full-time RSS member who propagates the ideology of Hindutva and enables organizational expansion.

Punya: Spiritual merit.

Runa: Debt.

Samaj: Society.

Samskara: Moral values.

Sangathan: Literally means 'organization'; a movement aimed at consolidating Hindus by imparting training in self-defence, which became popular in the early 20th century.

Sangh Parivar: Literally means the 'family of the Sangh'; refers to the RSS and all its affiliate bodies.

Sangh: The RSS is usually referred to as the Sangh by the *swayamsevaks*.

Saraswati Shishu Mandir: RSS school.

Sarsanghchalak: The chief of the RSS.

Seva: Service.

Shakha: The smallest organizational unit of the RSS.

Shuddhi: A movement started by Arya Samaj to reconvert the Hindus who had embraced other religions.

Swayamsevak: Member of the RSS.

Tabligh: Literally means 'propagating the message of Islam'. Used in the book to define Muslim conversion movements in the early 20th-century India.

Yogi: One who has mastered the philosophy of yoga and who is considered to be at an advanced spiritual stage.

Preface

What can one say about the Rashtriya Swayamsevak Sangh (RSS) that has not been already said before? Over the past few decades, scores of books and articles have been dedicated towards understanding India's perhaps most controversial organization. Many of these are in-depth accounts of the organization's genesis, its leadership, its modus operandi and its interface with politics. Therefore, for those looking for additional 'information' about the Sangh, as it is popularly known, this book will be a disappointment. What this book does attempt to do though is to bring a fresh perspective into the workings of the Sangh. I go about doing this by interrogating its humanitarian activities, particularly in the realm of disasters.

It has been a while since I have been intellectually fascinated by the RSS and its larger Parivar. The primary motivation for writing this book however stems from the fact that I now strongly feel that if there is any time to seriously engage with the Sangh, intellectually and even otherwise, it is now. This is partly because I see the growing popularity and influence of the RSS as part of a larger phenomenon worldwide, that is, the resurrection of 'sacred forms' in modern societies. I elaborate more on the idea of the 'sacred form' in my introductory chapter, but I must add here that the term 'sacred' should not be equated with religiosity, although it does draw upon certain aspects of religion. Since the early 1990s, there seems to have been a resurgence of sociocultural/religious movements across the world that allude to this phenomenon of 'sacred forms'. These movements have been enormously influential in not only shaping public policies but also lending a sense of purpose and identity to millions of people who seem to be struggling with the anomie imposed by a modern rational and largely secularized world. A few important examples that come to mind are the Gulen movement which originated in Turkey and gradually acquired a transnational character, the Hezbollah in Lebanon, the Soka Gakkai movement that started in Japan and the Muhammadiyah in Indonesia. The remarkable similarity in all these cases is demonstrated in that they all have massive networks at their disposal, conduct a vast array of humanitarian work and enjoy enormous following both in their countries of origin and among diasporic communities settled outside their countries of origin.

The other and more important reason why I think we need to take the Sangh more seriously than we have before is because of the acute religious/political polarization that we have come to witness in contemporary times. In the history of Indian politics, there has seldom been a moment such as this when the country has been so divided in terms of their world view with regard to the most normatively significant questions. Subjects of secularism, liberalism, citizenship and minority rights are being contested like never before. These contestations, which are amplified on the news hour slots of various television channels, often manifest as polemics without being backed by any substantive intellectual rigour. What is also evident from these debates is a discernible fault line between 'conservative' and 'secular' thought. The imagination that frames this binary discourse seems to emanate from an insipid understanding of reality, an understanding that the realm of the 'rational' and the 'irrational' can be clearly distinguished.

This book is a small step towards rupturing this certitude. It nudges the reader to re-examine 'conservative' thought with a little more generosity than we have accorded it so far. I do this by interrogating the cultural appeal of the category of *seva* (service), one of the foundational pillars of the Sangh. I argue that to derecognize the realm of the 'non-secular' and 'non-rational' as intelligible sources that influence public life is to do great disservice towards building a more nuanced understanding of contemporary India. Given the enormous popularity of the RSS today and the fact that it has millions of followers across the world, it is time we let go of our own inhibitions and 'fundamentalist' ideas that we accuse the 'other' of harbouring, in order to better understand the Sangh. As Andersen and Damle (2018) remind us in their recent book, to understand India requires an understanding of the RSS.

Acknowledgements

The process of writing this book has not been an easy one, especially because it revolves around themes that immediately evoke strong political sentiments among people. In the extremely polarized political climate in India that we have come to inhabit, I have often been accused of being a 'right-wing apologist'. Despite their harsh criticisms on the project, I remain ever indebted to my critics, as they have only made me more resolute and determined to write this book.

I have also been fortunate enough to receive critical appreciation and support from several quarters for attempting to tell a new story about the Sangh by diving into the heart of our political divide.

I would like to begin by expressing my gratitude to SAGE for their enthusiasm and belief in my book. Special thanks are due to Rajesh Dey, Commissioning Editor at SAGE, for his extraordinary support and proficiency in handling my project. Thanks to Safia Hassan for her enormous hard work in proof setting.

Professor Pralay Kanungo, my MPhil and PhD supervisor at Jawaharlal Nehru University, New Delhi, has been my first mentor in this project and has always been a perennial source of support and guidance. Despite several intellectual disagreements we have had, he has had a very important influence on my work and continues to inspire me to do better. I am also grateful to all my professors at JNU who allowed me to find my own voice and helped me become the person that I am today.

Special thanks are due to Prasanta Roy, Professor Emeritus at Presidency University, for introducing me to the love of politics. His classes on Marxism at the NS Building in Presidency University and his warm demeanour have in many ways contributed towards my choice of becoming a teacher.

The book has benefitted enormously from my association with the Asia Research Institute (ARI) at the National University of Singapore (NUS). Participation in two fantastic conferences at ARI, organized by the Religion and Globalization cluster, and a short fellowship in the summer of 2018 have helped me situate my work in a much larger (Asian) framework. I am immensely grateful to R. Michael Feener, Sultan of Oman Fellow at the Oxford Centre for Islamic Studies, and Philip Fountain, Senior Lecturer, Victoria University of Wellington, both prolific scholars and wonderful human beings, for inviting me to ARI and for being extraordinarily generous with their critical appreciation of my work. During my stint at ARI, I was fortunate to have had very fruitful conversations with Ronojoy Sen and Annu Jalais that have provided important insights into the book.

Azim Premji University, Bengaluru, has been my second home for the past six years. Several friends, colleagues and my supervisors here have been instrumental in supporting me to complete this work. I am particularly grateful to Sudhir Krishnaswamy, who has been a fantastic mentor and a very supportive supervisor to me since the past few years. Over the years, I have had numerous conversations with several of my colleagues at the university that have helped me revisit my own positions and refine my arguments further. I would like to thank Vishnupad, Sitharamam Kakarala, Arun Thiruvengadam, Moyukh Chatterjee, A. Narayana, Srikrishna Ayyangar, Siddharth Swaminathan, Purnendu Kavoori, Gayatri Menon, Sreeparna Chattopdhyay, Himanshu Upadhyay, Ruchi Ghosh and Nazrul Haque.

I remain grateful to the senior management at Azim Premji University for their consistent encouragement. Special thanks to our Vice Chancellor, Anurag Behar, for his excellent insights into this book project. I would also like to thank our COO, S. Giridhar, who has always been super supportive of my work and this book.

I am particularly grateful to the entire library team of Azim Premji University, especially my former colleagues Suresh Balutagi and Udrina Dafton, and to Sachin Tirlapur, Aditya Ranjan and Praveena C. S. for their enthusiastic and timely support to locate numerous articles, books and monographs for my study. I am also grateful to the library staff at JNU, the Nehru Memorial Museum & Library, New Delhi, and the Central Library at NUS.

The book has benefitted from the courses I have taught (and teach) on 'Religion and Development' and 'Religion, State and Governance' at Azim Premji University. I am thankful to all the students who took these courses for numerous stimulating conversations and their contribution to a variety of debates in the classroom. I am hopeful that this book will open up several new strands for research that will perhaps be pursued by some of my students in the future.

During the course of conducting research in Gujarat and Odisha, I have been the recipient of numerous hospitalities from members of the RSS, Seva Bharati (Gujarat), Utkal Bipanna Sahayta Samiti (Odisha), Vishwa Hindu Parishad, community members of villages in rural Kutch, and those in Erasama and Tirtol blocks of Jagatsinghpur, numerous journalists, civil society activists and government officials who shared their valuable time and information. I am thankful to Prafulla Ketkar, Editor, *Organiser*, who helped me access the archives of the *Organiser* for conducting research. I am grateful in particular to Shyam Parande, International Coordinator of Sewa International, for providing me with important leads and contacts for conducting this study. I am also grateful to Swadesh Singh, Assistant Professor at Satyawati College, for his support in providing me with several important leads.

My dear friends Bampi, Payel, Piyali, Meera, Sudarshan, Suhas, Aparajita, Rukmini, Manasi, Anindita, Dipanwita and Shreya have steadfastly stood by me through my highs and lows in the past few years. Thank you, I am blessed to have you in my life. Thanks to Arvind Pandey, my friend and brother for his affection and particularly his support in developing the maps for the book.

I would also like to thank my journalist friends Ajaz Ashraf and V. Kumara Swamy for their support and good wishes in helping me complete this book.

The extraordinary support and love of my family has been a steady source of encouragement in helping me complete this book. I am grateful to my sister, Maitreyee Bhattacharjee Chowdhury, my brother-in-law, Debojit Chowdhury, and my niece, Suhasini Chowdhury, for their affection and love. My cousin Partho Bhattacharjee has been a perennial source of inspiration. Thanks to my aunt Professor Mukta Biswas and uncle Professor Ranjan Biswas for their love and blessings always. Thanks are also due to my parents-in-law, Mrs Asha Bose and Mr Ajay Bose, and my brother-in-law, Siddharth Bose, for their good wishes always.

My parents, Mrs Shikha Bhattacharjee and Mr Bisweswar Bhattacharjee, have been instillers of confidence, courage and hope in my life. Their belief in my abilities, unconditional love and affection, and enduring encouragement have kept me going in times when things seemed bleak. I am particularly grateful to them for lovingly taking care of my little daughter since her birth and keeping her engaged for a good part of the year, so that I could complete this book.

I am blessed to have my daughter, Mishka, who brings so much joy to our lives that words can never describe. Despite being of such a tender age, she has displayed remarkable patience and understanding in letting me have my time to complete this project.

Finally, this book would have been impossible without the love, good humour and incredible support of my husband, Subhash. His presence in my life has in many ways redefined notions of love and friendship.

To my dear parents and husband, I dedicate this book.

May 2019   **Malini Bhattacharjee**
Bengaluru

Introduction

The display of barbarity within the various districts of the Punjab and N.W.F. Province has become too patent to be related here to a Hindu again and again....

The brethren of our have been made a prey to such a violent flow of fanatic fury for the simple reason that they profess the *Hindu Dharma* and that they belonged to the *Hindu Samaj*. As such, we, Hindus owe a solemn duty towards them. It is incumbent on us to provide these kin of ours with such assistance and means as would enable them to stand on their own legs and settle down once again in life in our midst....

—*Organiser* (1947, 10)

The above epigraph is an excerpt of an appeal for funds by the Hindu Sahayata Samiti, an affiliate body of the Rashtriya Swayamsevak Sangh (RSS) that was formed soon after the Partition to provide relief to Hindu refugees who had fled from Pakistan. As is evident, far from being a mere fundraising technique for the refugees, the appeal bears clear political overtones in seeking to consolidate the Hindus against the 'other'. In contemporary times, it is unlikely that one would come across an RSS fundraising appeal that invokes Hindu solidarity so explicitly. However, what remains unchanged is that the humanitarian work of the Sangh continues to be a political exercise, a creative strategy to advance the idea of building a strong Hindu Rashtra (Hindu nation). Since its establishment, the RSS has been rendering an array of humanitarian services in disaster and conflict situations, and these activities are broadly referred to as *seva* (loosely translated as service).

In contemporary India, the RSS is perhaps one of the most controversial organizations that has continuously attracted the attention of political analysts, academics and media agencies for its perceived role in being the ideological backbone and mentor of the Bharatiya Janata Party (BJP) that formed the government in the Centre after the 2014 elections with an overwhelming majority and subsequently formed state governments in several states across the country. The BJP is the political affiliate of a larger cultural movement that endorses the idea of Hindu nationalism (Hindutva). The RSS is the foundational organization for the formation of the Sangh Parivar (literally meaning the 'family of the Sangh') which refers to the array of organizations that represents the Hindu nationalist orientation in modern India. The RSS was founded in 1925 in Nagpur by Keshav Baliram Hedgewar who was convinced that the only reason Hindus had succumbed to the enslavement, first by the Muslims and then by the British, was because they lacked national consciousness. The founding of the RSS was an attempt to resurrect a national consciousness that would ultimately lead to the creation of a strong Hindu Rashtra. Since its inception, the RSS has been banned thrice (in 1948 after the assassination of Gandhi by an ex-RSS person, during the National Emergency from 1975–1977 and in 1992 after the demolition of Babri Mosque) and repeatedly attacked by centrist and leftist political forces in India for its alleged role in inciting communal violence, unleashing anti-minority propaganda and for attempting to 'saffronize' history and educational curriculum at large. And yet, the popularity of the RSS has been steadily growing. It is indeed phenomenal that an organization that started with only five persons in 1925 is now one of the world's largest non-governmental organizations (NGOs). In their recent book on the RSS, Andersen and Damle (2018, xi) mention that as of 2016, an estimated 1.5–2 million people regularly participate in almost 57,000 daily *shakhas*,[1] 14,000 weekly *shakhas* and 7,000 monthly *shakhas*, taking place across 36,293 different locations. The organization has about 6,000 full-time workers (*pracharaks*[2]) and around 6 million alumni and affiliate volunteers (Andersen and Damle 2018).

What does it mean for a cultural group like the RSS to provide *seva* in a crisis situation? How does the provision of *seva* help in consolidating solidarities across religious groups and ethnicities? What is the relationship of the 'secular' state vis-à-vis cultural organizations like the RSS? How do the beneficiaries of *seva* 'repay' this debt?

This book focuses on the political implications of the humanitarian work of the RSS in disaster situations. Humanitarianism in the most parts of the world is imbued in politics and therefore this is not a dimension that is novel to the RSS. However, what is interesting to observe is that, in recent times, the realm of humanitarianism has seen a resurgence of religious/cultural groups that are usually considered illiberal and conservative by several analysts.[3] In this particular context, ancient Hindu traditions such as *seva* (service) have acquired a new potency and are filled with new meanings as their practitioners compete with more secular aid providers. Even though religious/

---

[1] *Shakhas* usually form the smallest organizational unit of the RSS. These are primarily assemblies of *swayamsevaks* conducted in an open ground on a daily or weekly basis to impart physical and 'moral' training on Hindutva.

[2] *Pracharaks* are full-time workers of the RSS, who play a very important role in propagating Hindutva at the grassroots level. They are usually unmarried and not paid any remuneration by the Sangh. Their accommodation, food and travel expenses are usually taken care by the RSS unit to which they are assigned.

[3] For a detailed analysis of the intersections between religion and disaster relief, see Bush, Fountain and Feener (2015).

cultural groups were active in providing welfare much before the advent of the modern state in India as elsewhere, what are the reasons for a renewed popularity and resurgence of these organizations in humanitarianism which has undoubtedly become more complex now? How does the resurgence of religious nationalism with little regard for conventional understandings of tolerance shape social participation in the world's largest democracy? The book attempts to answer these questions in the backdrop of the meteoric rise of the ideology of Hindutva in contemporary India.

To argue that the rendering of *seva* serves a political agenda is far from being an interesting claim. As I have mentioned before, the realm of humanitarianism has always been political and all conceivable actors that participate in it have an agenda to further. In this sense, the RSS's invocation of *seva* too is at least partially instrumental and its strategy of enlisting support through *seva* is not novel. The interesting puzzle that presents itself before us therefore is why are seemingly 'rational' people enamoured by the idea of *seva*? Why is the Indian diaspora contributing their wealth towards furthering the *seva* activities of the Sangh? Surely, *seva* in its etymological sense cannot be conflated with more legal-rational forms of giving that are valorized in the contemporary humanitarian world. Then wherein lies its cultural appeal? One of the primary themes that this book interrogates is to find out whether there is something to be salvaged conceptually, intellectually and empirically from the heritage of the term *seva*. In light of the criticisms levelled against the Sangh Parivar, as being advocates of an irrational nativism, I seek to understand if the category of *seva* is merely irrational, paternalistic and morally vacuous or is there something more to it. How does 'progressive' thought, influenced by modern rationalist filters, limit our own understanding of such terms and their cultural currency? I attempt to investigate these questions, to use Mbembe's (Spivak 2007) phrase, by 'restituting intelligibility' to *seva*. I am arguing that the idea and practice of *seva* needs to be analysed in its own idiom and within a framework that does not place 'conservative' thought in a hierarchically inferior position than the 'secular rational'. I am thus not only asking how does *seva* help mobilize support for the RSS, but in itself what does the invocation of *seva* do to common people, who could be either beneficiaries or donors.

There is perhaps no better time to meditate on the above questions than now. Perhaps because the Indian political tradition of valorizing secularism has never been challenged as much as it is being done now. Contrary to the expectations of the advocates of secularization thesis, similar to other modernizing societies, economic development and democratic governance have not been a deterrent to the rise of religion in the public sphere in India. The stupendous victory of the BJP in the 2014 parliamentary elections in India under the leadership of Narendra Modi and successive wins in several state assembly elections are testimony to this. More importantly, current national debates have now begun to centre around the relevance of secularism in India, on the grounds that the word 'secular' was inserted only in 1976 during the period of National Emergency and hence the claim that it was not a value that was built on consensus.[4] Other members of the Sangh Parivar highlight that the idea of *vasudhaiva kutumbakam* (the world is one family) already entails the essence of tolerance and harmonious co-existence and hence 'foreign' categories like 'secularism' are irrelevant. The visibility of religion in the public realm is also manifested through the enormous popularity of religious/spiritual gurus, the rising rate of 'pilgrimage tourism', ostentatious celebration of religious festivals in public spaces and the significant presence of religion on the Internet and television channels. Religion features centrally in

[4] Academic scholars too have debated on the relevance of secularism to India, albeit to make a different argument than that proposed by Hindutva politicians. See Madan (1987) and Ashish Nandy (1998) in this regard.

court cases and judgements where the validity of traditional religious norms is constantly challenged. The recent judgment on the entry of women in the Ayyappan temple at Sabarimala is an important case in point that has violently divided people between those who support the judgment vis-à-vis those who oppose it.

Hindutva's Expansion in the Social Realm

Hindu Nationalism's advancement from the periphery to the centre of Indian politics explains its remarkable adaptability to the changing sociopolitical landscape of the country. Over the years, it has experimented with various forms of mobilization in an effort to capture the Hindu masses. This expansion has been made possible by the endeavours of several affiliates of the RSS, such as the Sewa Bharati (service wing), Vidya Bharati (educational wing), Vanavasi Kalyan Ashram (VKA; service organization dedicated to tribal welfare), Vishwa Hindu Parishad (VHP; World Hindu Council), Bharatiya Mazdoor Sangh (BMS; a trade union) and others, which work in coordination, and sometimes even in isolation, thus making ground for Hindutva. The scale of the Parivar is overwhelming. Today, it runs more than 15,000 educational projects under different denominations, close to 20,000 health projects, over 20,000 projects on empowerment and over 19,000 social projects (Rashtriya Sewa Bharati Annual Bulletin 2016–2017). Besides these, it runs a series of Sanskar Kendras (cultural centres dedicated to the promotion of Hindu culture), literary associations, publishing outfits in several languages and temple renovation committees. Together, these organizations have pervaded every possible sphere of civil society, and their presence is continuous and uninterrupted. With the creation of these affiliates, the Sangh Parivar's social welfare and cultural activities increased manifold from the 1960s onwards.

The aforementioned phenomenon however needs to be situated within the larger context of how the development scenario has been changing in the recent past in India. While the State in India has been regarded as the primary driver of development since Independence, the past few decades have seen a plethora of non-State actors who actively partake in development, either on their own or in partnership with the State. Of these non-State actors, religious and cultural groups form a significant number. This is not surprising, as most religious and cultural faiths have a long history of engagement with ideas of service that shape more contemporary forms of giving. Many Hindu organizations, such as Ramakrishna Mission Seva Pratishthan, Mata Amritanandmayi, Radha Soami Satsang (Juergensmeyer 1991) BAPS Swaminarayan Sanstha and Bharat Sevashram Sangha, that prefer to identify themselves as 'secular', claim to be deeply inspired by ancient Hindu philanthropic traditions and values such as *dana* (offering) and *seva* (Beckerlegge 2006; Warrier 2005; Williams 2001). Further, neo-liberal reforms and globalization, the emergence of a reckonable Indian diaspora and the growth of the Internet in recent times have contributed to bringing these organizations to the forefront in the domain of development and accorded a sense of legitimacy to them that was lacking before. What is also interesting to note here is that there is an increasing rise in the number of Hindutva affiliated groups which actively partake in service or welfare activities. While many of these organizations (such as the RSS) are not religious per se, they claim to be deeply inspired by the Hindu tradition of *seva* too. Far from being a neutral spectator, the 'secular' state is often seen as being an active supporter in this enterprise. This has led to the proliferation of certain discourses that are increasingly favouring a 'Hindu model of development'. The recent controversies around 'beef ban' are an illustration of this. The contribution of these religious and cultural organizations to development, often in partnership with the State has blurred the distinctions between the 'sacred' and the 'secular' (Clarke and Jennings 2008). What is equally interesting to observe is also how the realm of the 'sacred' and the 'secular' are gradually getting transmuted by each other's influences.

While the secular state in India is increasingly invoking the sacred, religious and cultural institutions are actively importing several secular practices and idioms in an effort to revamp their image and expand their respective constituencies.

The approach of this book stands in contrast to the dominant approaches that have framed the study of Hindutva so far. While a considerable amount of scholarly work (Andersen and Damle 1987; Basu et. al 1993; Hansen 1999; Jaffrelot 1996; Kanungo 2003; Zavos 2000) has contributed towards our understanding of the origins, organizational structure, spread and political character of the Hindu nationalist movement, most of these studies have not paid much attention to its service or *seva* activities, especially in the context of disasters. Two critical civil society reports (Awaaz 2004; IDRF 2002) however do discuss the humanitarian activities of the Sangh Parivar and allege that the enormous funds raised by the Sangh Parivar in the aftermath of disasters such as the Odisha Super Cyclone of 1999 and the Bhuj earthquake of 2001 were used to provide sectarian relief and further the agenda of Hindutva.

Moreover, a large body of literature on the RSS has highlighted the confrontational aspects of the movement and have used labels such as 'fundamentalist', 'communal' and even 'fascist' to describe the same.[5] What is inadequately addressed in these studies, however, is an in-depth analysis of how new supporters and allies are 'won over' in micro localized contexts through the RSS's day-to-day service activities. In what ways have the organization's *seva* activities 'sidestepped' or 'circumvented' the State, without really confronting it? In what ways has the Sangh's participation in humanitarian activities helped the organization in winning new allies, supporters or even cadres? This study in some ways also tries to reverse the lens through which we view Hindutva and examines its

[5] For a detailed analysis of various criticisms of the RSS, see Kanungo (2003, 13–23).

appeal from the point of view of its benefactors. Moreover, as Davis and Robinson (2012, 3) remind us, there is a need to recognize the 'compassionate side' of religiously inspired movements[6] that provoke comparisons with 'ineffective, corrupt or indifferent current governments' and attract supporters with different local sensibilities, interests and concerns. In a different context, Melani Cammett's (2014) book which explores the political motivations of the provision of social welfare services by Christian, Shia and Sunni Muslim political parties in Lebanon is an important work in this direction.

Seva and the RSS

In the Hindu tradition, *seva* broadly denotes 'selfless service'; *seva* could be directed towards society, an individual, one's parents, towards God or towards one's guru (Warrier 2003, 265). As Chapter 2 of this book will demonstrate, in specific social and historical contexts, the meaning and orientations of *seva* have undergone changes. In the RSS tradition too, the institution of *seva* keeps evolving and acquiring multiple shades under the aegis of its different leaders. What remains more or less unchanging however is that *seva* serves as a political stratagem in the Parivar by performing two important roles: First, it helps in consolidating the Hindu community by subsuming its internal differences; second, it mobilizes support for the Sangh by earning the gratitude and the loyalty of its benefactors. As Jaffrelot (2005, 211) suggests, Hindutva largely owes its success not only 'to its ability to alternatively mobilize support in the streets on ethno-religious issues and to make alliances with regional partners' but also to its earlier grassroots work. These 'on-the-ground activities', he maintains, are centred on 'a strategy of social welfare' or *seva*, which has not received much

---

[6] Although the RSS is not a religious movement, its political ideology of Hindutva appropriates certain traditions, customs and rituals of the Hindu religion.

attention, as this form of engagement is least expected on the part of a movement dominated by a high-caste elite.

A reading of the RSS history tells us that *seva* has always been at the core of Hindutva praxis (Reddy 2011, 413). Since its inception, an important aspect of the organization's work revolved around providing service in the form of relief during natural and political calamities such as the Partition of India in 1947, the Assam earthquake of 1950, the Punjab Floods in 1955, the Tamil Nadu cyclone in 1955, the Anjar earthquake in 1956, the Andhra Cyclone of 1977, the Latur earthquake of 1993, the Odisha Super Cyclone in 1999, the Bhuj earthquake in 2001, Koshi River Floods in 2008 and most recently the Uttarakhand Floods in 2013. Apart from creating a humanitarian and compassionate image for itself, relief interventions after these disasters also provided opportunities to the RSS to undertake cadre building and consolidate its organizational network.

Seva, however, has not remained limited to the realm of emergency relief alone. It attained an institutionalized footing under the leadership of M. S. Golwalkar, the second *sarsanghchalak* (organizational chief) of the Sangh, who sought to salvage the respectability of the organization after the lifting of a ban in 1948, following the assassination of Gandhi by an ex-RSS member (Hansen 1999, 96). A series of affiliates such as VKA, VHP, Vidya Bharati and Seva Bharati which were set up under the leadership of Golwalkar and Deoras, adopted *seva* as an important strategy in furthering the agenda of Hindutva. The affiliates of the Parivar have over the years focused on the expansion and institutionalization of social welfare in the field of education, health, rural development and livelihoods.

The provision of *seva*, however, was never a thoughtless exercise. Recipients of service were strategically chosen. Thus, while in tribal dominated regions, *seva* was used effectively to counter Christian missionary welfare activities and co-opt tribals under the Hindu fold, targeted *seva* to Dalits helped in building alliances with the erstwhile untouchable community. Since the 1950s onwards, therefore, the RSS grew into a vast network of organizations, many of which were engaged in rendering some or other form of *seva*. Deoras, in particular, according to Andersen and Damle (2018, xiv) led the RSS on a 'much more intense activist path' than before as he acknowledged the fact that the organization's Brahmanical moorings was not attractive to the non-elite. Overseas aspirations of Hindutva led to its expansion outside India, especially in countries where the Hindu diaspora formed a significant number. Many *swayamsevaks* in these countries initiated branches of the Sangh Parivar which also engaged in different forms of *seva*, including the provision of relief post calamities. *Seva* thus slowly grew and consolidated itself as one of the strong pillars of the Sangh Parivar by enabling mobilization in different realms of society and brandishing the image of the *swayamsevaks* as benevolent actors who are capable of doing good work. According to a databank established by senior workers of the RSS in 1997, there were 22,866 recorded *sevakaryas* (units of *seva* activity) operating across the range of Sangh-inspired organizations and reaching 7 per cent of India's population (Beckerlegge 2003, 36). By February 2007, this increased to 93,533 *seva* activities (*Sewa Sadhana* 2007, 7), thus indicating a massive leap in the number of social welfare projects. By February 2013, the total number of Sangh inspired *seva* projects stood at 133,397 (*Sewa Sadhana* 2013, 11) and to an estimated 165,000 by 2015 (Sewa Kunj 2015, 5).

There is a reasonable body of work that examines the political/instrumental orientation of the Sangh Parivar's *seva* activities. Deepa Reddy (2011, 413) notes that the 1990s models of *seva* are 'more-and-less assertive tactics' of 'Hinduization' and include activities such as 'synchronizing adivasi religious and cultural practices with those of mainstream Hinduism' and organizing reconversion ceremonies. Dyahadroy (2009) shows how the women's wing of the Dnyana Prabodhini, an educational initiative in Pune started by an RSS *swayamsevak*, uses the notion of *seva* to construct the image of an 'ideal woman' as one who is *seva* oriented and differs from the feminists who extol individualism. Tariq Thachil's (2011) work on VKA in Chhattisgarh has shown that the provision of *seva* works as an electoral tactic that helps Hindutva to make inroads among lower-caste voters in Chhattisgarh. Thachil further argues that far from being just another form of clientelism, the provision of service works as a strategy revolving around quotidian social interactions that helps to win political support through a depoliticized framework. Devika Bordia's study (2015) demonstrates how the concept of *des seva* was used by the RSS and the Vanvasi Kalyan Parishad in the Ayodhya and the Shabari Kumbh movements to discipline tribal leaders. Despite being rigorous, these studies do not tell us anything about why the specific category of *seva* is so powerful. What explains its frequent deployment on the ground and from where does it draw its moral and cultural life force? A few other studies that have attempted to explore the institution of *seva*, albeit in the context of non-Sangh Hindu organizations such as Mata Amritanandamayi (Lucia 2014; Warrier 2005) Ramakrishna Mission (Beckerlegge 2006) and Bharat Sevashram Sangha (Voix 2011) also do not address these questions satisfactorily. My work in this field has led me to believe however that on the ground things are far more complicated than we are led to believe. The motivations for rendering *seva* often stem from a complex combination of altruistic, instrumental and compassionate sensibilities. There is no single logic or motivation of *seva* shared by all donors.

Seva and the 'Gift'

Another body of work that has inspired this study enormously is the literature around 'gift making'. In his landmark work, *The Gift*, Marcel Mauss (1925), a French sociologist, had argued that in pre-market societies, the institution of gift exchange was central to social relations. More importantly, the 'gift' necessarily entailed a relationship of reciprocity between donors and recipients. Moreover, although gifts appeared to be voluntary, they were obligatory and interested and created a hierarchy of status based on honour. Thus, a gift that was not requited created an unequal relationship between people and constituted a debt which constrained the recipient to act deferentially towards the donor. Mauss also suggested that far from being a mere economic activity, the institution of gifting had a social, religious, magical and moral significance especially because gifts were never impersonal. The gift relationship provided the basis of mutual ties and enhanced solidarity between groups, as it fostered balance and mutuality in society. Mauss's central argument therefore was that there is nothing called a free or disinterested gift. In his celebrated work, *Given Time*, Derrida (1992, 137) goes a step further to even deny the possibility of a gift. According to him, any 'gift' is part of an economic cycle, thus making it an impossibility. He points out that the only real gift is one which can neither be identified nor returned and that 'pure gifts' are neither regulated by institutional rituals nor morally obligated.

Several other scholars have built on Mauss's work and some have also relied on his framework while analysing institutions like *dana* in the Indian context. Many of them have also suggested that Mauss's emphasis on reciprocity is exaggerated, and, in certain contexts, gift making may not entail any exchange or an expectation of any reward. In her study of *dana* in New Delhi, Erica Bornstein (2013, 14) has suggested that *dana* is a 'liberating mechanism that releases the giver of social obligation and eventually frees the giver of the constraints of the material world'. Bornstein however acknowledges that when a gift is regulated, it becomes instrumentally rational. Thus, contemporary *dana* becomes instrumentally rational when it is facilitated by NGOs regulated by the State or when donors receive tax benefits for their donations (Bornstein 2013, 4). Similarly, Laidlaw (2000) has also challenged Marcel Mauss's central thesis of gift making by arguing that the idea of reciprocity, to the extent that it exists in *dana* (in the context of Jainism), is not 'this worldly' and that there are no social obligations between donors and recipients.

The debate on gift making and its parallels with *dana* has important implications for the category of *seva* too. An important connection that may be drawn from Mauss's analysis of gifting is that any form of *seva* leads to an intimate relationship between the donor and the recipient and provides a site for nurturing religious, social and cultural relationships. Moreover, as Heim (2004, xx) suggests, despite their reputation for being complimentary, 'gifts are rarely tossed out blindly with no thought to where they land'. Thus, while acts of service may be projected to be selfless, non-obligatory and spontaneous, in reality, they are far more strategically conceived and implemented. The relationship between the donor and the recipient therefore is imbued with economic, social, cultural and political dimensions. This has important implications in the way we understand more contemporary forms of philanthropy in modern India.

While *seva* in its classical form essentially entails the notion of 'selflessness' or the idea of 'giving without any expectation', this study shows that there is an inherent tension between this capacious understanding of *seva* and its articulation in specific contexts. Organizations like the RSS are aware of this and therefore deliberately attempt to downplay the instrumentalist nature of their humanitarianism by constantly appropriating the more expansive notion of *seva*. Part of the reason why the beneficiaries and even the performers of service are enamoured by the idea of *seva* is because they truly believe that as an ideal type, *seva* is truly devoid of reciprocity.

Religious Aid Agencies and Disasters

The French anthropologist Didier Fassin (2011, 6) has argued that a new 'moral economy, centred on humanitarian reason' has been dominating public imagination since the last few decades of the 20th century. He uses the term 'humanitarian government' to describe the intermeshing of moral sensibilities in contemporary politics that creates an obligation to offer support and assistance to those in need. He goes on to explain that the expression 'government' refers to the set of procedures that have been established at national, international and local levels in order to administer support for the existence of human beings and includes both State and non-State agencies. This proposition makes absolute sense when one analyses the rising number of humanitarian actors the world over who actively raise funds and intervene whenever an opportunity arises, in situations of crisis. The story in South Asia is pretty much the same.

For anyone interested in the field of disaster aid, the decade of 2000s is particularly important, especially in the context of South Asia which experienced several catastrophes claiming millions of lives. The year 2005 marked the adoption of the Hyogo Framework for Action by 168 governments at the World Conference on Disaster Reduction in Kobe, Japan, which made the State a central actor in the humanitarian field. In India, the government also enacted the National Disaster Management Act (NDMA) which provided a blueprint of the State's responsibility for handling disasters at various levels. In the backdrop of these events, a series of intriguing media reports captured the role of religious and politico-cultural groups in disaster relief. Post the Bhuj earthquake in 2001, for instance, RSS *swayamsevaks* and VHP activists emerged as saviours, who rescued people from under rubble, treated the injured and cremated the dead. Post the Kashmir earthquake in 2005, local Islamic extremist groups were among the first to respond to the need of affected people (McGirk 2005). Evangelical and voodoo priests were seen to be providing spiritual and material aid to the homeless and injured after the Haiti earthquake of 2010 (Philips 2010). The Tohoku earthquake of 2011 and the resulting Tsunami also witnessed several religious groups (Tenrikyo, Soka Gakkai, Rissho Kosei Kai and Shinnyoen, Aleph and Buddhist temples,

Shinto shrines), mounting extensive aid campaigns (Ambros 2011).

The participation of these groups in the aforementioned disasters is not by chance. For centuries, civil society actors have often been the first providers of aid in emergencies. These actors range from small neighbourhood groups to large humanitarian movements. The nature of these groups, however, may range from being 'secular' to 'religious' or even 'politically conservative', with blurred boundaries between them. What is important to note, however, is that just like the State, these groups too have distinct ideologies and agendas that are manifested during the provision of aid. These ideologies may either be aligned to or even sharply opposed to that of the State. In certain cases, these ideological affiliations may be towards governments or movements outside of the nation state. Disasters thus become a stage where a range of actors enact their part and strive towards mobilizing the affected communities.

It is important to note here that disasters create situations that are very different from normal times. Disasters usually witness a complete breakdown of local government machineries and societal bonds that endure community living. The shock of the catastrophe and the death and displacement of loved ones gets compounded by damage to property, breakdown of regular means of communication, lack of food, water, shelter and electricity. In sum, at the very time when the needs for social support are most severe, the 'normal protective and helping processes are inoperative or disrupted' (Bunker 1957, 110). Given the extraordinary circumstances that disasters create, victims often become 'soft targets' of various kinds of mobilization which form part of relief activities.

Despite the presence of several relief agencies, there are certain factors that particularly make religious and politico-cultural actors popular during disasters. Disasters often provide occasions for contemplation on deeply existential questions, thus making victims particularly vulnerable towards any form of indoctrination that assists in meaning making of the disaster. Meaning making often alludes to 'miraculous' survival of places of worship or objects that are considered to have sacred significance. One such instance of a 'miracle' that captured the imagination of people recently was that the 1200-year-old Kedarnath Temple, its statues, the lingam inside the Lord Shiva temple and the statue of Nandi (the bull) had survived the Kedarnath Floods of 2013 while everything around it was destroyed (*The Times of India* 2013). That survivors would be attracted towards a transcendental explanation of a catastrophic event is not surprising. In contrast to a slow, apathetic, unfamiliar and bureaucratic State, politico-cultural and religious groups that are more embedded in society provide both emotive and material support to the affected. Research on the preparedness of religion to respond to disaster events has shown that religious organizations have made significant contributions to emergency planning, relief, rehabilitation and reconstruction, thus forming the 'backbone of community support at the grassroots level' (Penuel and Statler 2011, 582–583). Edward Simpson (2004, 164) thus suggests that new religious movements commonly flourish after large-scale national disasters. He cites the example of Muslim Brotherhood and Islamic Front for Salvation, which gained immense popularity, following the earthquakes in Egypt and Algeria respectively.

By and large, most of these organizations have large resources at their disposal, such as huge memberships, access to several volunteers and a steady annual income derived through systematic fundraising, that give them the ability to design, deliver and sustain community development services. Moreover, disaster situations also provide opportunities for massive fundraising to these groups as the motivation to donate time, money or even participate as a volunteer is deeply connected to one's faith. Individual donors who are often suspicious of the intentions and the efficiency of the State channel their funds through religious or cultural bodies that they are affiliated to.

Further the presence of these organizations on the ground and their familiarity with the terrain, even in the most remote parts of a country give them an edge over State agencies. With regard to the role of local Islamic groups (such as Lashkar-e-Taiba, Jamat-ut-Dawa, Al-Khair Trust, Al-Khidmat Foundation, etc.) after the Kashmir earthquake in 2005, for instance, Jan McGirk (2005) has pointed out that several factors worked in favour of these groups in managing relief, such as their former experience in managing disasters, general familiarity with the rough terrain of the region, their adeptness in transferring relief materials faster than the government to far-flung villages and their access to sophisticated technology. A similar story unfolded in Aceh, after the 2004 Tsunami, when local Islamic groups such as the Islamic Defenders' Front and Lashkar Mujahideen were among the first to bring help to the victims (Burke, 2005). Subsequently, these groups also played an important role in resisting the alleged proselytizing attempts of several Christian aid groups who participated in relief work. While it is widely acknowledged that the RSS is not a religious organization, there are several important parallels that one can identify from the above cited literature on the ways in which religious groups capitalize political gains through their relief work in times of disasters. The obvious Hindu leanings of the RSS and its affiliation with religious groups such as the VHP, provide it with similar advantages that religious groups possess especially in disaster situations.

In recent times, considerable attention has been given to modes of political mobilization that lie outside the electoral process. Many scholars have acknowledged the role of civic associations as important mobilizers of political action (Amenta et al. 2010; Skocpol 2003). In this regard, religious, social, cultural and political voluntary organizations have also been recognized as important players in creating or amending public policy. This acknowledgment has become particularly relevant in light of the resurgence of transnational movements that are driven by the instrumental deployment of religion, such as the rise of radical Islam, fundamentalist and Pentecostal forms of Christianity or Hindu Nationalism. Their forms of enlisting support are not substantially different from that undertaken by the State and, at times, may even coalesce with that of the State. However, these groups mobilize their primary constituencies on explicit ethnic or religious lines through activities such as yatras/processions, public celebration of religious festivals or more institutionalized mechanisms such as desecration or construction of places of worship, demanding special rights and privileges for a particular religious/ethnic community, etc.

What is important to note however is that outside of these conventional forms of mobilization, political actors engage with their constituencies through a host of other and sometimes unconventional formats. Situations of conflicts and disasters offer interesting contexts in this regard. In recent times, a growing body of work (Fountain et al. 1998; Simpson 2014) has explored the role of ethnic and religious mobilization in the realm of disaster relief. The context for this study is influenced by this framework. While this study is essentially interested in understanding the growth in the popularity of the Hindu nationalist movement, it uses the context of disaster relief in order to explore if the modes of mobilization employed in this context are any different from those during normal times.

Conceptualizing 'Disasters'

From being conceived as 'acts of gods' to events which are political and even 'man-made', the conceptualization of disasters has travelled a long way. The discourse on disasters typically tends to demarcate between disasters which are considered 'natural' (e.g., floods, earthquakes and cyclones) and those that are 'anthropogenic' or man-made (e.g., wars). While the focus of this book is on the former, the author does acknowledge that such a demarcation is artificial and problematic. The fundamental problem with this categorization is that it is built on the assumption that 'natural disasters' being outside of human control are more straightforward and fundamentally apolitical in contrast to 'complex humanitarian emergencies'. In recent times, however, catastrophes such as the 2004 Indian Ocean Tsunami, the 2005 Hurricane Katrina, the 2011 Tohuku earthquake and Tsunami which caused severe damage to the Fukushima Daiichi Nuclear Power Plant and the 2013 Uttarakhand Floods have shown that 'natural disasters' are not any less complicated than any other kind of catastrophe. They also point towards the fact that human collusion is discernible in the causes, impact and the response to a disaster. Political ecology approaches to vulnerability (Smith and Hoffman 1999) have suggested that social vulnerability, marginalization and a variety of risks are the main causes of disasters. While the cause of a disaster may be attributed to a natural hazard, the disaster is absolved of all 'naturalness' as soon as it interacts with the human society in which it occurs. Moreover, recent research is also acknowledging that even so called 'natural' hazards have a human hand, as is evident when analysing the reasons for climate change.

The political dimensions of all disasters become even more evident in the response period. Typically, the aftermath of a disaster sets the stage for a range of actors, each with their own distinct agenda, to plunge into providing relief, rescue and rehabilitation. In this immensely complex space, decisions relating to the extent of the disaster's impact, where and how should relief be provided, questions relating to the distribution of compensation and rehabilitation plans are deeply contested. These decisions are made through an interplay of variables that are enmeshed in a nexus of cultural, political, economic and religious concerns. This process is accompanied by a proliferation of different forms of mobilization that are undertaken by the various relief agents which includes the State, religious and political groups, international and even transnational actors. The nature and purpose of these mobilizations may be very different. As Fountain (2012) has argued, secular organizations may insist on the separation of 'religion' from 'normal' life by refusing to fund religious aid agencies, thus resembling active proselytization.

The above account underlines the need to consider disasters as events that involve a range of stakeholders who in turn shape its impact. Drawing from this framework, this study considers disasters as political events that occur in political spaces and affirms that they often have long-term consequences on the social-political, economic, cultural and religious ecology of a space. Any attempt at understanding the influence of a particular donor agency on the beneficiary community therefore has to consider these issues after the passage of a reasonable length of time.

Methodology

The theoretical framework of the proposed study is inspired by Gordon Lynch's (2012) idea of the 'sacred form'. Contrary to popular belief, Lynch argues that although we live in a secular age, we do not live in a 'desacralized' one, and that sacred forms, in the guise of the 'religious' and the 'secular', play an important role in shaping social life in the modern world. Simply put, 'sacred forms' entail certain specific symbols and discourses that provides a moral framework to make sense of human society. The concluding chapter of the book reflects on this in detail and attempts to explain how the ideology of Hindutva has shaped itself as a 'sacred form' in our society and what are the implications of this phenomenon. It also reflects on how the rise of Hindu nationalist politics can be explained in terms of the social processes of moral meanings. The author believes that an analysis of Hindutva in contemporary times has to move away from a straightforward interpretation of how religion is 'making a comeback' and instead identify new forms and structures of societies that are actively assimilating the 'sacred' within the 'secular'.

There are multiple ways in which one can analyse the social welfare activities of the Sangh Parivar. Given that there are several thousands of RSS-led or RSS-inspired *seva* activities that are scattered across India and even in overseas territories, it is not possible to provide a generic understanding of their work. I have therefore only focused on two prominent disasters in India where the RSS played an important role in providing relief and rehabilitation: The Odisha Super Cyclone of 1999 and the Bhuj earthquake of 2001. I use these cases to analyse their social welfare strategy and the impact that this has had on the daily lives and world views of its beneficiaries. On the basis of these findings, I put forth a few reflections that I feel have not been touched upon in previous scholarly writings on the RSS. The frame of reference for selecting the two cases—Gujarat and Odisha—is as follows:

- Both the states have experienced major disasters in which the RSS played an active role during the response and relief period.
- Gujarat and Odisha have often been referred to as laboratories of 'Hindutva' by academic scholars and mainstream media.
- The political configuration of the two states is interesting, encompassing a situation where in one case (Gujarat) the BJP has been the undisputed force since 1995 while in the other (Odisha) it has struggled to set up base through a regional alliance with the Biju Janata Dal (BJD).
- The religious landscape, although similar in terms of both being Hindu majority states, has important regional variations in terms of the manifestation and practice of Hinduism.
- Both the states have had a history of communal riots (involving Hindutva groups), of which two major riots have grabbed national and international attention in the recent past, namely, Godhra (2002, Gujarat) and Kandhamal (2008, Odisha).
- Economically, Gujarat has always been among the top five states with a high GDP growth rate while Odisha has always

been amongst the bottom five with extremely high levels of poverty.[7]

The differences in social, economic, political and cultural structures were expected to have important implications in the ways in which nationalist discourses such as Hindutva seek to find their feet and expand their influence.

The study combines both conceptual and empirical insights on the idea and practice of *seva* in the RSS. It draws its data from primary literature comprising newspaper reports, archives of the RSS mouthpiece, *Organiser*, newsletters, annual reports and pamphlets of the RSS and its affiliates, independent reports written by civil society activists and agencies, government of India reports and individual reports of a variety of aid agencies. Apart from this, secondary sources such as books, journal articles and research papers have been consulted for developing a theoretical framework and validating the findings from the primary sources.

A critical examination of the said literature is supplemented by a brief fieldwork undertaken in Cuttack, Bhubaneswar and Erasama and Tirtol blocks in Jagatsinghpur district of Odisha and in Bhuj, Anjar and Nakhatrana blocks of Kutch district of Gujarat by the author between September and November 2012. The main stakeholders interviewed across the two states included the members of the RSS, BJP, Sewa Bharati, Gujarat, and Utkal Bipanna Sahayata Samiti (UBSS), volunteers involved in relief work, government officials, media persons, survivors of the Bhuj earthquake and the Odisha Super Cyclone, NGOs and other cultural groups involved in relief work and the local community of the affected villages. Qualitative techniques such as structured/semi-structured

[7] According to Human Development Index Report of 2011, Gujarat ranked 11 with a rating of 0.527 (much above the national average of 0.467) while Odisha ranked 22 with a rating of 0.362.

one-on-one interviews, group interviews and observations were employed. The names of all interview respondents have been changed to pseudonyms, wherever requested.

Chapterization

There are five chapters in this book and, together, they accomplish three different objectives. The first chapter foregrounds the context of disasters as a site for contested ideologies, where an entire gamut of actors, both State and non-State,[8] vies to gain political mileage by providing their services to beneficiaries. This discussion is carried out in the specific context of India through a historical framework of the evolution of disaster relief since pre-colonial times. The RSS's role in disaster relief is introduced within this historical framework. More importantly, this chapter problematizes the term 'disaster' by interrogating the several definitions and meanings that have historically been ascribed to it in the course of its evolution and examines how these different definitions are imbued in politics. Chapters 2 and 3 undertake an analysis of the institution of *seva* and its practice in the RSS. This is because all of the RSS's humanitarian activities, including that of disaster relief, are carried out in the name of *seva*. In Chapter 2, I attempt to examine the religious, cultural and intellectual heritage of the institution of *seva* in order to understand it as a form of humanitarianism. The evolution of *seva* is traced from the Hindu notion of

[8] The term 'non-State' is typically used in the study of International relations to denote non-sovereign entities that exercise economic or political influence at the national and international level. In this chapter, however, the term 'non-State' has been used more broadly to include any actor that functions outside the formal apparatus of the State. The researcher is aware however that there is an inherent contradiction in classifying certain kinds of organizations as being strictly 'non-State' especially when they are established or supported by the State to meet its own interests. One of the primary intentions of this chapter therefore is also to interrogate the boundary lines between the State and the 'non-State'.

dana, practices of the medieval Bhakti period and the Hindu socioreligious reformist and revivalist movements of the 19th- and early 20th-century colonial India. The chapter also briefly touches upon the contribution of Vivekananda and Gandhi in shaping the idea of *seva*. Chapter 3 critically examines the conceptualization and practice of *seva* in the RSS tradition and explores its evolution as a political strategy. This chapter also outlines the organizational structure and networks for implementing *seva* and discusses the work of a few of its key affiliates. Chapters 4 and 5 provide a detailed overview of the RSS's relief and rehabilitation activities after the Odisha Super Cyclone in 1999 and the Bhuj earthquake in 2001 respectively. Chapter 4 undertakes a detailed analysis of how the RSS and its primary affiliate group, UBSS, responded to the Odisha Super Cyclone and how their participation in relief and rehabilitation activities enabled organizational expansion and acceleration of welfare activities in coastal Odisha. Chapter 5 focuses on how the rendering of *seva*, in collaboration with the state government of Gujarat, through rehabilitation projects after the Bhuj earthquake entrenched Hindutva in rural Kutch. In the Conclusion, I offer a summary of my key arguments and attempt to put forth a few perspectives. In this chapter, I also critically reflect upon the phenomenal growth and popularity of Hindutva as an ideology and argue for a new framework of analysis to research on this movement further. In doing so, I revisit the theoretical framework of the 'sacred form' used by Lynch (2012), which is mentioned above, to bring my argument to a closure. I provoke the larger question of whether there is a need to move beyond the stereotypical understanding of Hindutva as a challenge to liberal democratic principles to one that is focused on understanding the cultural logic of its appeal. More importantly, I attempt to nudge the reader towards some of the limitations of the 'secular' and the repercussions of the political project of secularism to suppress and derecognize the non-secular experience. I also put forth a few questions that can be taken up for further research.

A primary claim of this study is that disasters offer politico-cultural organizations like the RSS a creative entry point to undertake a creative form of mobilization by engaging with a range of stakeholders such as community, donors, partner organizations and the State. Humanitarian projection and engagement through service and rehabilitation projects in the post-disaster period facilitate the organizational expansion and ideological entrenchment[9] of the RSS. In a break from previous scholarly work that has primarily investigated the various modes of communal mobilization undertaken by the Sangh Parivar, which are often accompanied by violence, this book forms part of a new strain of literature that examines certain 'neutral forms of social action' undertaken by Hindutva to 'conquer new loyalties'. I argue that contrary to its characteristic forms of communal mobilization which typically take the form of yatras, hate speeches, riots, reconversion etc., the broader context of social welfare and the specific context of disaster relief allow the Sangh Parivar to engage in more nuanced forms of enlisting support. Participation in relief and rehabilitation paves way for what Thachil (2011) has called an 'embedded' form of mobilization that is seemingly unthreatening as it is subtle, non-violent and clothed in humanitarianism in contrast to the more virulent forms of mobilization. It is important to note however that this seemingly benign humanitarian strategy carries the potential of assuming a more potent form in favourable sociocultural and political contexts. This becomes particularly relevant in the context of disaster rehabilitation and recovery when relief agencies get an opportunity to initiate long term relationships with their beneficiaries.

[9] The idea of 'entrenchment' is borrowed from Daniela Berti's use of this category in her edited volume titled *Cultural Entrenchment of Hindutva: Local Mediations and Forms of Convergence* (2011). Berti mentions that the notion of 'entrenchment' refers to 'a multiplicity of processes, mechanisms and even paradoxical dynamics of assimilation by way of which Hindutva penetrates different regional contexts, both at the urban and rural levels, thanks to the mediation of different social actors' (Berti 2011, 2).

The work of the Sangh Parivar in the aftermath of the two disasters discussed in this book, involved a complex interplay of religion–culture–politics in ways that are not easily disentangled. One of the reasons why scholars have found it difficult to categorize the Hindutva movement is because it escapes the conventional framework of other religious movements. Unlike the VHP, for instance, there is no direct invocation of religion in the RSS imagination. The focus is rather on the 'nation', which is built on the lines of the Hindu culture. And yet, despite this, religion cannot be completely dismissed while analysing the growth of the Sangh Parivar. It lurks in the shadows and makes an appearance whenever a congenial moment arrives. The idea and practice of *seva* needs to be understood in this specific context. It represents a certain resurrection of a religious tradition in the world of humanitarianism. What is interesting to note however is that it does so unthreateningly by embracing the secular ethos. Saba Mahmood (2004, 9) has argued that secular liberalism cannot be understood merely as a State doctrine or a set of juridical conventions; it is a 'life form'. Adapting to this entrenched life form has been one of the key reasons for the success of the Hindutva movement. As in other realms, in the world of humanitarianism too, the Sangh Parivar has managed to revive some form of the sacred (which some contend, very superficially) in an essentially secularized space.

I

Disaster Relief in India
'Religious', 'Secular' and Those 'in Between'

In a fascinating book named *Sacred Aid: Faith and Humanitarianism*, Barnett and Stein (2012, 8) have argued that the twin values and processes of secularization and sanctification are 'enduring aspects of humanitarianism'. While secularization, they suggest, is demonstrated by the growing involvement of states and political agencies, increasing bureaucratization and professionalization, sanctification is evident in the construction of a sacred space that is separate from the profane and in the invocation of a humanitarian ethic that triumphs over everything else. An analysis of the history of humanitarianism in India indicates that the twin processes of secularization and sanctification have been enduring features here too. While one may be tempted to imagine that the 'sacred' may have been more powerful in pre-modern times, this chapter surprisingly reveals that it continues to exercise considerable influence in the space of humanitarianism even today. This is evident in certain kinds of idioms, values and ethics that are deployed to interpret, analyse and respond to disasters. The sanctification of human-itarianism is as a much a political exercise as the process of secularization. It is however important to bear in mind that it is becoming increasingly difficult to neatly demarcate the 'sacred' from the 'secular' aid providers as both these actors have undergone transformations in their characters and have imbibed the qualities of the other through prolonged interaction.

This chapter sets the context to this study and investigates two primary themes: the meaning of a disaster and the politics of relief that surrounds the role of both State and non-State actors in the specific context of India. Through an interrogation of the various understandings of a disaster, I demonstrate how the conceptualization and framing of a disaster can have profound implications on determining the trajectory and form of mobilization that a particular relief actor may pursue. I also argue in this context that far from being 'natural', disasters are inherently social, cultural and political phenomena that manifest multiple power dynamics particularly in their aftermath.

Meaning Making of Disasters

Ashok Singhal, a senior VHP leader, said,

> People staged protest against the hydro power project and opposed the idea of uplifting the statue. Despite this the Dhari Devi idol was removed from her temple on 16 June and placed at the platform created. The goddess exhibited her anger and Kedarnath and other parts suffered damage. The Dhari Devi wanted to teach the atheists ruling this country a lesson and tell them don't touch the Himalayas and its rivers. (Gusain, 2013)

Further to that, K. S. Valdiya, a Himalayan geologist, suggests,

> [H]eavy rain and cloudbursts were natural, the tragedy that followed was entirely man-made…. These tectonic faultlines,

which are active and see back-and-forth movements, have been cut in many places by roads. More dangerously, roads are built along the faultlines at many places. As a result, tiny seismic movements in the faultlines weaken the rocks at the base of the roads, making these stretches susceptible to cave-ins and slides. (Bhattacharya, 2013)

Question: Don't you think it was a man-made disaster?

Answer: Not at all. Do you think the cloudburst at Kedarnath happened because of wrong or commercial construction on the river beds of Haridwar? ... Kedarnath doesn't even fall in the eco-sensitive zone and the dhabas on the walk path couldn't have triggered calamity of this magnitude. (Aron in an interview with Vijay Bahuguna, ex-chief minister of Uttarakhand, *Hindustan Times*, 24 June 2013)

It is often understood that political mobilization ensues only when the dynamics of relief and rehabilitation come into the picture. While that is of course evident, what is equally impor-tant to bear in mind is that conceptualizations of catastrophes in themselves can lend themselves to political mobilization, even before the dynamics of relief actually set in. As I have argued elsewhere (Bhattacharjee 2015), this is especially impor-tant, because the ways in which disasters are constructed and represented have important implications in determining the nature and form of relief and rehabilitation.

The aforementioned quotations allude to three different narratives regarding the same event, that is, the Uttarakhand Floods of 2013 which caused the death of nearly 5,700 people (*Fox News* 2013). The juxtaposition of these three different impressions: The first attributing the tragedy to the wrath of the local Goddess Dhara Devi due to the shifting of her statue from an ancient temple, located near Srinagar (Garhwal) for a hydel-power project, the second pointing towards 'natural' and 'man-made' activities as being responsible for the disas-ter, and the third, completely denying the role of any human activity, powerfully points towards the variance in the range of conceptualizations about a disaster. While one may argue that the first and the third quotations, instead of being statements of belief, were deliberately made to give a political twist to the tragedy, it cannot be discounted that such narratives form an important part of popular imagination in understanding the causes of disasters.

In light of the above, it becomes interesting to interrogate the various definitions and understandings of the term 'disaster' itself. Perhaps one of the earliest forms of understandings about disasters is that they are 'acts of gods', or a manifestation of retribution for the sins of non-believers. This attribution to divinity can be found within the tradition of three major monotheist religions: Judaism, Christianity and Islam (Dynes, 1998). The *Encyclopedia of Disaster Relief* (2011, 275) suggests that many early natural disasters became the basis for myths which were assumed to be manifestations of the 'whims and moods' of the gods rather than acts of a physical natural agent. It also points to the fact that several Mesopotamian, Indian and African religious sources speak of a flood that covered the whole of the earth, which could have been inspired by an ancient tsunami. Chester and Duncan (2010, 85–95) have argued that in the Christian tradition, theological analysis of disasters did not end with the close of the Biblical era, but that it has continued throughout the Christian history and a number of so called 'Leibnizian philosophical models of theodicy'[1] have been developed. One of the most important examples in this regard is the case of the Lisbon earthquake of 1755, which had struck on All Saints' Day, thus triggering several conjectures which suggested that the disaster was a consequence of God's fury (Bassnett 2006, 322).

[1] G. W. Leibnitz was the first person to introduce the word 'theodicy' into philosophical discourse, which refers to an attempt to reconcile the idea of an omniscient and loving God and the concurrent existence of evil and suffering (see Chester and Duncan 2010, 85).

The divine interpretation of disasters is common practice even in the contemporary times. Soon after the Aitape Tsunami in Papua New Guinea, 1998, for instance, the Combined Churches Organization pastors maintained that God had caused the tsunami to punish Roman Catholics for their lack of Christian faith (Fountain, Kindon, and Murray 2004, 341). The pastors also maintained that the local beneficiary community's strongly anti-Christian attitude and conduct of *pasinnogut* (wrong behaviour) had led to the disaster (Fountain et al. 2004). Claudia Merli's (2010) research in Southern Thailand reveals how local discourses in the Muslim Satun province were characterized by religious interpretations of the 2004 Tsunami. She highlights that the consideration of the Tsunami as Allah's punishment was a prevalent idea among the local people of Aceh. Other scholars (Daly and Rahmayati 2012; Feener 2013) have commented on how the same Tsunami was differently perceived by different stakeholders; while some saw it as a pre-ordained divine event, others interpreted it as divine vengeance for the sins committed by people. Similarly, after the Kashmir earthquake in 2005, local Islamic groups involved in relief operations actively promoted the idea that it was a manifestation of divine retribution (Naseem 2007). After the Bhuj earthquake in 2001, the Shahi Imam (high priest) of the Fatehpuri mosque in Delhi said that natural calamities such as earthquakes, cyclones, floods, droughts, etc., are a result of 'oppression of poor and minorities' (Datt 2001). Accusing the BJP government (which held power in the central government during that time) of oppressing the minorities, the leader urged the government to run its machinery 'in the true spirit of secularism and to be just, fair and honest'.

The attribution of disasters to some form of divinity is also practiced by the seemingly secular State representatives. Levi McLaughlin (2012) states that on 15 March 2011, Tokyo Governor Ishihara Shintarō reacted to the Great East Japan earthquake by characterizing the disaster as 'divine punishment' for the 'egoism' of the Japanese people.

The above account is revealing of certain possibilities of why religious explanations are frequently invoked in times of calamities. The first possibility is that given its place in scriptural texts, certain stakeholders naturally gravitate towards theological understandings of disasters, and, in doing so, they may be actually convinced of this justification. The second possibility could be that religious leaders and groups use these unscientific explanations to exercise power and mobilize the victims of disaster for a specific political agenda. The third possibility for resorting to superstitious beliefs could stem from the normative need to achieve a larger good. Gandhi, for instance, who was a devoutly religious man, would frequently allude to superstitious explanations for what he believed could be a cure for the eradication of social evils such as untouchability, sectarianism etc. Soon after the 1934 Bihar earthquake, which had led to the death of thousands of people, Gandhi remarked that the disaster was a divine retribution for the sin of untouchability that existed in Indian society. Tagore, who was an equally vehement critic of untouchability, however, felt that Gandhi's comment in this regard was outrageous and feared that he was taking India back to the Middle Ages. Gandhi, on the other hand, perhaps hoped that if superstitious Indians were made to believe that the disaster was God's punishment for practicing social evils such as untouchability, this could lead to social reform (Chakraborty 2008). Irrespective of the motive, however, it is important to note that supernatural or divine interpretations of disasters occupy an important position in the imagination of people. Disasters often inspire deeply reflective existential questions as its victims try and rationalize the reason for their sufferings. During this hour, the act of 'meaning making' which alludes to a divine intervention, therefore, is effective in bringing solace to victims.

The second understanding of disasters revolves around the idea of its 'naturalness' where humans have little control in causing or preventing them. Thus, for instance, Burton and Kates have referred to disasters as 'natural hazards' which according to them are those 'elements in the physical environment, harmful to man and caused by forces extraneous to him' (1964, 413). The consequence of this understanding, according to Katiuscia Fara (2001, 48) was the emergence of a 'technocentric' approach, which identified science and technology as the only means of coping with natural hazards. Thus, efforts were directed towards the research of 'environmental triggers' with emphasis on climatological and geo-tectonic dimensions. The understanding of disasters as 'natural' was placed sharply in opposition to those which were 'man-made' or anthropogenic. Therefore, while floods, tsunamis, earthquakes and cyclones have typically been categorized as 'natural' calamities, incidents such as the Bhopal Gas Tragedy (1984) or the Chernobyl Nuclear Disaster (1986) are considered unambiguously 'man-made'. The obvious advantage of such a neat classification is that it absolves humans of all responsibilities in the causation of disasters. As the quotation by the ex-Chief Minister of Uttarakhand, at the beginning of this chapter, demonstrates the denial of the Uttarakhand tragedy as being 'man-made', served the purpose of absolving the state of all responsibility in preventing the disaster. Anu Kapur (2005) has persuasively argued that in India, the tendency to attribute disasters to 'natural' causes has led towards an insensitive attitude of the government in preventing, mitigating and even responding to disasters efficiently. She suggests that the reason why development plans did little about disasters in India is possibly because the 'stranglehold of the natural' has always been so powerful.

Recent disasters such as the Indian Ocean Tsunami of 2004, Hurricane Katrina of 2005, the Tohoku disaster in Japan and the Uttarakhand Floods of 2013 have reinforced that the categorization of disasters as 'natural' and 'anthropogenic' is problematic. It is increasingly being argued now that there are social, cultural and political dimensions to the causation and impact of 'natural disasters'. The growing recognition of social and political dimensions of disasters has led to a more radical re-conceptualization of the term itself. This theorization argues that disasters are primarily social rather than physical phenomena. Davis and Seitz (1982, 547) remind us that disasters are more than extraordinary physical events and that they attain human significance through the sociopolitical contexts in which they occur. Quarantelli and Dynes (1977, 24) have suggested on similar lines that with this shift in understanding of the term 'disaster', the focus is now not so much on the hazard but on the social consequences of the hazard. Moreover, the concept of vulnerability has acquired traction, particularly in the hands of anthropologists who study disasters. Wisner et al. (2003) for instance have pointed towards the fact that disasters are inevitable manifestations and reflections of vulnerabilities, long-standing unequal social power and the accumulations of risks. They also suggest that a disaster is necessarily related to a broader failure of entitlements as this enhances the vulnerability and ability of the poor to cope with the effects of a disaster. An illustration of this approach may be found in Amartya Sen's (1981) work on famines in the colonial India, which shows that far from being 'natural', famines are an outcome of man-made inequalities built into mechanisms of food distribution. Aguirre et al. (2005, 2) have suggested that social inequalities, corruption, poverty, etc., are the real disasters while hazards and other events precipitating disasters are only catalysts. Nibedita Ray-Bennett's (2009) study in coastal Odisha alludes to a similar argument when she mentions that social determinants such as caste, class and gender play the most important role in impacting the coping strategies of beneficiaries in surviving multiple disasters such as cyclones and floods and therefore the outcomes of disasters are differently experienced by different people.

Drawing from the same conceptual framework, anthropologists Susanna Hoffman and Oliver Smith (1999) have examined disasters as processes of continuity rather than abrupt change. In this understanding, disasters are approached, not as sudden and extraordinary events that disturb an existing social equilibrium, but as phenomena that sharpen, compound and perpetuate social and economic vulnerabilities, inequalities, residential patterns and ideological frameworks. Anthropologist Jacques Henry (2011) in his study on hurricane Katrina, for instance, has shown that significant continuity persists in risk exposure, inequality and residential patterns and ideological frames and the possibility of significant social change is limited. The notion of disasters as events that emphasize continuity rather than change is also explored by Sanjay Sharma (2001) in his work on famines in 19th-century India. Sharma (2001, 4–5) argues that although, in most of the official definitions, famines are perceived as unusual events, in practice, however, in most societies, a famine is 'an aggravation of familiar adverse circumstances'. He suggests that it is the failure of the apparatuses of the modern State that turns it into a famine.

An acknowledgment of disasters as political spaces helps us situate human complicity not only in the causation of disasters but also in the impact and processes of relief and recovery. In this regard, Rita Jalali (2002, 121) suggests that if disasters are not perceived as disruptive, extreme or unpredictable events, then how states and civil society institutions respond to such calamities, provides important insights about the political nature of their relationship.

History of Disaster Relief in India

While it is intuitively evident that disasters provide fertile grounds for ideological contestations to take place, it is necessary to be familiar with the larger historical context within which such mobilizations take place. Every disaster is unique and deeply embedded in the social, cultural and political structures of a given place. In the specific context of India, the world of humanitarianism has been populated by a range of State and non-State actors, which include the secular, religious and cultural groups which have shaped its historical evolution in dynamic and sometimes conflictual ways. As mentioned in the introduction to this chapter, this section draws attention to the twin trends of secularization and sanctification in the realm of humanitarianism in India and explains how these trends have enabled disasters to become contested sites.

The State

In the ancient and medieval times, the most devastating disasters in India comprised famines so much so that the very idea of disaster relief became synonymous with famine relief. Jean Dreze (1988, 12) mentions that one of the earliest accounts on famine relief by the State was written by Kautilya in *Arthashastra*. Kautilya mentions that in times of famines, a good king should commission the building of forts and ensure the provision of food and water supply or entrust the country to another king. Before the advent of British colonialism, indigenous rulers would respond to famines by distributing free raw grain through opening up of public grain stores to the people, run community kitchens and give remissions on revenue (Srivastava, 1968). Famine victims were also employed in public works through 'food for work programmes' for the construction of river ghats, temples or digging wells. The construction of the Imambara of Lucknow, for example, was commissioned by the Nawab Asaf-ud-Daula after the devastating famine of 1785 to help people find employment in exchange of food. These efforts however were mostly sporadic and limited to territories of individual kings and rulers. Famines became more frequent and severe in magnitude with the advent of the British in India and the ensuing colonization of India—the Bengal famine of 1770, being one of the most severe. The relief efforts of the British, however, were at best lukewarm and ineffective.

Sanjay Sharma (2001, 170) mentions that in 1837–1838, India experienced one of the worst famines of the 19th century and the first one in which the colonial State organized relief on 'modern principles', whereby the idea of 'public utility' became central to the relief process. Sharma argues that the State 'seized the opportunity' provided by the famine, by engaging the starving population to work as 'free' labourers in constructing roads, tanks, canals, wells, hospitals, jails, court buildings, etc. More importantly, he claims that the incorporation of public works into relief mechanisms went hand in hand with the colonial ambition of strengthening its empire 'downwards' and administering its newly acquired territory at lower levels, thus reconstituting its relationship with the local centres of power in a fundamental way. In this regard, he explains that the State merged the relief process with the ongoing process of mapping the unknown terrain and the application of superior technical skills of the industrial revolution to bring about progress and peace. In 1880, the British established the first Indian Famine Commission. A series of famines which began towards the end of the 19th century, from 1876 onwards, may have been the immediate trigger for the institution of this Commission. Dreze (1988, 14) suggests that the Famine Commission was perhaps driven by the political motives of preserving a stable political and revenue base, a feeling of obligation towards the people stemming from the harmful effects of colonial expansion and the concern with the colonial administration's image in the eyes of the British public. The Famine Commission laid the foundation of India's relief system, called the Famine Codes which were the first concerted efforts at famine prevention in India.

The Famine Codes provided guidelines to the local administration on 'anticipation, recognition and relief of famines and other natural calamities, including floods and cyclones' (Ray-Bennett 2009, 288). Based on these model codes, each state was required to come up with its codes in keeping with their local circumstances. The Famine Commission envisaged both direct and indirect forms of relief. Direct relief was provided in the form of employment for building public works projects, opening of relief kitchens, poor houses and giving of cash to women, the sick and the elderly. Indirect forms of relief consisted of remissions from land revenue and agricultural loans.

After the Bengal Famine in 1943, the Famine Codes were modified substantially. However, the famine relief policy was the only form of disaster management policy that existed for all other types of disasters up to India's Independence in 1947. Famine codes were renamed to the Scarcity Manuals and Relief Codes in Independent India. Following this, a 'paradigm shift' was brought about in the approach to disaster management, based on the conviction that development cannot be sustainable unless disaster management is built into the development process (Misra and Mathur 1993, 20). This was reflected in the successive five-year plans. Measures for flood mitigation were taken from 1950 onwards. Likewise, every major disaster contributed in bringing about qualitative improvements to disaster management efforts and thus created a fairly robust design of institutional and policy mechanisms for carrying out response, relief and rehabilitation. In 1948, soon after the India–Pakistan partition, Prime Minister Nehru established the Prime Minister's National Relief Fund with public money in order to help people who had been displaced from Pakistan. This fund, which continues to exist even today, and is wholly supported by public contributions, is primarily used to provide relief to victims of disasters.

In India, relief after disasters has traditionally been seen as the responsibility of state governments. Despite this, the central government does participate in relief efforts in times of severe calamities. The dimensions of this response are determined in keeping with the existing policy of financing relief expenditure and considering other factors such as the gravity of the disaster, the scale of the relief operation, etc. (Ray 2005, 4877). At other times, it is also shaped by purely political considerations arising out of complaints by the states ruled by the opposition. The subject of disaster management received some importance in the 1990s when the National Disaster Management Division was established in 1994 under the Ministry of Agriculture. In 1995, this institution was upgraded and renamed the National Centre for Disaster Management under an Act of Parliament. A landmark policy in the arena of disaster management in India was the enactment of NDMA in 2005 which was triggered by a series of calamities such as the Odisha Super Cyclone in 1999, the Bhuj earthquake of 2001 and the Indian Ocean Tsunami of 2004, which cost several lives and caused enormous damage to property. NDMA laid down a comprehensive three-tier system of disaster management which formulated a national-, state- and district-level disaster management authority with horizontal connections with several government departments and ministries. Each of these authorities is entrusted with the responsibility of formulating national-, state- and district-level plans respectively, for disaster mitigation and response.

Despite the passage of this Act, and several other policies and regulations, the state of affairs with regard to the implementation of disaster management in India is very poor (CAG 2013). Even now, the State's immediate response to a disaster is the deployment of armed forces, as demonstrated most recently in the Uttarakhand floods of 2013, the Koshi River Floods in Bihar in 2008 and in the Kerala Floods of 2018. Even where the state engages in relief and rehabilitation work, its action is often a function of the political will of individual politicians or state–centre dynamics. Thus, the inability of the State to deliver in times of crises may be attributed to several factors including lack of political will, prevalence of corruption, absence of accountability regimes and weak State capacity at large. This inadequacy and inefficiency of the State, opens up opportunities for a gamut of non-State agencies to not only participate in relief and rehabilitation but also on certain occasions achieve more visibility than the State.

The Non-State

The role of non-State agencies in providing humanitarian relief, especially in times of disasters, is much older than that of the State and continues to play a significant role even in contemporary times. There is enough evidence from various countries that point towards the involvement of community groups, religious, secular and even transnational actors in providing relief to people in times of crisis.[2] Even before the State arrives on the scene, it is the local communities that undertakes search and rescue operations, feeding the homeless and clearing the roads. The vital importance of these bodies in disaster situations can be attributed to the fact that the State, its institutions and public policies have proved to be insufficient and even inefficient at times to address the host of issues that arise after disasters (Zahir-ud-din 2005, 4667). Rita Jalali (2002, 123) suggests that the civil society performs multiple roles post disasters, such as creating social capital (cooperation and trust), providing an interface between the State and the victims, raising issues in the public arena and demanding public action.

In the context of India, following is a broad classification of the range of non-State actors that typically participate in disaster relief and rehabilitation:

- Secular voluntary organizations (e.g., Action Aid, Save the Children)
- Religious groups (e.g., Caritas, BAPS Swaminarayan Sanstha)
- Politico-cultural organizations (RSS)
- Corporate bodies/foundations and charitable trusts (Confederation of Indian Industries, Sir Dorabji TATA Trust)
- Multilateral organizations (World Bank, International Monetary Fund)

[2] For a detailed analysis on the role of civil society actors during disasters, see Jalali (2002).

Typologies by their very nature are not helpful beyond a point as the empirical world is far more complex than we imagine it to be. The above typology therefore has to be appreciated with the said caveat and an acknowledgment that the boundaries between the various categories are not watertight and there is considerable overlap between them. This is particularly significant while analysing the differences between 'religious' and 'secular' actors. As mentioned earlier in this chapter, processes of secularization and sanctification can no longer be ascribed exclusively to any one kind of group/s as the characteristics of the secular and the religious have been adopted by aid providers across the board. What is perhaps more problematic here is the essential politics behind normalizing a pervasive secular–religious dichotomy. As Philip Fountain (2013) has persuasively argued, the demarcation of 'religious' NGOs from the 'secular' groups is a result of a deliberate construction of religion as an essentialized, universal and ahistorical entity that needs to be set apart from the secular world. This particular construction of religion has resulted in the perpetuation of a 'myth of religious NGOs' that conveniently conceals the value-laden nature of mainstream development.

While I do elaborate further on the complexities of the secular-religious dichotomy and its implications for my work in the subsequent chapters, in the following section, I adhere to the simplistic typology provided above, in order to chart out the broad contours of the humanitarian world and provide a sense of the kinds of organizations that inhabit the same. I discuss the role of only the first three categories here ('secular', 'religious' and 'politico-cultural' groups), as they have a direct bearing on this study. These categories largely comprise the arena of what is typically called the 'voluntary sector' or, more broadly, the 'civil society'. Also known as non-profit institutions, these organizations can entail a range of actors from small neighbourhood clubs to large transnational NGOs. It should however be noted that corporate groups and multilateral organizations are no less important in the contemporary world of humanitarianism. In fact, their influence seems to be growing by the day.

Secular Voluntary Organizations

Within the voluntary sector, the group that shares strong resemblances with secular democratic states, at least theoretically, is perhaps secular organizations. By 'secular organizations', I refer to those bodies that do not represent the interests of any particular religious group or sect. These groups often, although not always, work closely with the State and even receive support from the State. Given their large volunteer base, organized processes and experience of working at the grassroots level, the State has frequently acknowledged the potential of secular voluntary groups in disaster relief. The Preamble of the National Policy on Disaster Management, for instance, recommends the involvement of National Cadet Corps and the Boys Scout in disaster management at the school level, NGOs and voluntary organizations such as the Red Cross in training and building awareness at community levels and in the process of reconstruction after disasters. NDMA also favours the involvement of youth voluntary organizations such as the Nehru Yuva Kendra Sangathan, National Service Scheme, etc., in disaster mitigation and preparedness activities.

The genesis of secular organizations in India may be traced to the 19th-century colonial period when sociopolitical groups emerged to initiate a national movement for freedom from the British rule. In addition to organizing the Indian masses for social and political action against the British, these groups actively advocated for the improvement of lives of Indians, steeped in poverty, disease, epidemics and famines. It must be noted that the period between the end of the 19th century and the early 20th century was marred by a series of famines and an outburst of diseases such as malaria, plague, cholera, tuberculosis, dysentery and diarrhoea, etc. Ira Klein has noted that between 1896 and 1901, famines alone took close to five million lives and played an important role in population reduction (Klein 1973, 642–643). From the 1890s to 1921, malaria accounted for about twenty million lives, while the influenza epidemic 1918–1919 wiped out around twelve–thirteen million lives (Klein 1973). One of the earliest secular organizations to take up the issue of famine prevention and relief in the late 19th century was the Poona Sarvajanik Sabha (1872) which actively criticized the revenue and famine policies of the government of Bombay (Bayly 1998, 106). The Sabha initiated several self-help associations in order to handle the severe famine of 1876 and presented several reports that contested the fairness of the Bombay settlement reports (Bayly 1998). Other voluntary organizations that came up during this period and actively partook in famine relief towards the end of the 19th century were the Deccan Sabha and the Friend-in-Need Society (1858) and the Satya Shodhak Samaj (1873). Apart from their role in advocacy for greater public welfare, these organizations collectively contributed towards creating a culture of volunteerism.

Georgina Brewis (2010, 903–904) mentions that between 1897 and 1900, several thousands of Indians, mostly belonging to the professional middle classes, volunteered in various famine fund committees and memberships of such committees were considered a symbol of status and patriotism. The Servants of India Society, founded by Gokhale in 1905, the Depressed Classes Mission (1906), Sons of India (1908), Seva Sadan (1908), etc., were several other voluntary groups that emerged directly out of the famines of late 19th century (Brewis 2010, 914). Allahabad Seva Samiti's (1915) relief efforts during the Haridwar Kumbh Mela in 1915 was an important landmark that led to the proliferation of several other *seva* samitis across Punjab and Uttar Pradesh (Watt 2005, 216). A series of Boy Scouts associations started in the early 20th century, such as Annie Besant's Indian Boy Scouts Association, started in 1916, and Madan Mohan Malviya's Seva Samiti Boy Scouts Association, started in 1918, provided a permanent and year round supply of volunteers who undertook relief work during famines, fairs and outbreaks of cholera (Watt 2005, 117). Bombay Sanitary Association, founded in 1904, also participated in social service by raising campaigning for the prevention of plague and cholera by organizing lectures and distributing pamphlets during pilgrimages and fairs (Ramanna 2004, 4561). Stree Zarthosti Mandal, a women's Zoroastrian association, was founded in 1903 in response to the plague epidemic of 1896–1897, while Social Service League, founded in 1911 in Bombay, served as the chief organizer of the epidemic relief committee during the influenza epidemic of 1918–1919 (Ramanna 2004, 4565). Similarly, in Gujarat, Gujarat Sabha and Gandhi's Home Rule League aligned themselves during the Kheda Satyagraha and the famine and plague epidemic in 1918 (Mehta 2005, 297). During the First World War in 1914, the British Red Cross started its activities in India in association with St John Ambulance Association. By 1920, the Indian Red Cross Society was formed by a legislative Act of the British Government.

The culture of volunteerism received a further fillip with the arrival of Gandhi from South Africa to India in 1915. Gandhi actively propagated voluntary service for the upliftment of hitherto marginalized groups such as women, lepers, 'adivasis' (tribals) and 'Harijans' (Dalits) through his 'constructive work' programmes and established several ashrams which combined voluntarism with a political commitment. Gandhi also advocated for personal and public hygiene and sanitation through his constructive programme, particularly as a deterrent to plagues and other epidemics. He frequently wrote in the contemporary newspapers such as *The Harijan, The Amrit Bazaar Patrika* and *The Indian Opinion* to raise awareness about the importance of maintaining decent sanitary conditions (*The Hindu* 2002). Gandhi and his followers also actively raised funds during the 1934 Bihar earthquake, and Gandhi entrusted his associate Kumarappa to serve as the custodian of this relief fund (Gandhi 2007, 386). Soon after Gandhi's death, a loose federation of organizations known as Sarvodaya Samaj (Sarvodaya Brotherhood) was set up which was later strengthened by the founding of the Akhil Bharat Sarva Seva Sangh (All India Association for the Service of All) in 1949. Many of these organizations participated in disaster relief as part of their larger work in development and received enormous support from the State. The Assam branch of Kasturba Gandhi National Memorial Trust, for instance, provided support after the Assam earthquake of 1950. The hallmark of these organizations was that despite being deeply nationalist, their ideology was more inclusive and espoused a civic form of nationalism. Gandhi's advocacy of service in particular was aimed towards developing a sense of dignity and equality in the Indian society. While in this regard it may seem logical to categorize Gandhian volunteerism as secular humanitarianism, a closer look at his writings around *seva* reveals an almost paradoxical religious underpinning. While I discuss this in greater detail in the following chapter, suffice it to say that the term 'secular' should not be interpreted here to denote omni-partiality or neutrality, but in its classical sense as a realm that is separate from the arena of religion, superstition and non-rational.

Post-Independence, the Government of India acknowledged and encouraged the role of voluntary actors in implementing its social welfare and development activities. This was reflected in the First Five-Year Plan and the establishment of the Central Social Welfare Board in 1953 which aimed at promoting social welfare activities through voluntary organizations (Asian Development Bank, 2009). Moreover, Gandhian organizations were actively supported and involved by the government in training government officials in development projects in the realm of health and rural development (Sen 1999, 335). During this period, several secular international organizations also established work in India. Save the Children established the All Save the Children Committee in 1944 during its famine relief work in Bengal; OXFAM Great Britain started work in 1951 during the Bihar famine to launch its first full-scale humanitarian response in a developing country while CARE International started work in the mid-1950s in India.

The voluntary sector was rejuvenated majorly after Jayaprakash Narayan's anti-corruption movement, anti-Emergency struggle and Janata Party upsurge in 1977–1979. The 1970s witnessed a surge in the number of voluntary groups, especially secular groups, which were a product of social movements that emerged to protect the rights of hitherto marginalized communities such as tribals, Dalits, women, etc. (Aiyar and Malik 2004). Although the primary focus of these groups was the promotion of an alternative development paradigm through advocating human rights, gender rights, empowerment of adivasis, backward castes and ecological issues (Kochanek and Hardgrave 2008), many of these groups also got involved in disaster relief after floods, cyclones, earthquakes and even after the Bangladesh Liberation War of 1971 which led to the influx of several Hindu refugees from Bangladesh to India.

From the beginning of the 1990s and onwards, voluntary organizations assumed further prominence in social welfare with the help of State support and enormous foreign funding. The neo-liberal reforms of the early 1990s created a congenial climate for civil society movements to flourish. Terje Tvedt (2006, 688) argues that many of the most publicized books and reports that explicitly seek to promote NGO agendas have been financed or produced by institutions such as the World Bank, United Nations or by NGOs such as OXFAM, Save the Children, etc., donor states, state bureaucrats and diplomats who have had a vested interest in promoting the 'independent' image of the NGOs, since it is this conceived 'independency' that has made them useful politically and given the system a whole added legitimacy.

Religious Groups in Disaster Relief

Historically, the role of religious groups in mobilizing support through humanitarian service has been most prominent. Henry Allen Moe (1961, 141) has argued that religion is the mother of philanthropy, 'both conceptually and procedurally'. This is hardly surprising as all religions regard charity as a sacred element of their faith. This can be inferred from references to the Hebrew word *tzedakah* in Jewish texts, the Latin word *caritas* in Christian theology, the Arabic word *zakat* in the Quran and the Sanskrit words *dana* in the Hindu, Buddhist and Jain scriptures, all of which underline the importance of giving to the needy. Erica Bornstein (2009, 623) mentions that the giving of alms is considered important in most religions; while in Islam it is 'one of the five pillars of the faith', in Hinduism, Buddhism, Confucianism and early Christianity and Judaism, it is considered 'good work'. The religious injunction to give and serve has often been manifested in times of crises when religious voluntary groups have participated in providing relief to victims of disasters. Many scholars have drawn attention to the contribution of religion to the history of development (Barnett 2011; Fassin 2012; Rist 2014). As Elizabeth Ferris (2005, 313) has noted, even before international humanitarian law was formalized in treaty law, members of faith communities provided assistance to those afflicted by disasters, persecution, displacement and war. This assistance, however, often went hand in hand with evangelization, particularly by Christian congregations. As Roland Anglin (2004) has stated, many contemporary development projects have their origins in the desire of these people to propagate the Christian faith by building and funding a number of aid and developmental initiatives, including hospitals, schools and other formal and informal activities.

In India, the evolution of the voluntary sector in disaster relief may be traced to a phenomenon of contested religious/ ideological mobilizations in the 19th-century colonial India. Farquhar ([1915] 1998, 388) has drawn attention to the fact that the Indian philanthropic movement was primarily triggered by the service activities of Christian missionaries. During the famine years of 1876–1879, he writes, the service rendered by missionaries, in the form of raising funds, carrying out earthworks and finding employment for poor people, attracted thousands of 'down-trodden' people to Christianity. This led to the beginnings of an indigenous philanthropy movement initiated by Ram Mohan Roy. While there were several other factors[3] that propelled the emergence of an Indian philanthropic movement during these times, Farquhar is accurate in pointing out that Christian proselytization was indeed an important driver for the emergence of indigenous forms of service organizations. The colonial governments' depiction of Hinduism as a superstitious religion with little regard for charity triggered off a reformist and a revivalist movement that was led primarily by the Brahmo Samaj (1828), Prarthana Samaj (1867) and Arya Samaj (1875) respectively. These organizations sought to get rid of 'social evils' such as sati, child marriage and polytheism from Hinduism. For many of these organizations, engaging in social service therefore was an assertion of their religious and nationalist loyalties and a manifestation of their desire to 'uplift' their own masses.

Other religious and spiritual organizations that came up towards the end of the 19th and the early 20th century and gave social service a further fillip were the Ramakrishna Mission and Bharat Sevashram Sangha. Bharat Sevashram Sangha, which was founded in 1923 in Bengal, followed in the footsteps of Swami Vivekananda and immersed itself in social service (beginning with flood relief in Bengal) as one way of consolidating a militant Hindu group (Voix 2011, 210–211). From the mid-1940s and even after Independence, several other religious organizations also initiated work in India, primarily through disaster relief activities. Islamic organizations such as the Jamaat-e-Islami (established in 1941) actively participated in relief activities during famines, floods and riots (Hasan 1990, 57). Catholic Relief Services began working with a local Church in Bombay in 1946 to provide food to people affected by the Second World War. World Vision started work in 1958 in Kolkata while Caritas India began working in 1962. In the later years, another prominent Christian NGO named

[3] A detailed discussion on this is provided in the next chapter.

the Evangelical Fellowship of India Commission on Relief established their branch in India in 1978. What is important to acknowledge is the fact that although many of these organizations were strongly rooted in religious tradition, they were not necessarily sectarian or communal in their outlook.

A new wave of Hindu religious movements took birth in India from the 1950s and gathered momentum from the 1970s onwards, which also contributed to disaster relief activities. The Ananda Marg, Shri Saibaba Sansthan, the Chinmaya Mission, the International Society for Krishna Consciousness (aka, ISKCON), Mata Amritanandamayi Math and the Art of Living Foundation are a few of the most prominent organizations that emerged during this period. A common characteristic across all these religious movements was that they were/are all oriented towards the practice of *seva* or religiously motivated service to humanity. Moreover, all of these organizations thrive under the devotion and patronage of their huge number of supporters, drawn mainly from the middle classes of India and the Hindu diaspora community, the world over.

From the 1990s onwards with the onset of globalization, religious organizations or those commonly seen as promoting the interests of a particular religious community have been on the rise. In India, this is visible from the series of Foreign Contribution by Voluntary Associations' (FCRA) annual reports prepared by the Ministry of Home Affairs. From the decade of 2000s, in particular, the 'Top Fifteen Donor Association' and the 'Top Fifteen Recipient Associations' have repeatedly featured religious organizations such as World Vision, Mata Amritanandamayi Math, Caritas, BAPS Swaminarayan Sanstha, Believers Church, etc. (FCRA Annual Reports 2000–2012). This phenomenon has received a further boost with the acknowledgment of religious groups as legitimate actors in the development world (Narayan et al. 2000) due to a variety of reasons (Clarke 2006; Helland 2007).

Politico-Cultural Organizations

The early 20th century was a period of turmoil in India; the Indian National Movement was at its peak following the Partition of Bengal in 1905, the Swadeshi Andolan and the introduction of the Montague-Chelmsford reforms in 1919. It was in this backdrop that a distinct strain of movement developed that assumed the shape of Hindu nationalism. Represented mainly by a political body, the Hindu Mahasabha (1915) and a politico-cultural organization, the RSS, this movement gradually came to occupy an important space in the voluntary sector. Although these groups were not religious in nature, they served an important political function by consolidating Hindus as a *sangathan* on modern principles. Both Hindu Mahasabha and the RSS played an important role in providing aid to Hindu victims of the Calcutta killings and the Noakhali carnage in 1946 and to Hindu refugees fleeing from West Pakistan after the Partition in 1947. Humanitarian service provided to Hindus, especially during the Partition riots, came as an opportunity for massive cadre building that deepened the polarization on religious lines even further.

What is unique about 'politico-cultural' groups like the RSS is that unlike the religious organizations, they neither practice any liturgical rituals nor adhere to any Church-like ecclesiastical order. However, it would also be erroneous to club them as 'secular' voluntary groups, as their modes of mobilization are centred on the protection of the 'Hindu dharma' with frequent allusions (no matter how superficial) to traditions, customs and rituals of the Hindu religion. The political rise of Hindutva in Indian politics since the mid-1980s has immensely benefitted these groups. They are closely allied to the political affiliate of Hindutva (i.e., BJP) and therefore exercise considerable covert political power in states ruled by the BJP.

Moreover, these groups have, in the recent decades, largely benefitted from an upsurge of 'faith-based organizations' in the larger space of development, as discussed in the previous section. Given its peculiar positioning in terms of a quasi-political and cultural movement, the RSS offers an interesting case for examining its role in the voluntary sector. A detailed examination of the philosophy, practice and implications of this movement's model of service, is examined in the following chapters.

Conclusion

The space of humanitarianism is a complex stage where a variety of actors contest with each other to further their own agenda. Given that disasters are by their nature deeply contested and political phenomena, the enactment of relief and rehabilitation by different aid providers is a mere extension of this politicization. A historical account of the realm of disaster relief in India reveals that it is populated by a host of actors that may be broadly divided into the State and the non-State. The category of 'non-State' is rather fuzzy and includes every possible group ranging from small neighbourhood clubs to large international NGOs. For a systematic enquiry of their role, this chapter has provided a broad typology of the non-State actors by dividing them under five categories: secular groups, religious groups, politico-cultural groups, corporate and multilateral agencies. While there are considerable overlaps between these categories and problems with the compartmentalization of these groups into neat categories, this typology is helpful in charting out certain broad ideological boundaries that exist between these groups. In particular, the chapter has focused on the first three categories of organizations which are together generally referred to as the voluntary sector in India.

The partaking of a range of actors, each with their own distinctive ideology, belief system and agenda, gives rise to a complex interplay that often leads to long term and decisive impacts on the people affected by disasters. A detailed examination of the history of disaster relief in India indicates that at various points of time, both state and voluntary actors have manifested their ideological positions through their participation in relief. On certain occasions, the boundaries between the State and the 'non-State' are found to be blurred. While voluntary organizations often emerge to fill in the space offered by a non-performing State, more and more 'non-governmental' actors are found to be allying with and even operating under the shadow of the State. This phenomenon has important implications for the broader domain of service delivery and the specific context of disaster relief as it is gradually fostering a culture of political clientelism that only favours groups with certain specific political affiliations. What political objectives are met through the service activities of non-State actors? In what ways do they promote or legitimize political ideologies through their humanitarian work? Chapters 3, 4 and 5 together attempt to find answers to these questions through a detailed examination of one such organization—the RSS—which lies between the margins of the State and the non-State.

II

Unpacking a Homonym

Seva *and Its Multiple Meanings*

Even though the genesis of humanitarianism is often traced to religion, the domain of development, at least in the initial years, treated religion as an untouchable entity. There were a variety of reasons for the same, but the most important reason perhaps was that the carving out of a space for development was itself a product of secularization. And the political project of secularization entailed that religion was not only kept separate from the political space but also that it was circumscribed to the private sphere because of the certitude that 'religion cannot produce neutral truths or a neutral medium' (Skaria 2002, 960).[1] In the case of India, Mahajan and Jodhka (2010, 12) have argued that soon after Independence, religion's role in development was undermined as it was primarily seen as a divisive force, especially in the backdrop of the bloody Partition. The discourse of development during this period, they argue,

---

[1] This idea has been extensively discussed in the works of Talal Asad (1993, 2003).

revolved around material and technological advancement and democratic citizenship, which were not the primary concerns of religious institutions. Thus, despite their contribution to social reform, religious groups were not accorded an important status in the arena of development. The task of development was primarily seen as the state's responsibility. The other important reason for the marginalization of religious and cultural traditions is due to the fact that their understanding of welfare is perceived to be essentially paternalistic and charity-based, as opposed to a rights-based idea of welfare adopted by the secular practitioners of welfare. Erica Bornstein (2009, 623) alludes to this in her study on *dana* in New Delhi when she argues that in the context of social welfare, impulsive forms of *dana* threaten to 'disrupt the regulation of instrumentally rational giving as the logic of capitalism attempts to regulate the gift'.

In more recent times however, there has been a drastic change in the relationship between religion and development, in that, religion now has come to be recognized as a legitimate and important entity that can meaningfully contribute to development. Several analysts trace this trend to a new world order that emerged after the end of the Cold War. The growing popularity of multicultural theories, the growing power of the Christian Right in America and in later years, the terrorist attacks of 9/11 in American soil had made it clear that the category of religion in public life could not be ignored anymore. More specifically, a series of initiatives launched during the late 1990s under the leadership of Wolfensohn, then President of the World Bank, and George Carey, then Archbishop of Canterbury, to launch a dialogue between the Bank and religious leaders further bridged the gap between the worlds of the sacred and the profane. Despite this recognition of religion however, it has also been observed that the balance of power has always been unfairly tilted towards the secular end. Religion is welcome to contribute to humanitarianism as long as it adheres to the rules put forward by the secular. Development policy makers are often seen to be selectively choosing certain types of religious organizations which they think fit into their sanitized secular framework (Denuelin and Bano 2009; Haynes 2007). Therefore, we observe more and more cultural/religious groups constantly negotiating their identities and modus operandi to simultaneously emulate and resist the secular to 'fit in' to the rational world of humanitarianism. The assertion of an alternative episteme by these groups, however, can be understood only when we interpret religion in a more expansive form.

I argue that an analysis of religion's entanglement with development can be better appreciated if we attempt to locate religion in covert and less explicit forms. As Peterson (2012, 130) has argued, '[O]ne cannot only look for religion in its conventional hiding places, but must be open to finding it elsewhere as well'. As mentioned earlier, it is not only the RSS, but several other Hindu organizations in contemporary India and elsewhere that are increasingly using indigenous categories such as *dana* and *seva* to mobilize support. One frequently encounters these terms now in the names of NGOs, their newsletters, flyers, annual bulletins, fundraising banners and several other publicity documents. The intriguing puzzle that poses itself before us is what makes the idea of *seva* so strangely powerful that it continues to be valorized in a rational secular space? Is it because *seva* too has become secularized? Or has the secular world of development, through its constant negotiation with the sacred, transmuted into a hybrid entity now that engulfs the sacred and the secular and hence accords greater legitimacy to categories like *seva*? What is the larger worldview that structures and articulates this category and the associated politics around it? In what ways does it pose a conceptual challenge to secular liberal thought? How do Hindu organizations appropriate and re-enact the idea for their own benefit? What if we discard the secular–rational lens for a while and ask a different set of questions about *seva*? RSS ideologues often claim that the reason why their welfare activities are deeply inspired by *seva* is because the tradition of *seva* is as ancient as the Hindu religion itself and that the act of selfless giving has been ordained by Hindu scriptures since time immemorial. In the following section, I explore the genesis of *seva* from the perspective of trying to understand the specific religious, spiritual, social and intellectual traditions that have shaped its conceptualization at various points of time in history.

Dana

Although the category of *seva* became popular mostly during the Bhakti movement in the medieval times, its closest predecessor may be traced to the ancient Hindu institution of *dana*. Broadly, *dana* refers to the 'act of giving, bestowing, granting, yielding and prestation, irrespective of what is being given and when' (Thapar 2000, 522). All religious ceremonies in the Vedic times entailed an act of giving and this is evident from a vast body of texts on *dana* found in various Hindu scriptures and law books (Nath 1987). Gifts of various kinds and donors have been highly eulogized in the Rigveda (Kane 1974, 837). The Bhagavad Gita characterizes a pure gift or *dana* as that which is being offered through desireless action (*nishkām karma*) (Bornstein 2009, 624). *Dana* is also frequently linked to *punya* (spiritual merit), thus implying that the gift is never really unreciprocated. In the Laws of Manu, *dana* is the principal component for gaining merit in the kali age (Anderson 1998, 61). S. C. Banerjee (1999, 254) mentions that it is in the Puranas (e.g., Agni, Matsya, Linga, etc.) that '*dana* is regarded as conducive to very great merit; so much so that, at some places, it has been extolled as the sole merit-producing act in Kali Age'. He further adds that the Puranic society (3rd–6th century AD) witnessed the phenomenon of a great spurt of gifts to Brahmanas.

Dana however has never been a static institution. As Thapar (2000, 521) mentions, the earliest literary sources of *dana* (*Dana*-stutis in the Rigveda)[2] refer to the giving of gifts to priests and Brahmanas with an elaborate itemization of the objects considered appropriate for each occasion. The event for gifts was generally a successful battle, cattle raid or victory over or destruction of the enemy. *Dana* therefore was made not so much in the spirit of charity but as a symbol of success and investment for future returns (Thapar 2000). Kings who abided by dharma were expected to shower gifts to Brahmans and the whole of society from time to time. Non-Brahmanas were also eligible for *dana* as long as they were 'worthy' persons (Thapar 2000, 523). At a later stage, *dana* assumed the forms of *ista* and *purta* in the Anusasana-parvan of the Mahabharata (Thapar 2000, 529). While *ista* is that which is offered to Gods, *purta* denotes work for public welfare like excavating wells, tanks, building temples, distribution of food etc. The concept of *purta* is especially significant in understanding the transition from *dana* to *seva* especially in the context of 19th-century colonial India. Thus, *dana* extended to both individual gifting and community welfare.

Over time, the idea of *dana* became a fundamental feature of all religions that had their roots in Hinduism. Buddhists and Jains adopted Hindu views of *dana* as a part of their religion. There is mention of *abhay dana* (a gift of fearlessness) *supatra dana* (a gift to a worthy recipient) *anukampa dana* (a gift given out of compassion) *ucit dana* (a gift given out of duty) *kirti dana* (a gift given to earn fame in the Jain tradition) (Williams 1963, 149–166). Laidlaw (2000, 619) mentions that giving *dana* is the 'paradigmatic religious good deed (*punya*)', and Jains actively give alms to renouncers. Giving *dana* and performing *seva* are listed as important activities in Sikhism too. Frequent references to *dana* and *seva* are found in the Adi Granth, Dasma Granth and popular Sikh literature and proverbs. The importance of giving is evident through various

[2] The *Danastutis* (eulogy of gifts) in the Rigveda are hymns in praise of those who make generous and handsome gifts.

activities of the Sikhs such as the maintenance of communal kitchens (*langars*) in which people of all socio-economic backgrounds are freely fed (Widgery 1929, 282).

It is important to note, however, that *dana* and *seva* are conceptually different categories. In the Hindu scriptures, while *dana* usually denotes the donation of material gifts such as grains, land, cattle or even gold, *seva* usually refers to some form of service. However, *dana* also may take the form of intangible gifts such as *abhay dana* (the gift of fearlessness) or *vidya dana* (the gift of knowledge) (Heim 2004). Despite these differences, it is important to acknowledge that, as an ideal form of giving, *dana* and *seva* share certain resemblances. In its classical and spiritual essence, *dana* is a gift without expectation of return. A 'worthy vessel' or recipient of *dana* is one who is extremely reluctant to accept the gift (Copeman 2011, 1063). It is also important that *dana* is imbued with *sraddha* (reverence). Like in Islam and in Christianity, in Hinduism too, *gupt* (secret) giving is stated to be conducive to greater merit than an open one (Banerjee 1999, 254).

Evolution of *Seva*

The Bhakti Period

Juergensmeyer and McMahon (1998, 267) have argued that *seva* as a form of giving owes its origins to a development in Hinduism later than the Vedas and the Dharmashastras. They trace the institution of *seva* to the practice of giving time and offering menial duties for the maintenance of temple deities during the Bhakti movement in the medieval period. They further suggest that the difference between *seva* and *dana* was not only between material gifts and gifts of service, but that, in the Bhakti understanding, *seva* was more of a spontaneous act of love and devotion, devoid of any obligation. However, similar to *dana*, the reward for *seva* was karmic merit. Several religious reformist movements in medieval India led by leaders such as Kabir, Guru Nanak and Chaitanya propagated *seva* as the dominant form of religious devotion. *Seva* could be rendered to one's guru, to one's parents, God or humanity at large.

Surendranath Dasgupta (1991, 351) mentions that according to Vallabhacharya, who wrote the Tattvadīpa-prakāśa, the word 'bhakti' is composed of the root 'bhaj' meaning 'love' and suffix 'kti' which means 'service'. He further adds that generally, the root and suffix together form a complete meaning in which the meaning of the suffix is dominant. Thus bhakti means the action of *bhaj*, that is, service (*seva*). Vallabhacharya has been credited with an important place to *seva* as a way of realizing God through love. Around 1500 AD, Vallabhacharya is said to have founded Pustimarg, a Vaishnav sect, that advocated for *seva* through the medium of recital of songs, prostrating in front of the statue, collecting flowers, ornaments and clothes as a demonstration of love to lord Krishna (*Brill's Encyclopaedia of Hinduism*, 2012). A similar trend was also evident in Sikhism during the medieval Sant movement, when loving service to Sikh gurus was prescribed as a medium for attaining salvation. This act of serving gods and goddesses or one's guru (teacher) has been referred to as the vertical tradition of *seva* (*Brill's Encyclopaedia of Hinduism* 2012). In subsequent years, and most importantly during the colonial period, the vertical tradition gradually gave way to the horizontal tradition, that is, *seva* directed towards community welfare. Beckerlegge (2006, 9) has argued that several elements within the Bhakti tradition can be identified as responsible for bringing about an innovation in the ideas of social justice that impacted the notion of service. One of the first Hindu organizations to have popularized a horizontal tradition of *seva* was the Swaminarayan movement. Raymond Brady Williams (2001) mentions how the ascetics of the movement were organized by Sahajanand for 'works of social welfare' such as digging of wells and reservoirs, building and repairing roads and temples and opening up community kitchens in times of famines and other disasters. This trend was further promoted by Swami Akhandananda and Swami Vivekananda of the Ramakrishna Math and Mission, who are said to have been influenced by the Swaminarayan movement's involvement in public welfare. The following section discusses the specific circumstances in the colonial period that facilitated this transition.

Colonial Period

The idea and practice of *seva* of the medieval times underwent a paradigmatic shift by the 19th century under the influence of several factors, the most important of which was the advent of British colonial rule. The colonial rulers since the 19th century onwards gradually introduced colossal changes to the subcontinent, such as creating the infrastructure for better transport and communication facilities, the printing press and Christian missionary activities. One of the most important developments was that of the decennial census, which led to the emergence of what Sudipta Kaviraj (1997, 330–331) has described as 'enumerated communities'. This was also a period when the Indian subcontinent witnessed several outbreaks of famines and epidemics such as cholera, influenza and plague which provided an entry point to Christian missionaries to actively seek converts through social service. As Sanjay Sharma (2001, 185–187) argues, famines provided an opportunity to the British to reinforce the superiority of European values and principles by mocking at indigenous forms of charity and marginalized the indigenous relief measures and looked down upon them as 'mofussil charity'.

The native Indian population perceived the Christian missionaries and the British colonial power as conjoined threats to their indigenous culture and, in an effort to combat this, ended up adapting Western organizational models (Gold 1992; Zavos 2000). In the process, Hinduism, just like the other religious communities, underwent a drastic transformation and became 'unified' and 'homogenized' from being 'a juxtaposition of flexible religious sects' in the pre-colonial period (Thapar 1985). This process was further facilitated by what scholars have referred to as the active 'construction of Hinduism' by the British (Cohn 1996; King 1999). Driven by their own mercantilist ambitions and in order to establish a better grasp over the local laws and customs, the British busied themselves in codifying religion. However, in doing so, they were influenced primarily by the Judeo-Christian faith and the resultant outcome was the construction of a Hinduism that was Brahmanical and one that relied on antiquity and textual history.

Hindu reform and revivalist movements that were born during this period interestingly emulated the same Orientalist tendencies of trying to sanitize Hinduism and free it of all 'social evils' by invoking a golden Vedic past. An assertion of the Hindu identity was manifested through the formation of several groups as *sangathans* (creation of a devoted and efficient organization of patriotic men) revolving around *gurus* (spiritual leaders) who attempted to constitute a new community of believers of Hinduism, 'to query the role of the colonial state on one hand and its dominant religion, Christianity, on the other' (Patel 2010, 105). Patel (2010) further argues that the Hindu *sangathans* emulated two key things that they believed were the strengths of Christianity: the process of building a Church like congregation which were called missions and the tradition of providing social service. This was manifested in the increasing participation of Hindu *sangathans* in providing social services in the form of famine relief, providing facilities during *melas* (fairs), opening of hospitals, orphanages, schools and even universities.

A wider range of voluntary and religious groups were involved in providing famine relief between 1896 and 1901 than before; thus, reflecting the trend of a rapidly growing civil society in urban India during this time (Brewis 2010, 900). The performance of this service therefore went hand in hand with the political agenda of asserting an omnibus Hindu identity. While, at a social level, it was expected to reform Hinduism by getting rid of its ritualism; at a political level, it was aimed at establishing sovereignty through displacing the colonial rule (Patel 2010, 106). This formulation of *seva* was an important landmark as it was to have a profound influence on the philosophy of organizations such as the RSS which emerged in the early 20th century and advocated for a specific kind of cultural nationalism.

Seva *and* Shuddhi*: Arya Samaj*

One of the first Hindu organizations that adopted this kind of a nationalistic social service was the Arya Samaj, which became one of the earliest non-Christian non-State actors to have started a movement for famine relief in 1897 and extended this until 1900 (Sharma and Rai 1992). Since the early years of its establishment, the Arya Samaj became involved in starting orphanages, schools, social service activities, promoting the practice of monotheism in Hinduism and 're-converting' Hindus who had gone 'astray' through the performance of *shuddhi* (Hardiman 2007, 8). *Shuddhi* activities acquired a special significance in the backdrop of the decennial Census which provided numerical counts of different religious communities. After the Census of 1891 reported an increase in Christian converts of 410 per cent from the previous decade, Arya Samajists expanded their programme of *shuddhi* (Jones 1994, 101). The *seva* activities of Arya Samaj received a further fillip in the backdrop of a severe famine that hit the western India in 1900–1901. Christian missionaries emerged as the saviour by providing relief to millions of people: They started food for work programmes, distributed free cooked food, clothes and medicines and started orphanages in different parts of Gujarat. They also used the famine as an opportunity to speed up conversion activities so much so that the total number of converts in Kheda, which was the worst affected district, went up from 500 in 1899 to 25,000 in 1901, the latter comprising 4 per cent of the total population (Yagnik and Sheth 2005, 138). The converts were mockingly referred to by high caste Gujaratis as 'Chhapaniya Christians', that is, those who converted during the 'chhapania kal' or 'famine of fifty-six' (Yagnik and Sheth 2005). Alarmed by this mass conversion, the Arya Samaj reacted by sending several volunteers from Punjab to 'rescue' Hindu orphans from the missionary homes and geared up its *shuddhi* activities in Gujarat. According to Yagnik and Sheth (2005), these initiatives were well-received by an already threatened Hindu upper-caste population which felt that Europeans and Americans were sponsoring missionary activities to gain converts and that Hinduism was under danger through famine and cow slaughter.

Seva *as Organized Service: Swami Vivekananda*

A key figure who played a central role in vociferously espousing *seva* towards the late 19th century was Swami Vivekananda. For a whole generation of Bengali and even non-Bengali middle-class youth, Vivekananda has been, and continues to be, the symbol of a true nationalist, a patriotic hero who is credited with resurrecting Hinduism (through yoga and the tenets of Vedanta) into a world platform. His speech at the Parliament of the World's Religions in Chicago in 1893, where he addressed the audience as 'sisters and brothers of America', is often cited with pride in several Hindu households even today. His ideas on *seva* in particular have been appropriated and re-enacted by many contemporary Hindu organizations that claim to draw inspiration from him. In the subsequent sections, I elaborate further on how Vivekananda became a towering influence on the RSS and its affiliate bodies.

Swami Swahananda (2015, 3) mentions that Vivekananda is said to have displayed signs of his commitment to humanitarian service from a very early age. He recounts that there are several episodes of his childhood such as one where he nursed a sailor and took him to a doctor after he got seriously injured while trying to fix a trapeze for him and his friends. There is another popular story about how the young Vivekananda is said to have rescued a boy from being overrun by a horse carriage.

Vivekananda's ideas about service were based on the philosophy of Advaita Vedanta which believes in the unity of existence. His espousal of the idea of 'practical Vedanta', or service imbued with religiosity, not only entailed an ontological shift from the earlier tradition of *seva* (inspired by the Vaisnav tradition) but also provided tremendous impetus to its popularity. By service, Vivekananda implied not only ameliorative service but all kinds of social action for overall welfare. The major thrust of his philosophy is best captured in the idea of *'daridranarayana'* which meant that serving the poor is equivalent to serving God. Thus, although *seva* continued to entail a spiritual dimension, Vivekananda was instrumental in adding a social dynamic to it. Further, what becomes repeatedly evident in Vivekananda's writings is that the idea of service or doing good to the world is a liberating act for oneself and not the recipient of the service. In his own words,

It is not the receiver that is blessed, but it is the giver. Be thankful that you are allowed to exercise your power of benevolence and mercy in the world, and thus become pure and perfect. (Vivekananda 2013, 1:96)

Perhaps the most important aspect of Vivekananda's idea of service was his delineation of the idea of *'seva* sadhana' that aimed at the spiritual awakening of the *sevak* (the one who rendered *seva*). He was interested in the spiritual rejuvenation of the Hindus and firmly believed that a masculine Hindu force could be built through *seva* or service to humanity in times of crises. The *sevak* was expected to strengthen himself physically and spiritually in order to perform the duty of ameliorating the conditions of the downtrodden. He gave a battle cry to the Hindu youth in India to commit themselves to the cause of *seva* by plunging themselves into relief activities post famines and plagues that were common during that time. The following excerpt is one among many of his speeches where this sentiment is reflected:

> Don't you see why I am starting orphanages, famine-relief works, etc.? Don't you see how Sister Nivedita, a British lady, has learnt to serve Indians so well, by doing even menial work for them? And can't you, being Indians, similarly serve your own fellow-countrymen? Go, all of you, wherever there is an outbreak of plague or famine, or wherever the people are in distress, and mitigate their sufferings. At the most you may die in the attempt—what of that? How many like you are being born and dying like worms every day? What difference does that make to the world at large? Die you must, but have a great ideal to die for, and it is better to die with a great ideal in life. (Vivekananda 2013, 5:396)

Beckerlegge (1999) mentions that Vivekananda advocated for a form of *seva* that was hitherto unknown to Indians: that of providing organized service to humankind. The Ramakrishna Mission Association's first participation in famine relief and orphan care took place in 1897 in Murshidabad. Subsequently, the Ramakrishna Mission actively participated in providing relief following a series of famines towards the end of the century. A number of 'Homes of Service' were started in various places such as Varanasi, Kankhal, Haridwar, Allahabad and Vrindavan, which gradually evolved in their tasks from providing immediate relief to adopting long term rehabilitation programmes such as taking care of orphans (Beckerlegge 1999, 160). The relief and larger welfare actives of the Ramakrishna Mission during this period was characterized by modern principles such as the use of public appeals for fundraising and adoption of a novel form of accountability, which was different from traditional forms of charitable action (Beckerlegge 1999). In subsequent years, other Hindu organizations like the Bharat Sevashram Sangha, which was established by Guru Swami Pranavananda Maharaj in 1916, also adopted community welfare as an important plank of their activities.

Several analyses of Vivekananda's idea of service draw attention to its novelty and the ways in which it differed from the Western notions of philanthropy. Swami Swahananda (2015, 63–64), for instance, differentiates Vivekananda's *seva* from philanthropic ideals of humanism or charity. He argues that while, in humanism, 'man is the centre and society the circumference', Vivekananda's view of *seva* has 'its centre in man-God and its field of work is the whole of humanity'. According to Swahananda, the ideal of *'daridranarayana'* takes away the concealed feeling of condescension. Instead, it is imbued with reverence and humility.

Associational Culture in the Early 20th Century

The emergence of service organizations in the 19th and 20th centuries however did not happen in vacuum. Carey Watt (2005, 30) mentions that following a shift from ideas of Christian charity towards more worldly forms of service, in the 19th century, organized philanthropy and social service became very popular and this was manifested in the form of regional associations in the West which organized relief efforts after natural disasters and raised funds to establish schools, hospitals and orphanages. Many of these organizations such as the Red Cross formed in 1863 by Henri Dunant and the Boy Scout Movement became transnational in character. In India, the persistence of famines, plagues, missionary conversions and the increasing British intrusion into Hindu holy places all helped to prompt the establishment of social service associations (Watt 2005, 43).

Watt (2005, 13) is however quick to point out that although the idea of *seva* was to a large extent influenced by the colonial rule, it also drew on indigenous ideas and practices of humanitarian service that had existed since the pre-colonial times. In building this argument, he refutes the claim of the Scottish missionary J. N. Farquhar ([1915] 1998, 388) who had provocatively argued that the Indian philanthropic movement was primarily triggered by the service activities of Christian missionaries. Watt, on the contrary, points out that the social service and associational initiatives of Indian groups in the early 20th century drew on deep rooted Hindu 'living traditions' such as *dana, karmayoga, sannyas* (asceticism) and *brahmacharya* (celibacy) as well as more general Indian notions and practices connected to physical culture, health and manliness (Watt 2005, 14). He argues that these 'living traditions' underpinned social service efforts, active citizenship and a culture of association. The 'foreign' ideas of social service, charity and philanthropy were negotiated by these Hindu traditions creatively (Watt 2005, 65–96).

Beckerlegge (1999, 188) has similarly suggested that the influence of Western colonial modernity was only one of the many influences that impacted the growth of an Indian form of philanthropy. Like Watt, Beckerlegge (1999, 175) also draws attention to the larger sociopolitical context that led to the transformation of the nature of giving in the Indian context. He argues that although a reliance upon neo-Vedanta principles has lent a distinctive character to the Ramakrishna Movement's practice of service, there is an obvious similarity between the adoption of organized service by the Movement and the kind of voluntary social service that took shape in North America and Western Europe in the latter half of the 19th century. The emergence of this new form of service in the Western context, according to Beckerlegge, was an acknowledgment of the fact that the earlier style of service which was based primarily on the Christian ethos of charity has failed. Also, given newer complexities generated due to industrialization and technological advancements required a different scale and form of service and therefore the earlier forms of charity dependent upon the impulse and largesse of a few individuals was no longer tenable (Beckerlegge 1999, 176). Despite this shift in the forms of giving, the individual charities of kings and rich merchants in the form of donating land and villages to Brahmins and other communities also continued.

An interesting study on gift making and philanthropy in Surat by Douglas Haynes (1987) points out that although acts of religious charity were employed by Hindu and Jain merchants to enhance their reputation and status in society, many of them began to contribute generously to a number of public welfare activities such as donation for schools, hospitals, libraries, etc., from the late 19th century onwards. This diversification of charitable patterns according to Haynes was aimed at 'accommodating' Victorian values of social welfare and 'progress' to build good relationships with the British and their community members. In this context, a deliberate and strategic effort was made by the colonial rulers to reiterate the older notion of *vidyadana* to facilitate the transition from traditional charitable giving to suit modern educational needs. Involvement in public philanthropy by Hindu and Jain merchants however continued alongside their traditional customs of gift making to temples and rulers.

Despite the contribution of indigenous traditions, it must be acknowledged, however, that the missionary relief work in India did introduce an important shift in the nature of indigenous service, in that the process of relief now came to be organized increasingly around what Barnett and Stein (2012, 13) call 'principles of rationality', which are characteristic of the modern organization. In the Hindu tradition, as discussed in the previous section, service had always been more in the nature of personal charity, best captured through the idea of *dana–punya* (charity that leads to gain of spiritual merit). Even though indigenous methods of service had existed before, mostly in the form of disaster relief (operationalized during famines) when rulers distributed free grain, opened public grain stores to the people, remitted revenues, etc., these were still limited to individual kingdoms and territories. In a break from this tradition, the Hindu reform and revivalist organizations that emulated the Christian missionaries focused their energies in establishing parallel institutions of social service which were similar to that of the missionaries. They also adopted more 'secular' philanthropic practices such as subscription-based systematic fundraising, bookkeeping and other modes of accountability that added greater transparency and respectability to their service projects. Thus, indigenous practices of giving were metamorphosed to a more secular form of service which acquired popularity as *seva*.

Gandhi and Seva

In the 20th century, *seva* acquired a renewed potency in the hands of Gandhi. As someone who was opposed to the Western idea of secularism (that emphasized the separation between religion and politics), Gandhi firmly believed that religion not only provided a 'moral basis' to politics but all human activities. Similar to Vivekananda, Gandhi also perceived *seva* to be a means of reaching God and attaining moksha (liberation). *Seva* to fellow beings was a means of identifying with a larger community and transforming society into a just space (Jacobsen 2012). His nationalist mobilization therefore went hand in hand with his idea of service and was a means towards achieving Purna Swaraj (complete Independence). Gandhi reiterated the fact on several of his writings that the word 'swaraj' entailed self-rule and self-restraint, and not merely freedom from a colonial authority which 'independence' denoted.

His advocacy of volunteerism through the idea of 'constructive programme' provided a new dimension to the idea of *seva*. In his own words,

Readers, whether workers and volunteers or not, should definitely realize that the constructive programme is the truthful and non-violent way of winning Poorna Swaraj. Its wholesale fulfilment is complete Independence. Imagine all the forty millions of people busying themselves with the whole of the constructive programme which is designed to build up the nation from the very bottom upward. Can anybody dispute the proposition that it must mean complete Independence in every sense of the expression, including the ousting of foreign domination? (Gandhi 1941, 2)

Juergensmeyer and McMahon (1998, 268) have argued that other Gandhian ideas based on *dana* and *seva* include *bhoodan* (gift of land) which advocated voluntary surrender of land for impoverished farmers, *gramdan* (gift of a village), in which a whole village could give itself for cooperative use and *sarvodaya* (service to all) for an egalitarian and just society. They also claim that Gandhi's interpretation of *dana* and *seva* made it possible for all, including wealthy Indians to think of such forms of giving not just as 'gifts' that aimed at enhancing the giver's power but as philanthropy, which encapsulated the general welfare of all (Juergensmeyer and McMahon 1998). Gandhi's ideas of philanthropy retained some of the critical features of *dana* such as an insistence on the purity of the act, the correct attitude of the donor and the recipient and the benefit of the process for the ultimate betterment of the world. The religious and moral imperative to give in order to cleanse and purify oneself and acquire spiritual liberation in the process proved to have a decisive influence on several members of the Indian elite such as G. D. Birla who generously donated for all nationalist activities (Juergensmeyer and McMahon 1998, 271).

In this regard, Srivatsan (2006) brings a very interesting perspective to the political role played by *seva* in the early 20th-century India. He argues that *seva* was a political and paternalistic ethic that became foundational to the reform of Hindu practice, and it helped in consolidating Congress, caste Hindu hegemony during the 20th-century freedom movement. Drawing attention to the conventional understanding of *seva*, Srivatsan argues that in Brahmanical imagination, *seva* is usually associated with a menial task that is carried out by someone who is considered inferior to the recipient of service by way of caste or class. He claims however that the Hindu social reform movement and the nationalist movement deliberately orchestrated a reversal of roles between the *sevak* (the one who renders *seva*) and the recipient of *seva* for achieving political ends. He traces the journey of *seva* as advocated during different stages of the freedom struggle; the ways in which it was conceptualized by the social reform movements of the 19th century, the Servants of India Society, by Gandhi in his early ideas of constructive work; by Christian missionaries and by Nehru. Srivatsan demonstrates how, in each case, the concept of *seva* was creatively articulated to represent a particular interest group's position. He also critiques the Gandhian idea of *seva* because his normative conception of *seva* does not advocate for an annihilation of the caste order like Ambedkar, but focuses instead on making the 'fallen individual' a better moral being. He therefore calls upon the 'upper caste' to reverse their social roles with the Dalits and make the latter the recipient of *seva* as a way of retribution for the former's sins. On similar lines, Ajay Skaria (2002, 957) points out that in Gandhi, the equal was met with *mitrata* (friendship), the subordinate with *seva* (service) and the superior with *satyagraha* (civil disobedience).

Srivatsan's criticism is powerful and cannot be dismissed easily. It is reasonable to argue that the national movement and the period leading up to the early years after Independence were characterized by a deeply paternalistic understanding of welfare. Niraja Jayal in her influential book *Citizenship and its Discontents: An Indian History* has argued similarly that in the early decades after India's Independence, social citizenship was characterized by its 'unselfconscious adoption of a charity perspective on poverty' (2013, 169). However, Srivatsan's analysis falls short of acknowledging the altruistic and affectual aspects of *seva* which may have been one of the reasons for its receptivity among the masses.

Hindu Nationalism: The Early Years

The early 20th century ushered in a new phase in the Indian national movement. Politically, this period was highly animated as the dream of Independence seemed to be realistic now and negotiations between the Indian National Congress and the colonial government had heightened. This was also a time when Gandhi's efforts at uniting the masses across caste and religious lines were met with fierce resistance from several quarters but mostly the conservative Hindu sections. At the same time, the religious divide between the Hindus and the Muslims started brewing in the backdrop of several events such as the enactment of the Morley-Minto reforms of 1909 which introduced separate electorates on religious lines, the Montague-Chelmsford reforms that reinforced religious representation, the perceived failure of Gandhi's Non-Cooperation Movement and religio-militant mobilizations such as the *shuddhi* and *tabligh* (propagation of Islam) led by certain Hindu and Muslim organizations, respectively. Hindu consolidation was expressed through the political symbolism of *yatras* (processions) and the public celebration of Hindu festivals such as Ganesh Chaturthi, which had so far been a private affair. Subsequently, communal riots between Hindus and Muslims broke out more frequently than before and acquired a scale and intensity that was hitherto unknown.

It was in this backdrop that the concept of *Hindutva* (Hinduness) as an idea was formally codified for the first time in 1923, when V. D. Savarkar in his book *Hindutva: Who is a Hindu?* Lay down three clear criteria for confirming the Hindutva of a person: geographical, racial and cultural. The 'geographical' factor implied that a Hindu is someone who lives in the land beyond the Indus, between the Himalayas and the Indian Ocean; the 'racial' implied that all Hindus have in their veins the blood of the 'Vedic fathers', that is, the Aryans; and the 'cultural' was defined by a common allegiance to shared rituals, ceremonies and rites that 'makes a land a Holyland'. Dr K. B.

Hedgewar, an admirer of Savarkar, who subscribed to this definition of a Hindu, founded the RSS in 1925 to espouse the idea of building a corporate and unified Hindu Rashtra. Hedgewar believed that the Hindus were a mighty and prosperous nation long before recorded history and that the only reason they had 'succumbed' to a handful of Muslims and then again to a handful of British merchants was because they lacked national consciousness and cohesion. Hedgewar was perhaps the first leader during this period to seriously shape the idea of *seva* as a means for constructing the Hindu Rashtra. For Gandhi and the Indian National Congress largely, nationalism was essentially a civic idea and transcended language, religion, caste and gender barriers. In this sense, as Ramachandra Guha (2007) has persuasively argued, India was indeed an 'unnatural nation', as there was no similar counterpart in the Western Europe where people of such wide diversities had come together to claim a nation. For Hedgewar, the imagination of the nation was diametrically opposite. Deeply inspired by Moonjee, who was an admirer of Musoolini's fascist military academies, Hedgewar was convinced that the physical and mental training of the *swayamsevaks* was the key to India's military regeneration and the only way to build a strong nation. *Seva* played a key role in this imagination.

An examination of the RSS literature and the speeches of its *swayamsevaks* reveal that they are frequently marked by a reference to the work and life of Swami Vivekananda. One also frequently encounters phrases such as *'daridranarayana'* in the pamphlets, bulletins and newsletters of RSS affiliates dedicated to *seva*. Following from Vivekananda, the RSS also claims that the primary purpose of rendering service is to make the beneficiary self-reliant. An excerpt from *Sewa Sadhana*, a Sewa Bharati publication, reads as follows:

> Through these projects an effort is made to make the beneficiary self-reliant on the one hand while on the other hand a feeling is injected into the mind and heart of the service providers that by serving these needy and deprived brethren

of the society they are not doing anything special but they are worshipping the God in the form of these downtrodden, wretched and deprived people. (*Sewa Sadhana* 2012, 12)

Vivekananda's popularity within the RSS has a strong legacy. Hedgewar was attracted by Vivekananda's ideas of creating a trained cadre of nationalist sanyasis who would be dedicated towards rendering service for the poor and underprivileged sections of society. This eventually led him to establish the *shakha*, where young men (known as *swayamsevaks*) were imparted with physical and moral training in order to resurrect the 'Hindu Rashtra'. From his early life, Hedgewar actively participated in social work. In August 1913, Hedgewar volunteered in the relief work organized by the Ramakrishna Mission to combat severe floods in the Burdwan district of Bengal.

An account of Hedgewar's service during the floods reads as follows:

The flood in 1913 was unprecedented and had uprooted the entire population of the Vardhaman district on the western bank of the river … Keshavrao joined the relief party sent forth by the Ramakrishna Mission … Their only mode of transport was by boats. In many places, one had also to wade through waist-deep water. Carrying beaten rice and other food articles for the needy, one had to negotiate long distances in damp and mire. (Deshpande and Ramaswamy [1981] 2015, 19)

Deshpande and Ramaswamy ([1981] 2015, 20) highlight that right on the 'heels of the flood' there was a cholera break out where Hedgewar was again found to be attending to the sick and providing medical care until 1:00 or 2:00 AM in the morning for days at a stretch. They also mention that during his six-year stay in Kolkata, Hedgewar provided public service on several different occasions, the most notable being the Gangasagar Mela which was most 'severely ravaged by cholera' (Deshpande and Ramaswamy [1981] 2015). Beckerlegge (2003, 41) mentions that Hedgewar 'associated the conditions of poverty, ignorance, disease, and oppression that afflicted Hindus as much with an inner condition as with external structural factors relating to British rule and its response to the Hindu and Muslim dimensions of the independence movement'. In this respect, says Beckerlegge (2003), Hedgewar was similar to Swami Vivekananda, although Hedgewar 'defined this inner condition in terms of apathy or 'emasculation' rather than spiritual impoverishment'.

Golwalkar's thoughts on *seva* and the profound influence of Swami Vivekananda and his guru Ramakrishna are revealed in the following excerpt from his *Bunch of Thoughts*:

> Such is the true servant of society who seeks not anything in return for himself but finds the joy of fulfilment in having suffered and sacrificed for the good of society ([1966] 2014, 436).

While there are criticisms galore about Golwalkar's hatred towards Muslims, Christians and communists, whom he identified as the three biggest internal threats to the Indian nation, interestingly in the same book, he decries any form of service that is discriminatory. In his words,

> This supreme vision of Godhead in society is the very core of our concept of 'nation' and has permeated our thinking and given rise to various unique concepts of our cultural heritage. That vision inspires us to look upon every individual; of our society as part of that Divine Whole. All individuals are therefore equally sacred and worthy of our service. Therefore any sense of discrimination among them is reprehensible. Thus, in our culture, the spirit of social service has been sublimated into worship of God. ([1966] 2014, 37)

In 1954, Golwalkar provided a philosophical foundation to the RSS's work by delineating the tenets of 'positive Hinduism' to a gathering of 300 *pracharaks* from all over India (Andersen and Damle 1987, 111). Golwalkar argued that contrary to the

Western ideals such as individualism and materialism, the philosophy of 'positive Hinduism' gives precedence to duty towards the community. Reiterating his belief in the idea that a person worships God through rendering service to society, Golwalkar asked his *pracharaks* to imbibe the same spirit (Andersen and Damle 1987). While it has been widely acknowledged that Vivekananda and his ideas of *seva* profoundly impacted the RSS, it needs to be noted that some scholars have alleged that the RSS and the larger Sangh Parivar have 'appropriated' Vivekananda's legacy of service and projected him as a hero of resurgent Hindu nationalism for the former's own political agenda (Beckerlegge 2003; Kanungo 2013). While there is a grain of truth in these arguments, it may be useful to exercise restraint in the usage of terms such as 'appropriation' which express a sense of dishonesty. As is evident from this chapter, there has been no static definition of *seva* that people across time have universally subscribed to. It has constantly been re-enacted and shaped in dynamic forms so much so that one even wonders if there is an 'essential core' that has remained unchanged.

Conclusion

What becomes evident from the above discussion is that the idea and practice of *seva* has been ever changing. It acquired popularity as a distinct category during the Bhakti movement of the medieval times, although the genesis of its essence can be traced to the ancient concept of *dana*. *Seva* underwent a paradigmatic shift in the 19th- and the early 20th-century colonial India when it was transformed from an individualized and personal act to an act of secular public welfare. The chief factors which influenced this shift were the twin processes of colonialism and the proselytizing activities of Christian missionaries which denigrated the social 'evils' of Hinduism and actively sought converts from traditionally oppressed lower caste Hindus. Several Hindu reformist and revivalist organizations attempted to counter these problems by taking recourse to *sangathan* and *seva*, conceptualized as a form of service with the distinct aim of uplifting the downtrodden Hindu masses and liberating them from colonial rule. *Seva* thus contributed towards building a nascent form of nationalism. An important influence in this regard was that of Swami Vivekananda for whom service to the motherland became a medium of spiritual salvation. *Seva* was also creatively deployed by Mahatma Gandhi during the course of the national movement in order to drive the agenda of 'Purna Swaraj'.

Seva acquired a new political potency during the late 19th and early 20th century in the works of Hindu Mahasabha and the RSS. It is in this context that the influence of *seva* on the RSS needs to be situated. The RSS adopted the tradition of service from its predecessor Hindu organizations, to consolidate the Hindu community and in the course of its evolution, used it as a strategy to firm up the boundaries between the Hindus and the two primary 'enemies', Muslims and Christians. The following chapter undertakes a detailed analysis of the ways in which *seva* is conceptualized and deployed as a practice by the RSS and its affiliates.

Thus, the same *seva* may have different motivations in different circumstances: religious (in Bhakti tradition), moral (*seva* to parents and guru) and instrumental (as a nationalist ethic). Despite several new meanings that *seva* acquired in the course of its evolution, there is one feature that sets it apart from all other kinds of social action and that is the idea of 'selflessness'. As Maya Warrier (2005, 59) insists, despite its myriad forms and manifestations, in its 'ideal-type', *seva* is service that is performed 'impersonally and selflessly' without any expectations of 'reciprocity, reward, protection or patronage'. Moreover, the impulse of *seva* lies in its spontaneity, as opposed to more legal rational forms of giving. It is this imagination of *seva* that pervades the moral imagination of people at large and hence, it continues to be so powerful in drawing funds and human resources in the field of humanitarianism.

III

'Nation Building' through *Seva*

Conceptualization of *Seva* in the RSS

The Rashtriya Sewa Bharati is of the opinion that whosoever does the sewa work irrespective of his religious or other beliefs and associations, it should be for the benefit of the Indian people and India. These activities should arouse the strong feeling of national unity and swadeshi in the hearts of the people and it should do good to India and help in rebuilding of the nation. Sewa is a medium for this ultimate goal. Each one should perform sewa in this manner arousing the intense love for motherland which we say is Hindutva .... We want that all those engaged in sewa work should develop an attitude to work with one mind, one voice and one thought to make India a mighty nation in the world. We just want this.

—*Sewa Sadhana* (2012, 13)

The passage quoted above is an excerpt taken from an interview of Sitaram Kedilaya, former Akhil Bharatiya Sewa Pramukh and is one example from a host of writings and speeches of RSS leadership that frequently extol and propagate the practice of *seva*. The frequent allusion to *seva* in the RSS literature is in many ways an indication of the significant space it occupies in the imagination of the Parivar. An important aim of this chapter therefore is to interrogate the conceptualization and nature of *seva* in the RSS and the multiple different contexts in which it is deployed such as in the realm of education, health, livelihood generation and cultural regeneration. Another important purpose of this chapter is to explore the development of social welfare as a political strategy within the RSS and its specific adaptations to changing sociopolitical conditions that influenced the institutional trajectory of the organization. The chapter also outlines the organizational structure and support systems for implementing *seva* and discusses the work of a few of its key affiliates. More importantly, the chapter attempts to understand the ways in which *seva* works as a common idiom that binds the members of the Sangh together as a single collective.

The above epigraph is a useful entry point into this analysis as it unequivocally declares that *seva* is a medium for arousing the feeling of Hindutva. It provides us with an important pointer towards understanding the distinct and unambiguous nature of the RSS's service activities. *Seva*, like all other institutions within the Parivar, is not an end in itself, but a means to an end, that of creating a strong Hindu Rashtra, through the awakening of Hindutva. The above quotation is also indicative of an injunction to 'other' service organizations of different religions or ideologies that their activities too should be similarly aligned. The Parivar is also clear that the ultimate purpose of offering *seva* is the promotion of character building and discipline. In the words of Seshadri (2012, 160),

> In the Sangh's scheme of regeneration and consolidation of Hindu society, cultivating character and moral values is given a pride of place. Without this ennobling aspect of samskar, the other arenas of transformation like social harmony, social justice and improvement in living conditions are bound to remain unwholesome and often bereft of real benefit. A major focus of the man-making process of Sangh is on this aspect of character-moulding.

One may legitimately argue though that that there is no novelty to this argument and anyone who studies the RSS can gauge this almost intuitively, even without examining the speeches and the writings of its leaders. What remains under-analysed however are the ways in which this concept of *seva* is constructed as a distinctive category from other forms of giving. In the RSS tradition, *seva* has been eulogized and considered as one of the central pillars of the Sangh's work. Certain essential features of *seva* associated with notions of non-reciprocity, spiritual salvation and community welfare are constantly invoked in the RSS imagination of *seva*. Speaking of non-reciprocity, Eknath Ranade (2011, 89–95), an eminent RSS leader and the founder of Vivekananda Kendra, mentions in the vocabulary of *seva sangathan* that there is no word called *'pratifal'* (loosely translated as 'return). He stresses that such is the commitment and passion of the members of the Sangh that even after sacrificing everything one has for the service of others, there is no expectation of any gain in return. Although it may seem that an act of service makes the recipient a gainer in the process, it is however the donor who gains more, as *seva* is always rendered for spiritual contentment.

What is also observable in the Sangh's conceptualization of *seva* is a distinct tendency to extricate its meaning from more commonplace terms such as 'service', 'philanthropy' or 'charity'. In a *baudhik* delivered on the occasion of Vijayadashami in New Jersey, Shyam Parande (coordinator of Sewa International) emphasizes that *'seva* has no equivalent word in English just as there is no equivalent word for Dharma and Karma' (HSS n.d.). He further mentions that *seva* is neither charity nor service and that 'it goes way beyond that'. Parande explains that Hindus by birth incur four *runas* (debts): *Matru Runa*—debt to one's mother; *Pitru Runa*—debt to one's father and your ancestors; *Rishi Runa*—debt to sages; and finally, *Samaj Runa*—debt to one's society. *Seva*, he suggests is the fulfilment of this last *runa*. In another context, Parande remarks that *seva* is the manifestation of divine energy and that 'effortless service attained or offered provides a joy rightly expressed in Indian languages as *sat-chit-aanand'* (Parande 2012, 19).

The emphasis on the distinctive nature of *seva*, as opposed to other kinds of giving, needs to be understood in the larger context of attempting to resist the hegemony of the Western (largely Christian) secular dominant knowledge systems which find manifestation in expressions like 'charity' and 'philanthropy'. Building on the nationalistic sentiments of colonial India, the RSS today continues to assert the superiority of Indian (Hindu) values and institutions that contribute to its larger rhetoric of Hindutva. Post-colonial scholars studying India have however argued that this valorization of indigeneity is trapped within the very Western secular framework that it tries to resist. As Ashish Nandy (1998) and Partha Chatterjee (1998) have suggested, the project of Hindu nationalism is essentially 'modernist' and therefore perfectly comfortable with rational secularism. At the cost of sounding provocative here, I want to submit that despite the post-modern intellectualists' attempt to distance themselves from the Hindutva brigade, there are uncanny similarities between the two. In a fascinating essay, Meera Nanda (2004) draws attention to these similarities, albeit to make a different argument. She mentions that Hindutva ideologues often claim that the 'decolonisation of the Hindu mind' requires 'understanding science through Hindu categories'. A similar line of argument is evident when post-colonial scholars argue that the claim of universalism of science is nothing but a cover for Western dominance and that actual liberation is possible only through a resuscitation of authentic traditions of India. Irrespective of its source, this is an interesting intellectual position as it lies at the heart of questions of identity and nationalism. In arguing that *seva* is essentially an 'indigenous' institution, the RSS facilitates a huge ontological shift with regard to its perception as a superior form of ('selfless') giving, in the imagination of common people. It is an invocation of this capacious understanding of *seva*, which is set apart from 'modern', 'Western' ideas of philanthropy that contributes towards making it so attractive to contemporary donors and recipients.

Following from the narrative described above, another important aspect of *seva* that the RSS emphasizes on is the quality of being non-sectarian. This invocation becomes particularly significant in the face of several criticisms against the Sangh that label it as 'anti-minority' and 'anti-secular'. An excerpt of a letter (*Sewa Sadhana* 2007, 7) written by Golwalkar on 14 January 1970 to K. Suryanarayan Rao, organizing secretary of the Karnataka Provincial Conference of VHP, held in Udupi in December 1969, reads as follows:

> In this service no distinction should be made between man and man. We have to serve all, be he a Christian or a Muslim or a human being of any other persuasion: for, calamities, distress and misfortunes make no such distinction, but afflict all alike.

The literature of RSS highlights several illustrations of service offered to non-Hindus. One story in particular which is often narrated by *swayamsevaks* to establish their secular credentials is that of the humanitarian work undertaken by the organization after the Charkhi Dadri air-crash. This tragedy was caused by a mid-air collision of two aircrafts in November 1996 over the village of Charkhi Dadri, near New Delhi. The aircrafts involved were a Saudi Arabian Airlines and a Kazakhstan Airlines and the crash killed all 349 people on board both the flights. A report in the *Organiser* (1996, 11) claims that RSS *swayamsevaks* and local people were among the first to reach the spot. An excerpt of the story reads as follows:

> A few minutes after the disaster it became clear that most of the victims belonged to the minority Muslim community, but *swayamsevaks*, as is their training and tradition and also their age-old samskaras, did not discriminate among the dead. The strictly humanistic attitude of the *swayamsevaks* deeply impressed the minority community.

The same issue of the *Organiser* carries an appreciative account by Dr Zafarul Islam Khan, the Editor of Muslim and Arab Perspectives, on the work of the *swayamsevaks* in the Charkhi Dadri incident. An excerpt of this account reads as follows:

> During the recent tragic disaster of two aircrafts near Charkhi Dadri, the RSS people played a remarkable role despite the fact that the majority of the victims were Muslims. I saw and experienced this myself.... The RSS people at the civil hospital in Dadri were disciplined and dedicated and rendered all possible services to the relatives of the victims as well as to the media people, while except for a small presence of Jamaat-e-Islami Hind workers, there was no government or Muslim workers to take care of the relatives of the victims or the visitors.... I have been an open critic of the RSS for its anti-Muslim policies many of which are simply based on misunderstandings. It is a pity that such a dedicated group should be guided by negative attitudes...

The above account serves three purposes: First, it is a demonstration of the non-sectarian nature of the RSS; second, it seeks to illustrate the appreciation from the nemesis itself, a Muslim; and third, it demonstrates how the organization is even a step ahead of 'other' groups such as Jamaat-e-Islami Hind workers in providing service to Muslim victims. Despite these assertions, however, one does come across reports alleging that the RSS often discriminates against non-Hindus in providing relief. A recent story (Reghunath 2014) based on Swami Aseemanand of VKA, for example, highlights how the Swami himself confessed to have refused aid to a Christian woman in Andaman after the 2004 Tsunami.

It may be reasonable to infer from the above discussion that the provision of non-discriminatory *seva* is part of a strategic exercise to demonstrate the secular ethos of the Sangh in order to gain popularity. However, as the subsequent chapters will show, a deeper engagement with numerous *swayamsevaks* and volunteers of the RSS reveal that a large section of these people engage in *seva* because they truly feel that they are doing good work to make a better society and a better nation. It is only by acknowledging the authenticity of their belief systems that we can arrive at a fuller understanding of the motivations of service. However, this particular worldview about *seva* was not constructed by any one leader of the Sangh, nor was it inspired by a single text. As the following section will show, *seva* evolved in the RSS as a dynamic vector, drawing to itself myriad groups of people who may otherwise have nothing in common. It imparts a sense of common purpose and identity to people and helps them engage with each other as members of the same community. It also enables to bind various affiliates of the Parivar together.

Evolution of *Seva* in the Sangh: Role of Hedgewar

As mentioned in the previous chapter, unlike its previous avatars, *seva* assumed a new formulation under the aegis of the RSS which was formed in 1925. Hedgewar made humble beginnings by deploying *swayamsevaks* for providing service to Hindus during public festivals and celebrations, especially in those where there was a likelihood of confrontation with the Muslims. As an RSS account reveals,

> In 1925, an enquiry committee consisting of Motilal Nehru, Moulana Azad and Dr. Mohamed came to Nagpur to settle the 'communal issue'. It put forward a mutually agreed formula, as to when and where the music could be played before the mosques and when and where it was to be stopped. But so far as the Muslims were concerned the agreement remained only on paper. They continued to become more and more aggressive. Hindu ladies proceeding for religious festivities like Haritalika became subject to Muslim mischief. However, Doctorji promptly deputed batches of *Swayamsevaks* to such

places and the women devotees could thereafter breathe a sigh of relief. (Deshpande and Ramaswamy [1981] 2015, 88)

The RSS created positive visibility when in 1926 the young *swayamsevaks* monitored a local celebration of Ram Navami and helped establish orderliness. It was during this occasion that Hedgewar chose a name and a uniform for his new organization: Rashtriya Swayamsevak Sangh, which literally means 'a national organization of (self-motivated) volunteers', who wore white shirts, khaki shorts and black khaki caps (Andersen and Damle 1987, 35).[1] In doing so, Hedgewar's purpose was 'to demonstrate the value of discipline both to the volunteers and to the general public' (Andersen and Damle 1987): A year later in 1927, when communal riots erupted in Nagpur, another significant act of service by the RSS that attracted the attention of the public was when Anna Sohani, an associate of Hedgewar, organized several *swayamsevaks* into 16 squads to protect Hindus (Andersen and Damle 1987, 36).

Fortifying *Seva*: Golwalkar

In 1946, just a year before the Partition, several communal riots broke out between the Hindus and the Muslims in Bengal and north-western India. The RSS members emerged as 'messiahs' for the Hindus during this time. The Partition of the Indian sub-continent into two countries on religious lines in 1947 and the communal mayhem that followed provided the RSS with a fertile ground for communal mobilization. Under Golwalkar's leadership, the Sangh played a major role in organizing relief and protection for the Hindu refugees who were fleeing from East and West Pakistan. During this time, the RSS formed several relief committees across Punjab and Bengal, such as the Hindu Sahayata Samiti, Punjab Relief Committee and the

[1] Basu et al. (1993) have argued that the RSS uniform was inspired by the British Indian police and army. On 11 October 2016, the RSS changed its uniform from khaki shorts to brown trousers.

Bastuhara Sahayata Samiti, which distributed food, clothes and blankets in refugee camps to the Hindu refugees and even provided protection to Hindu families from Muslim attacks. This demonstration of 'dedication, sacrifice and organizational capacity' during the riots, enabled the RSS to 'establish its image as the 'saviour of Hindus' and helped it to expand its influence in Punjab, Jammu and Kashmir, Delhi and other parts of North India (Kanungo 2003, 55). The rescue operations left several beneficiaries convinced that the RSS was genuinely concerned about the welfare of the Hindus. A large number of these refugees were businessmen who prospered in the new country and who were indebted to the RSS; over a period of time, they became a reliable source of funding for the organization (Andersen and Damle 1987, 49).

This positive image of the RSS however received a severe blow after the assassination of Mahatma Gandhi in 1948 by Nathuram Godse, an ex-member of the Sangh. The RSS was banned by the government of India and several of its leaders were arrested. Consequently, all its public activities came to a standstill. Following a series of negotiations between senior leaders in the RSS such as Eknath Ranade and Golwalkar and Patel and Nehru in the central government, the ban on the RSS was lifted in July 1949, on the condition that the organization adopt a written constitution, maintain transparency in its activities and confine itself only to doing cultural work. The organization therefore maintained a low profile and the rapid expansion of *shakha* activities that had acquired momentum in refugee camps in northern India was briefly stalled. It was at this stage that Golwalkar 'reoriented the RSS by playing down its paramilitary past' and charted out a new form of social involvement for his organization (Beckerlegge 2003, 49). Between 1949 and 1954, the RSS participated in a range of varied social movements such as the *bhoodan* movement of Vinoba Bhave and the Satyagraha movement to liberate the Portuguese colonies of Dadra and Nagar Haveli while also continuing to offer relief after riots and disasters. After providing refuge to Hindus fleeing from East Pakistan in 1949–1950, in 1950 again, RSS *swayamse-vaks* participated in providing relief after the Assam earthquake. The situation was worsened by heavy floods in Brahmaputra River and its tributaries like the Dihing River. Many villages were completely washed away and crops were destroyed. The RSS took this opportunity to become actively involved in relief work in the region. The Marwari Relief Society of Calcutta (a close associate of the RSS) sent some workers for relief work. The Assam branch of the RSS organized the Assam Bhukamp Pidit Sahayta Samiti (the Assam earthquake sufferers relief society) and distributed food, clothes and provided shelter to several victims of the earthquake. Naturally, this elicited a lot of popularity from the local people (Madhukar Limaye, Personal Interview June 2006). The organization was also at the forefront of providing humanitarian relief after the Punjab Floods in 1955, the Tamil Nadu cyclone in 1955, the Anjar earthquake in 1956, the Bihar Famine of 1966, the Andhra Cyclone of 1977, the Latur earthquake of 1993 and several other subsequent disasters.

Jaffrelot (1996, 261) suggests that the social welfare strategy of the RSS also helped it find common ground with new political allies. He cites the example of Jayaprakash Narayan joining hands with the RSS in 1967 to collaboratively provide relief to drought victims in Bihar. He explains that one of the reasons for the Hindu nationalists to formally join the JP Movement in 1974 was because both the parties regarded 'social reform as a priority in comparison with work within the political arena'. The participation of the RSS in these various relief activities brought it in direct contact with a large number of people who were introduced to the concept of Hindu nationalism through either RSS *shakha* activities, camps or community discussions.

Institutionalizing *Seva* in a Changing Sociopolitical Context

The tradition of *seva* however did not remain limited to providing emergency relief alone, but from the late 1950s onwards, gradually extended towards more institutionalized welfare in the field of education, health and rural development. *Sarsanghchalak* Golwalkar particularly sought to consolidate the support of hitherto marginalized groups such as the tribals and the Dalits and certain affiliates such as VKA and Sewa Bharati were created especially to provide targeted service to these communities. Apart from consolidating these groups under the omnibus Hindu identity, *seva* activities of these affiliates performed specific political functions such as offering a counter to Christian proselytizing activities in the tribal areas, assimilating Dalits, re-educating and indoctrinating children through a parallel form of education (Sundar 2004) and inculcating values of national awareness and 'character building' to create a Pan-Hindu unity.

By this time, the RSS had gradually begun to spread its influence in various realms of civil society, including the political. The Rashtra Sevika Samiti, the women's counterpart to the RSS, was established in 1936. In 1948, the students' wing of the RSS, the Akhil Bharatiya Vidyarthi Parishad (ABVP) was launched under the leadership of Balraj Madhok, an RSS activist. The year 1951 witnessed the establishment of Bharatiya Jana Sangh (BJS), the political affiliate of the RSS. In 1952, the foundation of the education wing, Vidya Bharati was laid when the first Saraswati Shishu Mandir was established in Gorakhpur, Uttar Pradesh. In the same year, VKA was also established in Jashpur, Chhattisgarh. BMS, a trade union, was established in 1955 under the leadership of D. P. Thengadi, a Maharashtrian *pracharak*. Although not all of these organizations were launched to provide *seva*, their very presence in different realms of society provided a solid foundation to the activities of the RSS.

The breakdown of the Congress hegemony from the mid-1960s onwards facilitated the political rise of the Sangh Parivar as the BJS increased its vote share in the 1962 elections from 4 to 14. It was in this backdrop that the RSS launched one of its most important, and as Manjari Katju (2003, 2) aptly calls one of its 'noisiest' affiliates, the VHP, under the leadership of a senior *pracharak* named Shiv Shankar Apte. The establishment of the VHP was reminiscent of the 19th-century attempts of Hindutva to shape Hinduism into an 'organized creed' (Nandy et al. 1995, 87). The VHP was a religious conglomerate of *sadhus*, created with an aim to 'endow Hinduism with a church-like ecclesiastical apparatus to counter Christian proselyte activities (Jaffrelot 2005, 9). When VHP was formed in 1964, Dadasaheb Apte found an ally in Mysore Maharaja Sri Jayachamaraja Wadiyar who agreed to lead the Parishad as one of its Conveners (Rai n.d.). The VHP held its third national executive meeting on 27–28 May 1965 in the royal palace of the Mysore Maharaja. The head of the Pejavwara Matha in Udupi, Teertha Swami, a disciple of the second RSS *sarsanghchalak* Golwalkar, was another founder member of the VHP from this region, who had an influential role to play in promoting Hindutva in coastal Karnataka in the early years (Mondal 2015). Teertha Swami was associated with the Ram Janmabhoomi Movement right from the beginning. According to RSS veteran leader M. G. Vaidya, approval for allowing reconversion (popularly known as 'gharwapsi') in Hinduism was first given in Sri Krishna Math, Udupi, Karnataka in 1969, when shankaracharyas, mahants and several Hindu saints held a gathering (Bharata Bharati 2014). As an ardent supporter of the VHP, his Matha collaborated on several social welfare activities with the VHP, especially in the realm of education and health for poor tribals.

Since its inception, one of the primary agendas of the VHP has therefore been to counter the influence of Christian missionaries, particularly in states such as Assam, Nagaland and Odisha by setting up a parallel system of social welfare in the form of schools, health centres, etc. This agenda was akin to what Jaffrelot (1996, 50) has described, as a process of 'stigmatization and emulation' that has been a characteristic feature of Hindu organizations since the late 19th century. The VHP adopted an activist line from the early 1970s, when it expanded its schools, balwadis, yogashramas, student hostels and child *samskara* centres to Delhi, Karnataka, Andhra Pradesh, Madhya Pradesh, Tamil Nadu, Maharashtra, Kerala, Uttar Pradesh and Bihar. It was also successful in establishing a branch in Assam as early as 1966. Similar to the Christian tradition, this social welfare work was carried out locally by converting temples into centres of social work and relief (Hansen 1999, 103). Many existing trusts were 'activated and reorganized' in order to carry out social work in slums and rural areas (Hansen 1999).

Two other important affiliates of the Sangh Parivar that were established in 1972 were the Vivekananda Kendra and the Deendayal Research Institute. The Vivekananda Kendra initiated a sustained effort at social welfare since its inception and is focused on the provision of welfare, nutrition, education, community welfare, popularizing yoga and developing appropriate technology for villagers, particularly in tribal areas (Kanungo 2013). Deendayal Research Institute assumed prominence for its rehabilitation efforts after the Andhra Cyclone of 1977. After this cyclone, the RSS had engaged in reconstructing four villages, two of which (Madhavnagar in Krishna district and Sriramanagar in Vishakhapatnam district) were dominated by Scheduled Castes (SCs). One of the four villages, named Mulapalam, which had suffered maximum damage, was renamed Deendayal Puram after the senior BJS leader Deendayal Upadhyaya and monitored by the Deendayal Research Institute for a few years (Parvathy 2003, 120). Other important Sangh affiliates that were established around this time, which dedicated themselves to *seva*, were the Jana Seva Vidya Kendra (1972), Rashtrotthana Parishat (1965), Hindu Seva Pratishthana (1980) and the Hindu Munnani (1980). Yadav Rao Joshi, a prolific *pracharak* of the RSS, who was responsible for the strengthening the Sangh Parivar in Karnataka since 1941, had an instrumental role to play in the establishment of these organizations in southern India.

Golwalkar died in 1973 and was succeeded by one of the most politically dynamic *sarsanghchalaks* of the Sangh—Balasaheb

Deoras. Andersen and Damle (1987, 114) suggest that under the leadership of Deoras, the affiliates of the Parivar became more assertive and populist in their orientation. This was manifested in the RSS and ABVP's active participation in social and political movements such as the Gujarat Navnirman movement and Jayaprakash Narayan's anti-corruption movement in Bihar in 1974 and the campaign for the Janata Party alliance during the Emergency years of 1975–1977. After a temporary ban of two years during the Emergency, the RSS re-emerged as an important partner of the Janata Party alliance through its political affiliate, the BJS. However, as Kanungo (2003, 185–186) mentions, a foresighted Deoras consciously chose to keep the RSS away from overt politics and focused instead on consolidating the social welfare activities of its affiliates through the support of the Janata Party government. Under his leadership, *seva* activities of the RSS came to be organized under various umbrellas.

Vidya Bharati, a key affiliate of the Sangh Parivar was established in the year 1977 with its headquarters in Delhi. Responsible mainly for the implementation of elementary education, Vidya Bharati served as an umbrella organization for RSS-founded schools, popularly known as Saraswati Shishu Mandirs. As mentioned before, the foundation of this organization however was laid in 1952 when the first Saraswati Shishu Mandir was established in Gorakhpur, Uttar Pradesh, under the leadership of a Maharashtrian *pracharak* named Nanaji Deshmukh. Subsequently, the RSS also started schools in the names of Bharatiya Vidya Niketan, Gita Vidyalaya and Saraswati Bal Vidyalaya which laid special emphasis on religion, 'patriotism' and 'Indian culture' (Sarkar 2005, 200). These schools were initiated in some specific urban and rural tribal pockets of Bihar, Odisha, Andhra Pradesh and Chhattisgarh to counteract missionary educational influence. These schools also imbibe students with 'Hindu sanskars' such as deference to elders, patriotism, etc., through ritual and extra-curricular practices. Apart from its Shishu Mandirs, the RSS also started Ekal Vidyalayas which are single teacher schools for pre-school children where they are introduced to 'the rudiments of reading and writing, Sanskrit and sanskars'. Modelled on similar lines, Sanskar Kendras are another initiative of Vidya Bharati.

In 1977, Akhil Bharatiya Vanavasi Kalyan Ashram was established for coordinating all RSS *seva* activities with regard to tribals across the country. It brought several smaller tribal projects, which were under the VHP, under its wing. VKA's work is based on the foundational premise of the RSS that tribals are Hindus. Golwalkar firmly insisted on calling them *vanavasis* (forest dwellers) instead of *adivasis* (aboriginals), a trend which has been maintained by the Parivar. He also rejected the view that they are animists and not Hindus, on the ground that Hindus have always worshipped elements of nature such as Tulsi (plant) and Nag (cobra) (Golwalkar [1966] 1980, 471).

VKA had started its activities as early as 1952 in Jashpur, Chhattisgarh, to give a concrete shape to one of the RSS's priority areas—opposing the conversion activities of Christian missionaries. Jashpur in particular, provided a fertile ground for the initiation of VKA as it had a long history of Christian missionary activity (Sundar 2006). VKA, just like the VHP, began its work by starting a parallel stream of welfare activities in the realm of education, health and self-reliance. The organization's activities received a particular boost after the release of the Niyogi Commission report in 1956 which severely criticized the missionaries for evangelizing and even promoting separatism. Tariq Thachil's study (2011) in Chhattisgarh has shown that the provision of services by VKA over a sustained period of time has helped the political affiliate BJP recruit popular political candidates, party workers and influential teacher activists. In the course of time, VKA also expanded its activities to other states such as Odisha, Gujarat, Jharkhand and the north-eastern states such as Assam, Nagaland and Arunachal Pradesh. From social welfare, it also made forays into two other aspects: the 'promotion of tribal culture and tradition', and 'protection of tribal rights on water, forests and land (*jal*, jungle and *jameen*)' (VKA website). The 'promotion of tribal culture and tradition' mostly manifested itself in the form of an aggressive Hinduization of the tribals. The work of VKA in the Dangs district of Gujarat is a good illustration of this phenomenon where Swami Aseemananda revamped the Shabari tradition from a combination of local Adivasi folklore and the Ramayana and started a massive campaign against the Christian missionaries (Kanungo and Joshi 2009).

In 1979, the RSS established its first formal service wing, Sewa Bharati, in Delhi, under the leadership of an ex-RSS *pracharak* named Vishnu Kumar. Sewa Bharati was established with the explicit aim of assimilating Dalits and backward castes into the Hindutva fold (Jaffrelot 2005, 212). The organization started its work in the slums of Delhi mostly through its Sewa Basti initiatives and gradually expanded its work to the outskirts of the city. Its work mostly focuses on the eradication of untouchability, imbuing people with the spirit of service and unity and serving the economically needy and socially backward sectors by contributing to their physical, educational, social, moral and economic development. The emphasis however is on imbibing *samskaras* or a set of values that bring about a transformation in the language, behaviour and hygiene of people who reside in slums. A significant percentage of these communities are Dalits, who are oriented towards an 'ideal Hindu way of life' through discourses on religion, culture and patriotism (Jaoul 2011).

The agenda of co-opting lower castes within the Hindutva fold, received a fillip after a particular incident in 1981 when around fifteen hundred Dalits converted to Islam in Meenakshipuram, Tamil Nadu. Triggered by this incident, the VHP took upon itself the responsibility of becoming the vanguard of Hinduism and gave a clarion call to save it from becoming a minority religion. As an immediate reaction to the Meenakshipuram incident, the Sangh Parivar organized the Virat Hindu Sammelan, a huge assembly of Hindus that, among other things, adopted the abolition of untouchability as one of its five objectives. Soon after this, VHP organized its Seva Vibhag (Chauthaiwale 2008, 72). Jaffrelot (1996, 359) mentions that after the 1981 conversions, the Hindu nationalists accelerated their social welfare projects; with the experience it had acquired in helping tribals, the VHP diversified its activities and opened 867 schools in 1983, of which 374 were Bal Samskar Kendras which were established with the explicit purpose of 'shaping the character of the younger generation in childhood'. Another important aspect of this strategy was to build temples, of which about 100 were planned for Tamil Nadu alone, mainly in SC areas. In Gujarat, the RSS and ABVP made a special effort to win over Dalits in the mid-1980s by correcting their earlier stance of being opposed to reservation for the 'lower' castes and successfully co-opted them in the 1986 communal riots in Ahmedabad (Nandy et al. 1995, 102–104).

During the same period, the VHP also followed a policy of aggressive mobilization by conducting 'gharwapsi' (reconversion) of tribals, promoting traditional Hindu festivals and weaning away tribals from their own cultural rites and rituals.[2] The Sangh proudly claims that *seva* activities of the VHP have been successful in 'bringing several Hindus back' to where they belong, from the 'clutches of Muslims and Christians'. An article published in *Sewa Sadhana* proudly claims that the Banswara and Beawar projects of VHP in Rajasthan have proved to be 'hit', as these areas which once had the influence of Christians and Muslims, today echo with the slogans of 'Jai Shri Ram' and 'Bharat Mata ki Jai' (Chauthaiwale 2008). Under these projects more than 650 schools are being run in the tribal

[2] For a detailed understanding of the work of VHP in Maharashtra, see Thomas Blom Hansen (1999), and for Odisha, see Pralay Kanungo (2003, 153).

areas. According to the article, more than 70,000 people of these regions have 'returned home', that is, to Hinduism.

The vast network of social service projects targeted at tribals and Dalits helped the VHP to build a huge network of Hindutva loyalists across the country which was optimally exploited during the Ram Janmabhoomi Movement. In 1983, the VHP initiated the 'ekatmata yajna' and launched three processions throughout India with trucks carrying huge water pots filled with water from river Ganga (Davis 2005, 40). The water was distributed in villages and towns that the processions crossed by and the pots were then 'refilled from local sources of sacred water such as temple tanks and river bathing places (tirths), creating a Pan-Indian reservoir of holy water' (Davis 2005). Soon after this, the VHP developed a programme through which a mass appeal was launched to Hindus all over India to make special bricks, inscribed with the words Shri Rama, for use in building the new Ram temple. These bricks from throughout India were sanctified locally in a ceremony called the Ramshilan puja, then collected and transported from their points of origin to Ayodhya (Davis 2005). This mass mobilization eventually culminated in the demolition of the Babri Mosque in 1992. The act of demolishing the mosque was called *kar seva*, an appropriation of the Sikh tradition of community worship through work. Arvind Rajgopal (2001, 317) suggests that Hindutva's appropriation of the term *'kar seva'* (adopted by the VHP at a meeting in Haridwar on 23–24 June 1990) as a form of political activism was adopted after its use by Sikh militants in the mid-1980s.

Beneficiaries of Seva

As the above account has demonstrated, in the RSS tradition, Dalits and tribals are the two important target groups that have been the primary beneficiaries of institutionalized *seva*. Even contemporary *seva* projects of the Sangh Parivar primarily cater to these two categories. Balasaheb Deoras mentions that the problems of 'vanvasis' and Dalits will be solved through constructive works, not through agitations (Chauthaiwale 2008, 12). Recounting the *seva* projects of *swayamsevaks* for the tribals of Talasari region of Thane, Maharashtra, Deoras mentions the following:

> I realised that the *swayamsevaks* have mingled with the Vanvasi life of that region and it is due to that oneness that they now understand the problems of those people well. (Chauthaiwale 2008, 12)

Deoras goes on to explain that trying to resolve problems through agitations only makes them more complicated. Problems are resolved, he argues, when they are presented in the right perspective before the people, only through a creative outlook. This 'creative outlook', one may infer, is what inspires *seva*. On a similar note, Sadhvi Ritambara (Chauthaiwale 2008, 35) applauds the work of Sewa Bharati for starting Sewa Bastis in Delhi for the Dalits, as this leads to the 'unity of the whole Hindu society'. Taking recourse to mythology, she mentions that even Shri Ram had defeated evil forces with the help of the 'so-called lower sections of the society'. He could win over Lanka only with the 'blessings of Shabari and cooperation of Kevat, Nishad, monkies and bears'. The need of the hour, she reminds the *swayamsevaks*, is to 'embrace the last person of the society' in this spirit. The emphasis on a 'creative outlook' of *seva* that captures the central difference between *seva* and a rights-based approach to development which in fact promotes social movements that often lead to agitations.

Apart from the affiliates of the Parivar especially dedicated to *seva*, several *shakhas* also take up community service in various villages. A story of one such *shakha* in Nettancode, located in Kanyakumari, is recounted in an RSS publication (*Sewa Sadhana* 2013, 27). The RSS claims that before this *shakha* was started in 1981, the local people were living 'under acute terror of the missionaries' and that conversion was taking place openly. Apart from a few activities dedicated to improving the socio-economic condition of the people such as initiating a cooperative bank, a small-scale brush manufacturing unit, building a new road, organizing health and eye camps and inculcating saving habits through small saving schemes and recurring deposit accounts, the *shakha* focused more on 'cultural activities' such as initiating *bhajan* activities, initiating religious classes for children and conducting Gita classes for the youth. Senior religious saints such as Kanchi Shankaracharya and Thiruvaduthurai Adheenam were invited to attend the village temple events, an ashram dedicated to sadhvis was inaugurated and celebration of Hindu festivals such as Vinayak Chaturthi was initiated in a large scale. Soon, the *shakha* also facilitated the ABVP, the BMS and the Hindu Munani to open their chapters in this village. The RSS also claims that the *shakha* has so much influence in the village now that the villagers nominate their panchayat chief unanimously.[3] The rendering of *seva* is thus enmeshed with a process of politically consolidating the Hindu community around certain rituals and practices considered 'Hindu'. It has also succeeded in killing grassroots level democracy by encouraging informal forms of electing leadership.

There are numerous such examples of service activities started by the Sangh to counter the influence of Christian missionaries. The Kushth Ashram in Bulandshahr, monitored by the Dayananda shakha, was started to not only help lepers but also to keep the Christian missionaries out from this locality. The Vanvasi Ram Primary School was similarly started in Amera village, Chhattisgarh, to counter Christian proselytizing activities (*Sewa Sadhana* 2009, 73). Subsequently, the Mahavir Baiga Ashram and Buddhadev Primary School were also started to impart 'good *samskaras*' to the people. A Sangh *shakha* was started in the village in 2001 which initiated education and

[3] A similar practice was reported to the author while conducting fieldwork in rural Kutch. The idea of 'samras' villages is discussed in Chapter 5.

health-related service activities alongside other activities such as organizing Hindu religious festivals.

Organizing *Seva* Activities in the Sangh Parivar

Seva is rendered by the Sangh Parivar through a robust network of organizations; each assigned with a specific area of focus, but driven by the same ideological mission. All *seva* activities in the Sangh are organized under four broad categories: 'education', 'health', 'social' and 'self-reliance'. In 1989, the birth centenary of Hedgewar, the RSS made a special effort to coordinate and expand its *seva* activities. A dedicated body named Seva Vibhag was established to fulfil this. Seva Vibhag initiated a process of systematically documenting the various *seva* activities that were being conducted by the RSS and its front and affiliate organizations, and, by 1994, a databank named Seva Disha was established (Beckerlegge 2004, 127).

For purposes of overall coordination and to avoid overlap, the Sangh constituted the office of the Akhil Bharatiya Sewa Pramukh. The Sewa Pramukh is a member of the Executive Council of the RSS, Akhil Bharatiya Pratinidhi Sabha and heads the Seva Vibhag of the RSS. As Figure 3.1 indicates, Akhil Bharatiya Sewa Pramukh oversees the work of *kshetriya* (zonal) *seva* pramukhs, who in turn oversee the work of *prant* (province) pramukhs. Currently, there are 11 zones in all—Dakshina (Southern), Dakshina Madhya (South-Central), Paschim (Western), Madhya (Central), Paschim Uttar (North-West, which comprises Rajasthan), Uttara (Northern which consists of Uttar Pradesh, sub-divided into two parts, Poorvi [eastern] UP and Paschimi [western] UP), Bihar Kshetra (comprising Bihar and Jharkhand), Poorvottar Kshetra (comprising all North-eastern states), Purva (Eastern; comprising Bengal and Odisha). These zones comprise 41 *prants* (provinces).

The *prant seva* pramukh oversees the work of the *vibhag seva* pramukh (3 districts make 1 *vibhag* or division), who in turn

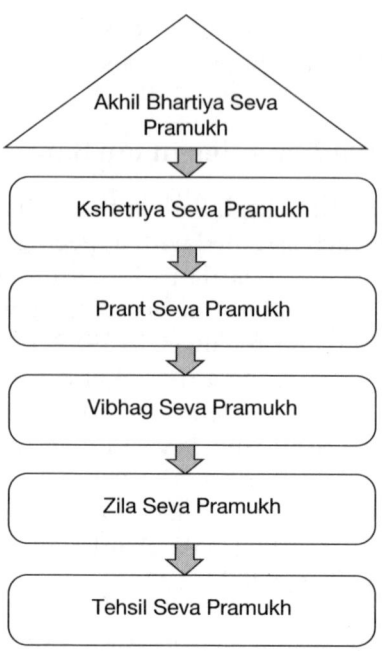

FIGURE 3.1. *Organizational Chain of Command for Implementing* Seva *Activities in the RSS*

Source: Interview with Shyam Parande, Head, Sewa International, Keshav Krupa, Shankarapuram, Bangalore, 24 February 2013.

monitors the work of *zilla* (district) *seva* pramukhs under him. The zilla *seva* pramukhs oversee the activities of the tehsil *seva* pramukh, who form the first level units in this entire chain. The primary task of these pramukhs at various levels is to encourage and promote *swayamsevaks* and even people outside the RSS to engage in *seva* activities. These pramukhs work directly with the people.

The administrative coordination of *seva* activities at each level is undertaken by a parallel chain of bodies which represent the Rashtriya Sewa Bharati (RSB). There are vertical and horizontal connects between these two structures. The RSB similarly operates at the national, zonal and state level. At the state level, it is known by different names also. For example, while in Gujarat it is called Sewa Bharati, in Odisha it is known as the Utkal Bipanna Sahayata Samiti, in Maharashtra it is called Jana Kalyan Samiti, and in Karnataka it is called Hindu Seva Pratishthan. This structure performs the enabling function and supports the implementation of *seva* through raising funds, performing audits, accounting and executing programmes.

The Rashtriya Sewa Bharati Trust was established in Delhi in 2003 to act as a larger umbrella body for all Sangh inspired organizations that were engaged in *seva*. The Trust was set up with the explicit aim of providing 'training in administration, office management, development of karyakartas, finance and accounts management to all the affiliated voluntary organisations' (*Sewa Sadhana* 2012, 10). Subsequently, RSB also started playing an important role in networking various voluntary organizations. The first attempt at this networking was the organization of Sewa Sangam in Bangalore in 2010, following which several similar Sewa Sangams were organized at the *prant* levels. The event in Bangalore was hugely successful and was attended by organization and 'eminent guests' such as both Sri Ravishankar and Baba Ramdev. The Trust also publishes publicity material for its affiliated organizations. The Trust grants affiliation to several registered voluntary organizations across the country. Currently there are about 500 organizations affiliated to the Trust (*Sewa Sadhana* 2012, 13) *Sewa Sadhana* (the annual bulletin of Rashtriya Sewa Trust) outlines four objectives of the Trust which are 'awakening', 'coordination', 'training' and 'research' (*Sewa Sadhana* 2012). 'Awakening' is implemented through organization of Sewa Sangams at the state and zonal levels where voluntary bodies are encouraged to share their work and develop a 'common minimum programme' to 'achieve the results in a particular frame'. The Trust also occasionally undertakes research on particular service activities undertaken by its affiliated bodies. However, it does not undertake any *seva* activities on its own.

The RSS today boasts of a variety of *seva* activities across the country, ranging from women's self-help groups, micro enterprises, forest conservation projects in Jharkhand, eye banks, initiatives dedicated to improving health (physical and mental), nutrition in tribal districts such as Raygada in Odisha, ashrams for the homeless, computer aided learning centres, organizations for the physically challenged, rural technology centres, vocational training programmes, veterinary welfare, awareness of drug abuse, etc. There are milk cooperatives (Kamdhenu Hitkari Manch, Namhol, Himachal Pradesh), projects dedicated to preserving medicinal plants in the Himalayas, environmental initiatives, a Gurukul in Kurukshetra, Haryana, a Rashtra Mandir (that promotes patriotism) in Agra, orphanages, destitute homes, a Jain bird sanctuary in Delhi, and Yoga Bharat Sansthans across the country.[4] In addition to providing service, these organizations are deeply concerned with the infusion of 'Hindu awareness and national discipline' (Jaffrelot 2005, 216), an ethic which binds them to the common umbilical cord of the RSS. They further help in achieving the broader political goals of the Parivar through an apolitical framework.

The RSS categorically maintains that all its front organizations work independently without any interference from RSB. However, given its ideological mission, it would be naïve to believe that the high command does not monitor its operational arms. In addition to the core RSS organizations, there are a set of *matrosansthas* or *vivedhakkshatras* which are sister organizations of the RSS. These include VKA, VHP, Vidya Bharati, Bharati Vikas Parishad and Rashtriya Sevika Samiti. The *seva*

[4] Information collected from several bulletins of *Rashtriya Sewa Bharti* 2007–2013.

heads of all these organizations periodically consult the Akhil Bharatiya Sewa Pramukh for guidance. Other bodies focused on *seva* that come within the ambit of the Parivar include Arogya Bharati, National Medicos Organisation (NMO), Deendayal Shodh Sansthan (Chitrakoot) and Vivekananda Kendra.

Currently, VKA runs around 20,199 service projects which are spread across 13,886 places in India (VKA website). Its current programmes are organized under four categories—education, economic development, health and sports. The VHP runs 115,043 *seva* activities which are clubbed under the categories of 'education', 'medical', 'self-empowerment' and 'social' (VHP website). Vidya Bharati today runs 13,067 formal educational projects which consist of schools from the primary to the higher secondary levels (Vidya Bharati Akhil Bhartiya Shiksha Sansthan website). These projects cater to 3,475,757 students across the country. In addition to this, it also runs 8,221 Ekal Vidyalayas (Single School teachers) and 4,397 Sanskar Kendras (Vidya Bharati Akhil Bhartiya Shiksha Sansthan website). A report, published by *Tehelka* (26 April 2011), a news daily, highlights that the RSS owns one of the fastest growing education projects, that too in the Maoist affected regions. The report claims that the *seva* activities of Sangh Parivar have ousted the Christian missionaries' decades-old dominance in the field of education and applauds the Sangh for reaching out to *adivasis* in Odisha, Chhattisgarh, Jharkhand and the North Eastern states. It also highlights that the Ekal Vidyalaya Foundation is the most successful of all projects that runs 34,343 schools which collectively have 962,485 students.

Seva in a Diaspora Context

The service activities of the Sangh Parivar have not been restricted to the Indianterritory alone. The consolidation of a strong Indian diaspora in North America, Canada, Western Europe and South East Asian countries since the past few decades, the growth of

Internet technology and the resurgence of religion the world over have helped the Sangh in establishing a network of Hindu organizations in several foreign lands. The Sangh Parivar's overseas ambitions received a fillip during the Ram Janmabhoomi Movement in the early 1990s when the RSS actively mobilized overseas Hindus, particularly those in the United Sates and UK, seeking support and raising resources for the building of a Ram Temple at Ayodhya. Hindu Swayamsevak Sangh (HSS), the overseas affiliate of the RSS, claims to have established contacts in more than 100 countries, out of which it has active branches in 34 countries where it runs over 500 *shakhas*, including the United States of America, England, South Africa, Fiji, Mauritius, Kenya and various countries in Africa, Caribbean and Europe. Other prominent organizations of the Sangh Parivar in America are Vishwa Hindu Parishad of America, Hindu Students Council, American Hindu Against Defamation (AHAD), India Development and Relief Fund (IDRF) and Overseas Friends of BJP (Kanungo 2011). Besides these, several countries such as the USA, UK, Canada and Australia have registered chapters of Sewa International from the 1990s onwards. To coordinate the service projects of these international bodies, a special affiliate named Sewa International was established in 1998.

According to a senior representative of Sewa International, the organization has a threefold objective (Interview with Shyam Parande, Head, Sewa International, Bangalore, February 2013). First, it works with the People of Indian origin and NRI society which 'feels for India' and 'wants to give something back to their home country'. Sewa International helps this community reach out to various voluntary organizations in India to contribute towards social good. Second, it encourages the diasporic Indian community to serve their present country of occupation by encouraging them to participate in local social welfare activities. In the words of the representative, "When you serve the local people, they will recognize your culture through that ... as a group as a society and as an individual'.

This objective seeks to promote volunteerism among Indians in foreign countries and coordinates with Indian voluntary bodies to respond with funds and volunteers during natural calamities abroad. With India on the footsteps of becoming a 'super economic power', says the Sewa International leader, 'we should send not only our volunteers, but also contribute funds for natural calamities abroad'. The last and most important objective of Sewa International was to demolish the myth that Indians or Indian traditions do not believe or engage in charity. The Sewa International representative stated that it is popularly believed that charity is synonymous with Christian missionaries. However, he noted that the Hindu tradition has always stood for charity and that India's history is replete with examples of service to the society. This, he added, 'needs to be brought to the notice of the world'. Sewa International promotes this idea through various international conferences and seminars.

In the recent past, Sewa International coordinated community-building efforts in Sri Lanka after Tsunami in 2004 and in the United States after Hurricane Katrina in 2005. Apart from the above-stated functions, Sewa International also supports several chapters of the Sewa Bharati in India by raising funds from the diasporic communities, providing support in planning and rehabilitation after natural disasters and coordinating the efforts of various units of Sewa Bharati. Sewa International currently works across 16 countries in the world through promoting volunteerism.

John Zavos (2015) has argued that *seva* operates as a critical diasporic currency for South Asian migrants as it facilitates the construction of local and global citizenship identities, and symbolizes positive social action, civic virtue and religious devotion. This, according to Zavos, enhances the 'model minority' status of Hindu communities. Thus, Hindu organizations located outside India deploy *seva* as a creative medium of interaction to engage with migrant communities in order to enhance the latter's own self-image in a foreign land where they are constantly negotiating their own identities vis-à-vis the other who refuse to accept them as one of their own. *Seva* thus enthuses pride and a sense of nationalism among the Hindu diaspora.

Conclusion

The idea and practice of *seva* assumed a novel dimension under the aegis of the RSS in 1925. In the hands of the RSS leaders, the idea of *seva* was constructed as a distinct and a superior category compared to the Western notions of charity and philanthropy. This has been achieved through a valorization of the classical notion of *seva* which entails selflessness and frequent allusions to the nationalist hero Swami Vivekananda who contributed enormously towards popularizing *seva* and conflating it with nationalism during the colonial period. This conceptualization has facilitated an ontological shift in the ways in which people perceive of *seva* today.

An examination of the actual practice of *seva* in the RSS tradition however reveals an unmistakable instrumental dimension. While its initial activities of service revolved around providing relief after natural and political calamities, *seva* gradually acquired an institutional character under the leadership of Golwalkar. Commitment to *seva* was a conscious strategy adopted by Golwalkar, stemming from the need to rehabilitate the RSS's image as a social and humanitarian organization as opposed to a communal and paramilitary body, after it was banned following the assassination of Mahatma Gandhi. A large number of affiliate organizations were commissioned from the 1950s onwards by Golwalkar which penetrated various realms of civil society through social welfare work. United by the single agenda of creating a Pan-Hindu unity by subsuming hitherto excluded groups such as tribals and Dalits, and countering the process of conversion to 'foreign religions', many of these affiliates used *seva* for strategic reasons. Thus, imitating the social welfare strategy of the missionaries, some of these affiliates, such as VHP, VKA and Seva Bharati, initiated a parallel system of social service that specifically targeted groups such as the Dalits and tribals. These activities were accentuated under the influence of certain important political events such as the 1981 Meenakshipuram incident. The political leadership of Deoras further helped in expanding and organizing the *seva* activities of the RSS. From the 1980s onwards, with the growth of transnational Hindutva, *seva* received additional stimulus and has played an important role in mobilizing the Hindu diaspora.

Despite this political dimension however, there is a certain materiality to *seva* that goes beyond its political ramifications. The most remarkable thing to acknowledge here is that the RSS's conceptualization of *seva* offers a resuscitation of an innate idiom, a common language, a common communicative structure, a common worldview that people (including performers and recipients of *seva*) instantly connect to because they recognize it as their own. The primary reason that this works is because people express themselves and understand each other best through this shared idiom and shared worldview. The following chapters reveal this in in greater detail in the context of disaster relief work in the states of Odisha and Gujarat.

IV

Seva after the 'Super Cyclone'

The Case of UBSS in Odisha

On the narrow dirt track that leads to Ersama—a large cluster of some 2,400 bustling coastal villages 110 km east of
Bhubaneswar—a group of bandanna-sporting RSS workers in khaki
shorts, yellow rubber gloves and gauze masks stumble on to eight
rotting bodies in a ditch. They get to work immediately, digging furi-
ously with their spades and shovels, tossing the bodies into faceless
wayside graves (sometimes two to a grave) and sprinkle them with
bleaching powder before moving on in search of more corpses.

—Biswas (1999)

On 29 October 1999, a super cyclone slammed the coast of
Odisha and caused extensive damage to lives, livelihoods, infrastructure and cattle in over 12 districts in the state. According
to government records, 9,885 people lost their lives while
15 million people were said to be affected (United Nations
Disaster Management Team 1999). It is undoubtedly one of the
worst catastrophes to have ever hit the region. Erasama block,
which is located at a distance of 25 km from the sea coast in
Jagatsinghpur district was hit by a 10-feet-high tidal wave and

suffered maximum casualties. As the above epigraph indicates, the RSS gained visibility as one of the important actors which was at the forefront in collecting and disposing off dead bodies in the aftermath of the cyclone across several villages in coastal Odisha.

Since the late 1990s, Odisha has been in the news on several occasions due to Hindu–Christian violence. One of the first incidents that had attracted media attention from all over the world was the ghastly murder of an Australian Christian missionary named Graham Staines and his two sons in a small village name Manoharpur in Keonjhar. Staines and his sons were sleeping in a station wagon outside a Church when their vehicle was set on fire. The perpetrators of the crime alleged that Staines was trying to gain Christian converts among the local tribal population through fraud and allurement. The prime accused in this incident, Dara Singh, allegedly belonged to Bajrang Dal, a Sangh affiliate organization. In 2008 again, following the killing of Lakshmanananda Saraswati (a Hindu monk) by Maoists who were allegedly in connivance with the Christian missionaries, ethno-religious riots broke out in the Kandhamal district of Odisha in which around 45 Christians were killed and extensive Church property destroyed.

While several scholarly studies and media reports have drawn attention to the role of the Sangh Parivar in exacerbating communal tensions in this state, there is surprisingly little attention paid to its role in possibly the worst possible disaster that Odisha faced in the 20th century. I argue here that the RSS's participation in the Super Cyclone of 1999 needs to be analysed more carefully as it was a significant moment in the entrenchment of Hindutva in the state. This chapter undertakes a detailed analysis of how this entrenchment was catalysed through the relief and rehabilitation activities of the RSS and its affiliate group, UBSS, in the aftermath of the Super Cyclone.

How did the rendering of *seva* in the aftermath of the Cyclone facilitate in the political project of building a Hindu

Rashtra? What were the larger narratives that were woven into the enactment of *seva*? How did this intermingle with the local sentiments and idioms of the donors and recipients of *seva*? Before embarking on this discussion however, a brief overview of the state is provided below. The subsequent section traces the evolution of Hindutva in this region, up to the period of the Super Cyclone in 1999.

A Brief Snapshot of Odisha

The state of Odisha is situated in the east coast of India, facing the Bay of Bengal. Known by various names such as 'Utkala', 'Kalinga', 'Kosala' and 'Udra' at various points of time in ancient history, the modern state of 'Odisha' came into being during the colonial period, when in 1936, the Odia-speaking territories

FIGURE 4.1 *Political Map of Odisha*

Source: Recreated from Administrative Atlas of India, Population Census of India, 2011.

Note: This figure has been redrawn and is not to scale. It does not represent any authentic national or international boundaries and is used for illustrative purposes only.

were united. Comprising 30 districts (Figure 4.1), the state consists of mainly two parts: the coastal area and the highland area.

The population of the state is 41,947,358 as per the 2011 Census of India. Scheduled Castes (SCs) comprise 17.1 per cent of the state's population while Scheduled Tribes (STs) form a significant 22.8 per cent (Census of India 2011). The ST population in the state is overwhelmingly rural, with 94.5 per cent residing in villages. The state has as many as 62 tribal groups, which constitute roughly one-fourth of its population. The tribal population is substantial in districts such as Malkangiri followed by Mayurbhanj, Rayagada and Nabarangapur.

Economically, Odisha is one of the poorest states in India and the proportion of people living below the poverty line is much higher than the all India average (Singh, *The Times of India*, 24 July 2013). The social indicators such as infant mortality and life expectancy rates, access to health and education, etc., remain abysmally low and regional disparities within the state are quite high (Haan and Dubey 2005; Planning Commission 2011). Politically, two main parties have historically dominated Odisha: Indian National Congress and the Janata Dal. In 1996, Janata Dal party member, Naveen Patnaik, took over the position of chief minister from his father, Biju Patnaik. Soon, he split from the Janata Dal, due to the party's failure to ally with the BJP, and in 1997 formed the BJD. Since that time, the BJD has maintained its stature as Odisha's most popular party. From 1995 onwards, the BJP emerged as a third force in the politics of Odisha (Table 4.1) by winning 9 assembly seats and improving its vote share in the 1996 Lok Sabha elections (Roy 1997).

The religious landscape of the Odisha has primarily been dominated by Hinduism, with Islam and Christianity comprising a miniscule percentage of the population. According to the Census of India 2001, Hindus comprise 95.5 per cent of the population while Christians comprise 2.4 per cent and Muslims 2.1 per cent of the total population (Census of India 2011).

TABLE 4.1	The BJP's Performance: Odisha Assembly and Lok Sabha Elections (1980–2000)						
	Odisha Assembly			**Lok Sabha - Odisha Seats**			
	Con-tested	**No. of Seats Won**	**% of Votes**		**Con-tested**	**No. of Seats Won**	**% of Votes**
1980	28	0	7.09	1984	4	0	1.18
1985	67	1	5.66	1989	6	0	1.28
1990	63	2	8.49	1991	21	0	9.50
1995	144	9	8.03	1996	20	0	13.42
2000	63	38	42.88	1998	9	7	21.19
				1999	9	9	24.63

Source: Election Commission of India.

Although, since ancient times, Odisha has been regarded as a 'Hindu province', it has also experienced the strong influences of both Buddhism and Jainism (Kanungo 2003, 3293). Over the years, Islam and Christianity also entered the province of Odisha through the advent of Afghans and the Mughals in the 16th century and Christian missionaries in the 18th century. While a strong 'Hindu–Muslim' syncretic tradition emerged over the 17th and 18th centuries,[1] evangelization by Christian missionaries, and denigration of certain adivasi customs, led to the brewing of an anti-Christian sentiment in certain tribal pockets during the 19th century (Kanungo 2014). Despite this, by and large, Odisha managed to keep communalism at bay. This situation gradually changed with the emergence of Hindutva in the state.

[1] Despite a strong Hindu–Muslim syncretic tradition, the image of the 'Muslim' started undergoing visible changes in popular imagination from the 19th century (see Pati 1997, 1393–1394).

The Sangh Parivar in Odisha: Emergence and Growth[2]

The emergence of Hindu nationalism in Odisha can be traced to the efforts of the Hindu Mahasabha which opened its first branch in the state in Puri in 1940. The political symbolism of this was significant as Puri, being the abode of Lord Jagannath, has always been a famous Hindu pilgrimage spot. In the 1940s, a non-Odia RSS activist, Anantlal Srivastava, started two *shakhas* in Ganjam and Sambalpur districts and was supported by Mukund Rao Moonjee, who started the Cuttack *shakha*. Following a temporary ban after Gandhi's assassination in 1948, the RSS emerged again in 1949 and picked up the momentum of its activities in Odisha as in other parts of the country. In 1949, Golwalkar deputed Baburao Paldhikar as the first RSS *pracharak* to Odisha and also acknowledged Odisha as a distinct *prant*. As in other regions in India, the organization's influence and spread in the early years was facilitated by its many followers who mainly comprised upper- and upper-caste notables such as lawyers, political leaders, educationists and Marwari traders of Odisha.

In 1964, Deendayal Upadhyay established the Odisha branch of the BJS in Jharsuguda and appointed Shridhar Acharya, an experienced *pracharak*, as the state organizing secretary. In the same year, the RSS also launched an Odia weekly named *Rashtradeepa*, to propagate its ideology. Further, the *gau raksha andolan* (cow protection movement) launched across the country in 1965–1966 helped in mobilizing more support for the movement, although in Odisha the Prevention of Cow Slaughter Act had already been passed in 1960. In 1967, the VHP established base in Odisha with Raghunath Sethi, a Dalit RSS pracharak, as its secretary. A year later, in 1968, VHP

[2] Due to paucity of sources, this section borrows substantially from Pralay Kanungo's work (2003) on the emergence and expansion of the RSS in Odisha.

organized its first state conference here. In 1968, the student wing of the RSS, the ABVP, inaugurated its branch in Odisha by organizing a conference in Puri.

In the subsequent years, several other affiliates were floated by members of the Sangh such as the Bajrang Dal, the Durga Vahini, BMS, Vanvasi Kalyan Ashram (VKA), Saraswati Shishu Mandir, UBSS and the Budakattu Krishna Sangh which have been mobilizing students, women, farmers, labourers, tribals and literary personalities. Moreover, periodic communal riots such as in Cuttack in 1992, Bhadrak in 1986 and 1991, Soro in 1991 during the Ram Janmabhoomi campaign worked to the advantage of the Parivar.

The underdevelopment of the state of Odisha has further facilitated the popularity of the Sangh in this region as many of its activities are directed towards providing welfare in the realm of education and health. These services have furthered the advancement of Hinduization in the state by targeting poor tribal people who have been most vulnerable to the proselytizing activities of the Christian missionaries.[3] In

[3] There have been numerous debates on the issue of religious conversions in India and a strong strand of criticism has been directed against anti-conversion laws legislated by the state governments that seek to prohibit conversion through 'force', 'fraud' and 'allurement'. The justification for such criticism has been that these laws not only contradict the fundamental Right to Freedom of Religion, guaranteed by the Constitution of India, but also that these are instruments to further the homogenizing agenda of Hindutva that also engages in similar conversion tribals who were never Hindus to begin with. While I acknowledge these legitimate criticisms, I also feel that the proselytizing activities of the Christian missionaries have not been subjected to sufficient critical analysis. A greater appreciation of the 'vulnerability' of those converted, will perhaps help one situate better the larger appeal of Hindutva, particularly among the downtrodden communities.

1969, VHP deputed Lakshmanananda Saraswati to the tribal district of Phulbani/Kandhamal which had been a stronghold of Christian missionaries for some time. Lakshmanananda aggressively pursued the agenda of countering missionary activities and 're-converting' tribals (Kondhs) who had converted to Christianity. By the early 1970s, he established base at an ashram at Chakapad and introduced a series of activities such as setting up schools, promoting 'indigenous' methods of agriculture, introducing Kondhs to Hindu modes of worship and customs and gradually weaning them away from their traditional rituals and practices. Mobilization of tribals and anti-Christian propaganda attained a violent colour from the 1990s onwards, especially in the tribal districts of Udayagiri, Keonjhar and Mayurbhanj where Christian missionaries were attacked, nuns were raped and churches were vandalized. In 1998, an SC convert was burnt alive in Udayagiri by an angry mob, and, as mentioned before, in 1999, an Australian missionary Graham Staines and his two sons were burnt alive in Keonjhar.

The entrenchment of the Sangh in Odisha was further facilitated by the rise of the BJP as an important electoral force in the state. While the BJS had an insignificant presence in Odisha, the 1990s witnessed the gradual electoral rise of the BJP. Its nine-year long alliance (1998–2009) with the BJD cemented the roots of the RSS and its affiliates across the state. The BJP and BJD entered into an alliance in 1998 and together contested the Lok Sabha elections in 1998, 1999 and 2004, winning the majority in the state. BJP's two consecutive terms in power, in alliance with BJD, provided a great boost to Hindutva activities. By 2003, the RSS *shakhas* in Odisha grew to around 2500, with a membership of 100,000 *swayamsevaks* while the VHP built a base of 60,000 in the state (Banerjee 2003). The Bajrang Dal had over 20,000 members who served in 200 akharas and the Durga Vahini had 7,000 members working in close coordination with RSS and VHP cadres (Banerjee 2003).

The Super Cyclone of 1999

As already mentioned, on 29 October 1999, coastal Odisha was hit by a severe cyclone that caused large-scale devastation to humans, animal life and property. Jagatsinghpur and Kendrapara were the worst affected districts with more than 8,000 casualties in the former district alone (Das 2002, 4784). The rural population which lived near the coast was affected the most and accounted for maximum number of human and cattle deaths, destruction of their kutcha houses and their crops and complete contamination of drinking water facilities. Debris of ruined houses and several dead bodies and animal carcasses were found floating in the water for several days after the cyclone. The cyclone also dealt a severe blow to the livelihoods of the coastal fishermen, shrimp harvesters, jute farmers, weaving communities and cashew and groundnut growers. Then Chief Minister of Odisha Giridhar Gamang put the damages caused at ₹1,000,000 millions (Chattopadhyay, *Frontline* 1999).

Despite Odisha's propensity to disasters and several high intensity disasters in the past, there was little that the state government had done in terms of preparedness or mitigation of disasters, except the construction of 23 Cyclone shelters in collaboration with the Indian Red Cross Society. A news article (Mohanty, *The Telegraph*, 13 January 2005) highlights that although meteorologists had warned of the impending Super Cyclone three days in advance, Chief Minister Giridhar Gamang had called in three astrologers and kept a personal vigil as 'they appealed to the gods to deflect the storm'. Although an anticipation of a formidable Cyclone had led the state government to make skeletal arrangements in the form of organizing evacuations, the sheer scale and magnitude of the Super Cyclone came in as a shock and left the state baffled. For almost a week, the administration was completely crippled and failed to provide any assistance to the survivors.

The chief minister of Odisha appealed for assistance from the central government to deploy defence and paramilitary forces. As in most other disaster situations in India, army, air force and navy were among the first agencies of the government to swing into action after the Super Cyclone. Several aircrafts of air force, and even the passenger carrier Indian Airlines, were pressed into service. The Odisha state government received a total of ₹828.15 millions from the National Calamity Relief Fund and ₹38.10 millions from the Prime Minister's Relief Fund (Sinha 2002, 3). In addition to this, several different kinds of civil society organizations comprising 51 NGOs, 11 international NGOs, 13 corporate groups and 12 religious organizations were involved in relief and rehabilitation work following the Super Cyclone (Behera and Sarkar 2003).

The aftermath of the disaster unleashed a wave of politics that involved partisan interests of political parties and centre–state dynamics. The incumbent Congress government's handling of the disaster was 'awfully inadequate' and therefore demolished the chances of the Congress's return to power in impending elections (Mohapatra 2000, 1353). The mismanagement of relief operations was politicized optimally and under pressure from opposition parties such as BJP and BJD, Congress Chief Sonia Gandhi removed the chief minister from office. An important achievement of the ruling state government amid all the chaos after the disaster, however, was the establishment of the Odisha State Disaster Mitigation Authority (OSDMA) in December 1999, as an autonomous 'nodal agency' (Niranjan Mohapatra, Interview, Odisha Relief Commissioner's Office, 28 October 2012) which was later renamed to Odisha State Disaster Management Authority in 2008. Chief functions of the OSDMA following the Super Cyclone were to coordinate the relief efforts of state agencies, multilateral agencies, the United Nations and NGOs.

The relief operation after the cyclone lasted for about three months, following which the state government got onto the task of conceptualizing a rehabilitation plan. According to government estimates, a total of 1.9 million houses had to be rebuilt; out of which, 0.8 million houses were completely destroyed (Samal and Meher 2005, 82). The government provided two types of housing assistance: free housing to 200,000 poor families through the Indira Awas Yojana, an ongoing social housing programme targeting the SCs and tribals and households below the poverty line, and loans to families above the poverty line through the Housing and Urban Development Corporation (HUDCO). Besides building houses, the state government offered many rehabilitation support mechanisms such as providing ex-gratia funds (₹75,000) to the families of the deceased, financial assistance for damaged houses, provision of livelihood equipment such as fishing nests, PDS rice at subsidized rates, waiver of school and college tuition fees, compensation for crop insurance and various food-for-work programmes (Samal 2006, 94). The government engaged in not only constructing houses but also commissioned a series of multipurpose cyclone shelters which were planned along the entire coastline of Odisha.

RSS Relief Efforts

A serious problem that arose in the aftermath of the cyclone, especially in Erasama, was the floating of putrefying dead bodies of humans and cattle. Superstitious local villagers, who were already traumatized after the cyclone, refused to touch the dead bodies for the fear of making contact with evil spirits and of contracting diseases. Things were made worse by the complete breakdown of communications as none of the external relief agencies could reach the most severely affected places for more than a week after the disaster. In the midst of this situation, two groups that took upon themselves the task of cremating dead bodies and corpses of animals were the RSS and the Ananda Marg. Given its experience in disaster relief, RSS *swayamsevaks* plunged into action with bare minimum equipment and organized themselves into a Shiv Sena Vahini. This sena simultaneously worked in the districts of Jagatsinghpur, Puri, Khurda, Jaipur, Balasore, Cuttack, Kendrapara and Keonjhar. By the RSS's own account, around 1,307 human bodies and more than 1,200 carcasses of cattle were either buried or cremated (UBSS 2000, 31–32).

In many villages of Erasama, local sadhus who were affiliated to the RSS's religious affiliate, the VHP, conducted prayer meetings for the survivors of the deceased. The VHP arranged a mass funeral oblation near Swargadwar at Puri sea beach with the chanting of Maha Mrityunjaya Mantra and recitation of the Bhagavad Gita (*Organiser* December 1999, 20). Special prayers were arranged in the Baisi Pahacha of Lord Jagannath temple under the leadership of VHP leader Swami Lakshmanananda Saraswati (*Organiser* December 1999, 20). These prayers were arranged for those who had lost their family members but did not get an opportunity to see the dead bodies or perform the last rites. It is important to note that funeral ceremonies are fundamentally emotive and deeply connected to one's faith. Providing support to the survivors of those who had lost their own family in the disaster thus symbolized an important gesture of solidarity. Moreover, the strategic choice of Puri, the abode of the most revered Jagannath and a famous pilgrimage spot for Hindus, for conducting these ceremonies gave the VHP and its activities considerable visibility.

The task of cremation of dead bodies earned the RSS considerable praise from community members and the media, as evident from the quotation cited at the beginning of this section. This was especially relevant in a context where neither the government nor any other NGO (other than the Anand Marg) undertook this difficult task. Apart from cremation tasks, the RSS *swayamsevaks* also engaged in relief activities such as clearing roads off fallen trees, electric poles and other debris, organizing community kitchens and arranging for medical care for the injured.[4] These activities were first mostly initiated by local *swayamsevaks* in small pockets of the cyclone ravaged districts. Interactions with community members in some villages (Kharagpur, Manijanga, Narua) of Erasama and Tirtol blocks in Jagatsinghpur revealed that the RSS was one of the prominent relief providers that came to their rescue even before the arrival of any government agency (interview with a group of villagers in Kharagpur village, Tirtol, Jagatsinghpur district, 4 November 2012). They buried the dead, cleared roads and opened community kitchens within a week of the disaster.

Interviews with some senior members (Amit Mohanty and Deepak Lohia, Interview, 29 October 2012) of the UBSS, the service wing of the RSS in Odisha, revealed that those towns and villages which had been running *shakhas* since the pre-cyclone days became the first centres of RSS relief operations as it was easier to mobilize the *swayamsevaks* there to organize aid. They also claimed that a series of community kitchens were started by 30 October 1999, which gradually increased to 568 centres by the first week of November wherein nearly 45,000 people were served food daily. This work continued for more than 25 days in the tidal wave affected areas. After that, as utensils started gradually being distributed, dry food such as rice, cereals, wheat flour, etc., were distributed in place of cooked food and communities were encouraged to cook for themselves. Besides this, around 424 doctors were deputed by the UBSS across more than 1,500 villages for providing primary healthcare to the survivors (Behera and Sarkar 2003, 132–133). Also, *swayamsevaks* at Sambalpur, Dhenkanal and Meramandali Railway Stations on the South Eastern Railway organized free food distribution for many passengers in trains which were stranded due to the cyclone. A BJP official

[4] Data for this section and the subsequent sections from here have been collected through numerous informal interactions with RSS members and community members of villages taken up for fieldwork.

in Bhubaneswar, Ajay Mohanty, mentioned in an interview (31 October 2012) that the district collector had requested him to provide some *swayamsevaks* and BJP party workers to help with packing relief boxes that were being prepared for air dropping. Soon after, 200 *swayamsevaks* were engaged in this job. A local businessman of Bhubaneswar (Praveen Lal, Interview, November 2012), who had been involved with the UBSS relief work after the cyclone, said that although several NGOs were engaged in providing relief, there was severe mismanagement in their administration. In contrast, distribution done by UBSS, according to him, was far more orderly as the needs of the affected population were assessed through surveys and records maintained.

The strength of the RSS network can be inferred from the way in which the organization's top brass mobilized its cadre, affiliates and partners after the Super Cyclone. The *sarsang-hchalak* during that time, Rajendra Singh and Sarkaryavah H. V. Seshadri, launched a nationwide appeal to the people in general and *swayamsevaks* in particular to treat the Super Cyclone as a national tragedy and come forward to provide all possible aid to those affected by the disaster in Odisha. Rajendra Singh donated ₹5000 from his personal funds for the relief of victims (*Organiser* 28 November 1999, 5). Meanwhile, the Delhi unit of the RSS launched a money and material collection drive in response to an appeal by senior leader H. V. Seshadri. In order to elicit support of the public and mobilize funding for its relief work, then Kshetriya Karyavah of the RSS for Andhra and Odisha and Saha Prant pracharak of Odisha, Ajit Prasad Mohapatra, undertook a trip to Mumbai and Delhi to meet with important functionaries of the RSS and other service organizations and trusts (UBSS 2000, 36–38). The Utkal Prant Karyavah Bipin Bihari Nanda urged people to donate generously. Deenanath Batra, then secretary of Vidya Bharati Akhil Bharatiya Shikhsa Sansthan, also sent a circular to all the Samitis affiliated to the Sansthan that money and other material be collected through the Shishu Mandirs and sent to Odisha immediately (UBSS 2000, 23).

In response to these appeals, people from all over the country donated in cash and kind; relief material came in the form of rice, clothes and medicines. *Swayamsevaks* in every *shakha* collected small and big donations in their localities and sent them through drafts. Children studying in Saraswati Shishu Mandirs (schools run by the Sangh's education wing, Vidya Bharati) also did their bit to collect donations. Overseas affiliates of the Parivar such as Sewa International appealed to the Hindu diaspora community in Singapore, USA, UK and Canada for support. Radheshyam Choudhuri, then member of Calcutta Stock Exchange and a representative of Friends of Tribal Society, shuttled between Calcutta and Erasama to mobilize maximum relief (UBSS 2000, 38). Members of Parliaments and legislators belonging to the BJP contributed one month's honorarium, while different units of BJP at different levels involved themselves in mobilizing funds for the UBSS. Vidya Bharati mobilized funds for the reconstruction of damaged schools from several agencies such as the Gem and Jewellery National Relief Foundation, the Bhansali Trust, the Free Trade Union Multipurpose Project Trust and Sewa International.

Several important leaders from the Sangh Parivar flew down to Odisha during this time, including then Prime Minister Atal Bihari Vajpayee; Kushabhau Thakre, who was then National President of the BJP; Pramila Medhe, then *karyavahika* of Rashtra Sevika Samiti; and Dineshananda Goswamy, then president of ABVP. The BJP unit in Gujarat extended support by sending a team of around 195 doctors in the second week of November. By the first week of December, this massive mobilization of relief, according to the RSS, resulted in the deputation of close to 8,000 *swayamsevaks* who came from different parts of the country to offer their services in Odisha (*Organiser* 5 December 1999, 9).

Establishing Mass Contact through Relief Programmes

An important aspect of the relief work carried out by the RSS was that it provided the Sangh with an opportunity to come in contact with a huge number of people who were affected by the disaster. It was during the course of the relief work that several new *shakhas* mushroomed in the villages of coastal Odisha, a territory which had had so far very little association with the RSS before. An ex-RSS *pracharak*, who was responsible for 13 centres during the relief phase, mentioned that out of around 2,000 *swayamsevaks* who had volunteered for the immediate relief work in Jagatsinghpur, around 350–400 *swayamsevaks* had stayed back for another two months (Tarun Das, Interview, 10 November 2012). These *swayamsevaks* were instrumental in organizing evening *shakhas* in those villages where they were working.

In his own words,

> The primary work of *swayamsevaks* is *shakha vistaar* (expanding the number of *shakhas*). And in *shakhas* we teach boys the importance of serving the country. In 1999, after the disaster, several hundreds of swayamsevaks came from all over India. Even though they spoke different languages, we all worked together to serve the people. After relief work would be completed for the day, we would assemble the village men and boys and run *shakhas*. Around 50 teams of *swayamsevaks* ran close to 100 *shakhas* in the coastal areas, between November 1999 and May 2000.

What is evident from Das's account is not only the fact that the relief process was strategically utilized to further a larger ideological agenda but also that it facilitated a certain bonding among *swayamsevaks* who had perhaps never known each other before this calamity. The fact that non-Odia-speaking volunteers plunged into conducting *shakhas* in a remote coastal region of a state they had probably never visited before, demonstrates not only their commitment and passion but also the power of the *seva* ethic that binds the Sangh together.

The relief centres were frequently visited by RSS leaders who used these occasions as political platforms to engage with people. In May 2000, K. S. Sudarshan, then *sarsanghchalak* of the RSS, visited Tirtol and Erasama blocks in Jagatsinghpur and addressed a crowd of about a thousand people on a football ground. This rally was attended by a host of *swayamsevaks*, community people and *sadhus* from various mathas. Among other things, Sudarshan pressed upon the need to be wary of elements that may try to convert people to other faiths through the course of rehabilitation. The obvious reference here was to several Christian NGOs who were active in Erasama.

The RSS also used their relief work as an opportunity to project a non-sectarian and humanitarian image for itself. With reference to its relief work post the cyclone, a UBSS publication states the following:

> The fact that food was served to all the affected people alike without any consideration of caste, religion or language, attracted all discerning eyes. (UBSS 2000, 17)

On the same page, a photograph of a community kitchen shows the banner of UBSS and volunteers in khaki shorts serving a Muslim community (evident from the skullcaps worn by the men). This was also verified by a field visit undertaken in a Muslim-dominated village named Chaulia in Erasama block which was completely ravaged by the cyclone. Community members named UBSS as one of the first agencies to have set up a community kitchen and also mentioned that it later undertook rehabilitation projects such as tilling the land and providing tools of livelihoods to the villagers (Group interview with villagers in Chaulia village, Erasama block, 7 November 2012).

The relief period witnessed a phase of solidarity between various affiliates of the Parivar. As evident from the previous chapter, commitment to *seva*, especially in times of crisis is an ethic that is common to most affiliates of the Parivar. Hence, mobilizing affiliate organizations was not a difficult task. The UBSS participated, supported and co-organized several projects along with its other affiliates. One of these was the distribution of educational kits by the UBSS and ABVP to 25,250 students of tenth standard who had lost their study material, over 11 districts (UBSS n.d.). ABVP also started several temporary hostels named Vidyarthi Kalyan Kendras for students preparing for board examinations the following year. They initiated another project named 'Jeeva Daya'; UBSS partnered with VHP to provide cattle fodder and veterinary treatment in over seventy villages (UBSS n.d.). The UBSS also strengthened its ties with various Hindu organizations such as Bharat Sevashram Sangha, Ramakrishna Mission Math, Mata Amritanandamayi, Chinmaya Mission, Swaminarayan Sanstha, Anukul Chandra and several mathas during this period. Swayamsevak Amar Rout (Interview, 25 November 2012) mentioned that association with these partners was either in the form of RSS volunteers escorting the relief trucks of these agencies to appropriate destinations or helping them distribute relief in an efficient manner. These partners along with other fraternal groups such as Sri Ravi Shankar's Art of Living Society and Patanjali Yog Samiti continue to have a good relationship with the Sangh and are invited during functions, seminars and training programmes organized by the UBSS. Swami Ananda Maharaj of the Ramakrishna Mission Math, Bhubaneswar (Interview, November 2012) validated this when he mentioned that despite their differences, a cultural, if not ideological convergence between the RSS and their own organization is not surprising as they both cater primarily to the Hindu population.[5] Apart

[5] An interesting analysis of the affinities between the Bharat Sevashram Sangh and Hindutva organizations has been conducted by Voix (2011, 227).

from these organizations, mathas are another important ally of the Parivar in coastal Odisha. In Kharagpur village (located in Tirtol block of Jagatsinghpur district), for instance, the local Lakshmi Narasimha Matha is a chief patron for RSS activities.

Mobilization through Cyclone Relief

Although the RSS has always contested Christians in the tribal dominated regions of Odisha, it encountered its nemesis in coastal Odisha in the form of Christian NGOs which established base in Erasama after the Super Cyclone. A local RSS activist (Rabindra Biswal, Interview, 8 November 2012) in Narua mentioned that after the Super Cyclone, Erasama witnessed a deluge of 'Christian NGOs', some of which have embedded themselves firmly into the locality. The rehabilitation efforts of World Vision, in particular, he alleged were accompanied with efforts at proselytizing the villagers. Around 20 Dalits in Deika village, in Japa Panchayat of Erasama, have allegedly been converted to Christianity. These claims were refuted by members of World Vision who mentioned that their primary tasks as part of Cyclone rehabilitation has been livelihood generation. Similarly, several members of the Dalit community in Deika also denied any attempts at conversion through either 'force' or 'allurement', although they did admit that World Vision had established a 'church-like' structure in the village which served as a meeting hall (Amar Kandi and Subhas Bhoi, Interview, 15 November 2012). A local RSS activist in Erasama claims (Ajay Sahu, Interview, 15 November 2012) that one of the primary tasks of the local Hindu *sangathan* here has been to arrest conversion by organizing awareness building programmes that urge villagers to protect their own culture and *sanskriti*. They are supported in this activity by the local mathas. Awareness building activities in this area have also culminated into more violent activities of reconversion.

This mobilization proved fruitful in later years when the Kandhamal riots broke out in 2008. Social activist Sudhir Pattnaik

(Interview, 30 October 2012) mentioned that hundreds of RSS activists and VHP affiliated *sadhus* of several mathas from coastal Odisha had contributed enormously in mobilizing communities to participate in the Kandhamal riots. According to him, the violence that was sustained for so long was not a spontaneous reaction of the local tribal Kondh community. The people who provided the fuel, energy, psychological support and material resources, he suggested were mostly from coastal Odisha.

RSS Rehabilitation Efforts

Angana Chatterjee suggests that the Cyclone of 1999 presented an opportunity to the Sangh Parivar to gain a foothold in coastal Odisha through massive burgeoning of its organizations (Chatterjee 2009, 158). She however does not dwell on the nature and scale of these organizations. An examination of the relief and rehabilitation processes carried out by the RSS after the Super Cyclone in Odisha points towards one unambiguous phenomenon—that of the consolidation and expansion of the RSS's service organization, the UBSS. The UBSS was founded by RSS *swayamsevaks* who had participated in relief operations after the massive 1982 floods in Odisha which had affected eight districts, leading to huge destruction of farm land and displacement of people. Although it was established in 1982, it was not until the Super Cyclone in 1999 that the organization attained some visibility. By the UBSS's own admission, the organization grew in size and activities only after 1999 (Deepak Lohia, Interview, 31 October 2012). A senior correspondent of The *Hindu*, Odisha, corroborated this when he said, 'They were never a known NGO before the Super Cyclone' (Sanjay Das, Interview, *The Hindu*, 1 November 2012). Thus, an organization which had for long remained a dormant body, between 1982 and 1999, positioned itself as the chief institution to coordinate the Sangh's relief work across the state after the cyclone.

The UBSS's rehabilitation activities after the Super Cyclone followed two distinct trajectories: the first focused on undertaking projects that were directly aimed at rehabilitating cyclone affected damages while the second undertook an expansion of RSS *seva* activities in areas which were unaffected by the cyclone. The second route was an outcome of the revamping and overhauling of the institutional structure of the UBSS itself. Both these different kinds of projects, helped in furthering the agenda of Hindutva in their own way.

Rehabilitation of Cyclone Affected Areas

Land Tilling and Orphanage Construction

One of the most popular and well-remembered projects of the UBSS is that of mass tilling of several acres of farm land, which had become inundated with saline water brought in by the tidal floods. With generous support from the Gems and

FIGURE 4.2 *Jashoda Sadan, Cuttack*

Source: Author (field visit).

Jewellery National Relief Fund, Mumbai, the UBSS claimed to have arranged for the tilling of 25,000 acres of land across 254 affected villages. Apprehensions of conversion of orphaned children by Christian NGOs after the cyclone led the RSS to focus their attention on adopting orphans after the Super Cyclone. This led to the establishment of an orphanage by the name of Jashoda Sadan (Figure 4.2) in Cuttack in collaboration with VHP. Senior VHP leader, Govind Ray (Interview, 17 November 2012), mentioned that a total of 72 children, who had been orphaned during the Super Cyclone, had been housed here. Over a period of 5–7 years, after these children had completed their matriculation, their distant families were traced and they were gradually sent back to their villages. Some of these children have also been adopted by some families in Cuttack. Jashoda Sadan is a spacious and clean building with a capacity to house 500 children. During the course of the fieldwork conducted in 2012, there were 65 children who lived there. It is interesting to note here that although this building had been built for the Super Cyclone survivors, it is now mostly inhabited by children from tribal dominated districts of Odisha. None of these children are orphans; they all stay here as their parents are unable to meet the expenses of their education. This destitute home provides an ideal environment for initiating these children into the ethos of Hindutva by introducing them to 'cultural, moral and spiritual lessons' through stories and parables.

Cyclone Shelters

The UBSS built two shelters or 'ashray sthals' after the cyclone. These two shelter houses are located in Narua (Jagatsinghpur district) (Figure 4.3) and Udala (Mayurbhanj district). Since their establishment, these shelters have served as *sanskar kendras* or 'cultural centres' where children are taught devotional songs dedicated to Bharat Mata, stories about patriotism and traditional values and culture of Indian society, such as love and respect for elders, etc. While in Udala, the shelter house

| FIGURE 4.3 | *UBSS Cyclone Shelter in Narua, Jagatsinghpur, Odisha* |

Source: Author (field visit).

serves to provide discourses on 'Indian culture' to tribal children; in Narua, it serves as a women's stitching and embroidery training centre in the evenings and as a meeting place for local Sangh activists.

Saraswati Shishu Mandirs

By the RSS's own account, a total number of 67 Saraswati Shishu Mandirs suffered damages due to the cyclone; while some required complete reconstruction, others required major renovation work. The UBSS along with Shiksha Vikas Samiti (the equivalent of Vidya Bharti in Odisha) undertook the repair and reconstruction of several such schools across Odisha with the support of Sewa International. In the course of reconstructing

FIGURE 4.4 *Keshab Dham in Gatirout Patna, Cuttack*

Source: Author (field visit).

these schools, some schools that had been partially damaged by the cyclone were completely revamped and upgraded in terms of infrastructure and facilities. One such residential school named Keshab Dham in Gatirout Patna (Figure 4.4), near Cuttack, has been completely revamped after the Super Cyclone.[6] The school which initially housed only about 170 students now has 430 students and is spread over a sprawling campus. The school had suffered major infrastructure damages during the Super Cyclone and all the trees were uprooted. The funding for the reconstruction and revamping of the school was provided by Sewa International, UK (Figure 4.5).

[6] Information on this school is based on the observation conducted during a visit conducted on 6 November 2012 and conversations with the Pradhan Acharya of the school.

FIGURE 4.5 *Keshab Dham Memorial Plaque*

Source: Author (field visit).

Being a residential school, its teachers reside with the students following the ancient gurukul system and play a major role in shaping the character of the pupils. Most of the *acharyas* (teachers) of this school are *swayamsevaks* and are the primary agents for imparting 'sanskar and sanskriti'. The school houses a massive auditorium which serves as a sociocultural centre where all functions, annual events and trainings are held. One wall of the auditorium showcases cardboard standees of Chaitanya (a 16th-century Vaishnava saint and social reformer), Subhash Chandra Bose (freedom fighter), Gopabandhu Das (an eminent 19th-century Odia social worker, reformer and freedom fighter) and Swami Lakshmanananda Saraswati (Figure 4.6). The positioning of Swami Lakshmanananda along with other leaders and martyrs is deliberate and seeks to act as a constant reminder of his assassination by the 'anti-national' Christians.

	Cardboard Standees of Religious, Nationalist
FIGURE 4.6	and Hindu Nationalist Heroes in the Auditorium
	of Keshab Dham, Gatirout Patna, Cuttack

Source: Author (field visit).

The significance of strengthening Saraswati Shishu Mandirs and education as a medium of mass mobilization cannot be underestimated. Chatterjee (*Asian Age* 11 November 2003) has argued that Shishu Mandirs, which are extremely popular in Odisha among the middle classes for their affordability and their emphasis on imparting cultural values to children, provide a congenial space for mobilizing young and impressionable minds into the ideology of Hindutva. The curriculum, pedagogy, the constant allusion to Hindu *samskaras* (values), rituals, festivals and traditions help in creating a collective and distinct self-identity among the students. Students of such schools, who go on to become service professionals in the future, are natural vanguards of Hindutva. The act of strengthening and expanding the educational apparatus after the Super Cyclone, keeping in mind future returns, therefore, was a political masterstroke on the part of the RSS.

Interviews with two teachers (Ashish Mohanty and Bishnu Pati, Interview, November 2012) in this school also reveal a spiritual Hindu orientation that motivates them to work. Both the teachers used words such as *samskaras* to describe their work. Ashish Mohanty, who has been associated with the school for over five years mentioned,

> Samskaras form a very important foundation for all work. All modern problems are because of lack of values ... we have more problems because of excess money, not because of poverty.

In a similar vein, Bishnu Pati, who has been associated with the RSS since his childhood, remarked,

> Unlike other organizations, the RSS emphasizes on building good 'samskaras' (values); if you instil the right kind of values in people, their plight will automatically improve. Development is not only about giving money and building toilets or schools.

Expansion of Seva Activities in Non-Cyclone Affected Areas

One of the biggest benefits that the UBSS derived from its participation in disaster relief after the Super Cyclone was the opportunity to strengthen its organizational base and infrastructure and expand the network of its *seva* activities. As mentioned before the Cyclone relief funds helped the UBSS establish itself as an organization, in terms of infrastructure, manpower and activities. This was also reflected in a shift in the nature of *seva* activities that the UBSS had been involved in. Over the years, from being an organization that only provided relief and rescue in times of disasters, it has moved in

FIGURE 4.7 *Sprawling Campus of UBSS Office, Bhubaneswar*

Source: Author (field visit).

the direction of providing institutionalized service. The UBSS, which operated out of the RSS *karyalay* (office) in Cuttack in the pre-Super Cyclone days, now has its own office on a sprawling campus in the Mancheswar industrial area of Bhubaneswar (Figure 4.7). The plot of land on which its new office has been constructed was made available in the year 2000 by K. V. Singhdeo of the BJP, who was the minister of Industry in the BJP–BJD government in Odisha. The Bhoomi Pujan was attended by then Sarsanghchalak K.S. Sudarshan (Figure 4.8)

The UBSS office is also equipped with a huge auditorium and lodging facilities for about 50 people. The portraits of Hedwegar and Golwalkar are put on display in several rooms of the building. The auditorium is used in the mornings for yoga classes. At other times, the hall is utilized for organizing

FIGURE 4.8 *Plaque Showing Details of UBSS Inauguration*

Source: Author (field visit).

RSS meetings, training programmes for various UBSS activities such as teachers' training workshops for teachers of Balmiki Shiksha Yojna, acupressure training, etc., and even conducting cultural events. In January 2007, a Bharat Mata *mandir* (temple) was inaugurated by Baba Ramdev (an influential yoga guru) in the presence of several hundreds of people who attended the function.

Apart from serving as the office of the UBSS, this two-storied building also serves as a multipurpose treatment centre named Seva which provides facilities of physiotherapy, naturopathy, homeopathy, acupressure and yoga. The treatment costs being reasonably lower than allopathic treatment, the centre has managed to attract a considerable number of patients from lower middle-class families.

A senior leader of the UBSS candidly admitted that most of the permanent projects of the UBSS unfolded around 2000–2001 as the organization had access to huge funds. He further mentioned that these projects were intended to build contact with newer areas and extend the UBSS network. In 2000, the UBSS started a project known as Balmiki Shiksha Yojana (Figure 4.9), one teacher school model, which is similar to the Ekal Vidyalayas run by VHP and Friends of Tribal Society in Odisha. A series of these schools were started in slums and rural areas for students between the age group of 5–14 years, who had either dropped out of regular school or were unable to enrol due to their circumstances at home. Some of these schools continue to operate even today. From 2001 onwards, five orphanages were started in different locations of Odisha. While one orphanage named Matru Nilaya was started in Cuttack in

FIGURE 4.9 *A Balmiki Shiksha Yojana in Cuttack*

Source: Author (field visit).

the year 2001, four others were established in quick succession by the name of Jagannath Niketan in the tribal dominated districts of Gajapati, Sambalpur, Rayagada and Mayurbhanj.

Besides, its work in education and childcare, the UBSS has also focused its efforts in the field of healthcare. In 2002–2003, the organizations started an initiative called Sushruta Swasthya Sahayata Kendra which literally means patient aid centres (UBSS n.d.). Starting with the first centre in Cuttack, these centres were gradually expanded to other districts such as Khurdha, Ganjam and Sambalpur. These centres are attached to a medical college or a hospital and are intended to serve the poor and needy patients who cannot afford medical and accommodation expenses. Another medical project that was begun after the cyclone was the Sushruta Swasthya Seva Parakalpa, which comprises operating mobile medical units in some of the remotest villages in tribal dominated backward districts. These mobile units are equipped with a doctor, attendant and a driver and have access to the remotest parts of the state where the government's presence is a pipe dream. This is especially true in places like Malkanagiri where no government vehicles dare to venture for the fear of getting kidnapped by Naxalites.

The above-mentioned projects go hand in hand with other activities such as health awareness camps about impending dangers of sun stroke, blood donation camps, free naturopathy and yoga treatment-cum-awareness camps in the villages, cleaning of hospital campuses, constructing additional bore wells in several villages, etc. The organization has also continued to conduct relief operations during several floods that have hit the state between 2000 and 2011 (UBSS Newsletters 2010–2012). In the recent years, it has also made efforts to provide relief to targeted Hindu communities by offering service during festivals such as Shivaratri and Jagannath Rath Yatra (UBSS Newsletter July–September 2011, January–March 2012) and even after communal riots such as the Kandhamal violence of 2008 (UBSS, n.d. 'Kandhamal Speaks'). These activities have enabled the

UBSS to come in touch with a sizeable number of middle-class Odia people and be favourably looked upon by the population at large. The process of building a compassionate brand image has been a soft and effective form of mobilizing support. Freely available to anyone, these welfare services enable the organization to build a network of sympathizers, supporters, well-wishers and perhaps even potential members. The beneficiaries of these projects also contribute generously to the UBSS. While rich businessmen (especially Marwaris) provide generous support, common people also donate on occasions such as birthdays, weddings and funerals. It is important to note here that the Indian administration has granted the UBSS the statutory registrations that exempt it from tax on the donations it receives and authorizes it to receive foreign funds. Donors also get a tax benefit for the contributions made to the organization.

Conclusion

An analysis of the humanitarian work of the RSS after the super cyclone reveals that the disaster provided it with an opportunity of revamping its image in the public eye. The UBSS strategically utilized the cyclone funds to expand RSS activities in several places across the state, including those which were unaffected by the Super Cyclone. This resulted in the reconstruction of orphanages, schools, shelter houses and hostels in strategic locations where the Sangh had already built a support base for itself while trying to counter Christian missionary activities. The cyclone occurred at a time when the BJP–BJD alliance had just ripened and when BJP was leading the NDA alliance at the centre. The miserable performance of the state Congress government in handling the impact of the Super Cyclone enabled the BJP–BJD alliance to form the government in 2000. Moreover, the Sangh Parivar managed to mobilize considerable resources (funds and volunteers) for undertaking large-scale relief in the coastal districts of the state of Odisha. It also used this opportunity to rejuvenate and consolidate its hitherto dormant service wing, the UBSS.

Although the RSS had gained some mileage during the period of relief operation by temporarily mobilizing communities through its *shakha* activities, this momentum could not be sustained for long in the absence of a formidable support base in the coastal region. It was perhaps an inkling of this lack of support that led the RSS to divert its cyclone rehabilitation funds to those areas where they had already established a base. Thus, tribal districts such as Kandhamal, Mayurbhanj, Malkangiri, Raygada, etc., witnessed a flurry of welfare projects. While a few rehabilitation projects such as tilling of farm land, construction of cyclone shelters and the establishment of orphanages did benefit the cyclone survivors, a substantial section of its funds were also used to revamp the institutional infrastructure of its own organization. Thus, from being a group that was hardly recognized in the pre-cyclone days, the UBSS emerged as a reckonable NGO with an ostentatious building of its own and sufficient funds to diversify its portfolio and carry out an array of *seva* activities. These activities obviously helped in mobilizing the Hindu community, and the RSS was aided in this endeavour by certain specific cultural, social and political factors that dominate the landscape of Odisha at large.

V

Building a 'Hindu' Rashtra in Post-Earthquake Kutch*

> Saffron scarves flung round their necks and pickaxes and shovels slung over their shoulders, the Hindu nationalist volunteers walk the streets of Bhuj, collecting the dead.... They belong to the RSS known for its discipline and efficiency.... The group has emerged as one of the leaders of the relief efforts in this devastated corner of western India where more than 10,500 people have been confirmed dead.... The effort has burnished the image of the RSS ...
>
> —Chris Tomlinson (2001)

On 26 January 2001, as India was getting ready to celebrate her 51st Republic Day, the state of Gujarat was hit by a severe earthquake which caused extensive destruction to lives and property. Around 20,000 people were reported to have lost their lives across the state and over 167,000 people were injured (EERI Report 2001). The towns of Bhuj, Bhachau and

* An alternative version of this chapter has been published earlier as 'Seva, Hindutva and the Politics of Post-Earthquake Reconstruction in Rural Kutch' (Bhattacharjee 2016).

Anjar, which lie in the district of Kutch, suffered the maximum impact due to their proximity to the epicentre. The total economic loss suffered by the state was estimated at US$5 billion (Jain et al. 2001, 1). This chapter explores the political ramifications of and broader consequences of rendering *seva* in three villages of rural Kutch in the specific context of the Bhuj earthquake in 2001. As evident from the epigraph stated above, the pro-active humanitarian response of the RSS in this case, helped the organizations earn enormous goodwill from various quarters and provided it with opportunities to undertake massive fundraising, direct mobilization and recruitment of new cadres.

In the popular imagination, Gujarat has always been perceived as a Hindutva bastion, mainly because the state has had uninterrupted BJP rule since 1995. But electoral politics aside, a closer examination of the emergence and growth of Hindutva in the state reveals that the Sangh Parivar had assiduously been building a base for itself in the region since the 1940s. Slowly and steadily, the Parivar managed to penetrate every possible realm of civil society and administration, so much so that the boundaries between the BJP government ruling the state and the larger Sangh Parivar which pervades the civil society has almost blurred. In this backdrop, it becomes interesting to examine how the RSS responded to the devastating Bhuj earthquake in 2001 and how the disaster made way for greater visibility and consolidation of Hindutva in the region.

Gujarat: A Brief Overview

The state of Gujarat was formed in 1960 when Bombay state was divided on linguistic grounds into Gujarat and Maharashtra. Gujarat is situated in western India and shares an international border with the Pakistani province of Sindh on the west (Figure 5.1). The population of the state is 60,383,628; SCs constitute around 6.5 per cent of the total population and STs constitute 14.8 per cent of the population (Census of India 2011). A majority of the population in Gujarat comprise Hindus (89.1 per cent) followed by Muslims, who

GUJARAT
POLITICAL MAP

Banas Kantha

Kutch

Patan Mahesana Sabar Kantha

Gandhinagar

Panch Mahals
Surendranagar Kheda Dohad
Ahmadabad
Anand
Jamnagar Rajkot Vadodara

Porbandar Bhavnagar Bharuch Narmada
Amreli
Junagadh Surat Tapi

Amreli Navsari The Dangs

Valsad

FIGURE 5.1 *Political Map of Gujarat*

Source: Recreated from Administrative Atlas of India, Population Census of India, 2011.

Note: This figure has been redrawn and is not to scale. It does not represent any authentic national or international boundaries and is used for illustrative purposes only.

account for 9.1 per cent. Jains comprise 1 per cent, Sikhs 0.1 per cent, and Christians 0.01 per cent of the population (Census of India 2011).

Economically, the state of Gujarat has always been counted among the top five most developed states in India with a consistently high GSDP (gross state domestic product) since the past two decades (Planning Commission Gujarat Report, 2012), enabled through massive industrialization and huge Foreign Direct Investments. However, several reports and studies in recent times have also criticized the economy of the state for promoting an unregulated neo-liberal agenda for exclusively benefitting only certain privileged sections of the society (Hensman 2014; Jaffrelot 2013; Sud 2005).

Politically, the state has been dominated by the BJP since the past two decades (Table 5.1). Since Independence in 1947,

TABLE 5.1	*The BJP's Performance: Gujarat Assembly and Lok Sabha Elections (1980–2002)*						
	Gujarat Assembly			**Lok Sabha – Gujarat Seats**			
	Con- tested	**No. of Seats Won**	**% of Votes**		**Con- tested**	**No. of Seats Won**	**% of Votes**
1980	127	9	14.02	1984	11	1	18.64
1985	124	11	14.96	1989	12	12	30.47
1990	143	67	26.69	1991	26	20	50.37
1995	182	121	42.51	1996	26	16	48.52
1998	182	117	44.81	1998	26	19	48.28
2002	182	127	49.85	1999	26	20	52.48

Source: Election Comrrission cf India.

when it was part of the Bombay state, Gujarat was governed by Congress. The Congress continued to be in power even after Gujarat was created as a separate state in 1960 and was ousted by an alliance of the BJP and the Janata Dal in 1990. In 1995, BJP won a decisive victory and formed the government under the chief ministership of Keshubhai Patel. From 1995 onwards, BJP has been consistent in retaining power in the state, despite a few skirmishes. It retained a majority in the state assembly elections of 1998, 2002, 2007, 2012 and 2017.

The RSS in Gujarat

One of the most important organizations that laid a footing for Hindutva in this region was the Arya Samaj which opened a branch in 1895 in Baroda and became involved in starting orphanages, schools, promoting the practice of monotheism in Hinduism and 're-converting' Hindus who had gone 'astray' through the performance of *shuddhi* (Hardiman

2007, 8). In 1940, Madhukar Rao Bhagwat, father of Mohan Bhagwat, current RSS *sarsanghchalak* in Rajkot, established the first branch of the RSS (Sud 2012, 123–124). The RSS first acquired popularity when it actively participated in the anti-cow slaughter agitations of 1950–1951 which resulted in a ban on cow slaughter by the Bombay government. In 1951, the first affiliate of the movement, the BJS was established in Gujarat, followed by ABVP, which also began its activities in the same year in the city of Baroda, although it registered itself only in 1964 (Chetas Malhotra, ABVP activist, telephonic interview, April 2014). In the subsequent years, the Sangh established other affiliate bodies that committed themselves to service. Soon after the Morbi Floods of 1979, the RSS set up the Gujarat Baadh Peedit Sahayata Samiti (Gujarat Flood Relief Association) Trust under the chairmanship of Dr P. V. Doshi, a *swayamsevak*. The prolific work is said to have won the RSS several accolades, including one from the then Prime Minister Indira Gandhi. This trust later transformed into the Gujarat Sewa Bharati.

The gradual polarization of the Gujarati society on religious lines due to the communal riots in 1946, 1953 and 1969 benefitted the Sangh in consolidating the Hindu community. The wars with Pakistan in 1965 and 1971 created widespread anti-Muslim feelings among 'upper-caste' Hindus which further benefitted the RSS with the support of organizations such as the Hindu Dharma Raksha Samiti (Committee to defend Hindu religion) (Shah 2002, 245). Another important political event that presented itself as an important opportunity to the Sangh Parivar was the Navnirman movement of 1974. Essentially a student-led movement against rising prices and political corruption, the crusade acquired a life of its own with huge participation from the civil society. The student's wing of the Parivar, ABVP, played a leading role in this movement and acquired enormous popularity and goodwill (Yagnik and Sheth 2005, 253–254). Subsequently, the Jan Sangh's participation in the anti-Emergency campaign and its alliance with the Janata

Morcha, in opposition to the Congress, provided further visibility to Hindu nationalists. The Sangh's participation in the anti-reservation riots of 1981 and 1985 enhanced its popularity in the public domain. It was also successful in gradually incorporating 'lower caste' Hindus within the Hindutva fold (Nandy et al. 1995, 104) and mobilizing tribals by strategically creating a rift between the so-called 'Hindu tribal' and 'Christian tribal' (Yagnik 2002). A few scholars and human rights organizations (Lobo 2010; Narula 1999; Venkatesan 1999) have mentioned that between 1997–1999, certain specific affiliates of the Sangh Parivar, such as the Hindu Jagaran Manch, VKA, Bajrang Dal and the VHP, perpetrated a series of attacks on Adivasi Christians in districts with significant tribal populations such as Dangs, Surat, Valsad, Rajkot and Nadiad and attacked Church properties.

These efforts became more organized in Dangs, from 1997, after Swami Aseemananda, a VKA leader, was deputed to the region. Aseemananda initiated an anti-Christian propaganda and aggressively pursued the project of re-converting Christian tribals to Hinduism (PUCL 2006). Like Swami Lakshmananda in Kandhamal Odisha, Swami Aseemananda also initiated a few social welfare initiatives such as provision of free schooling and hostels for children, but his major thrust however was on the 'spiritual upliftment' of the tribals (Reghunath 2014). Finally, the BJP's victory in the 1995 state assembly elections and its successive return to power in the consecutive elections have helped Hindutva to firmly entrench itself in the sociocultural and political imagination of the people.

State Response to the Bhuj Earthquake

The state's response to the Bhuj earthquake was unprecedented and phenomenal. Given that the BJP was in power in both the state of Gujarat and the centre during that period, it left no stone unturned in sending out relief. Within 24 hours of the disaster, the central government launched a massive rescue and relief operation by mobilizing the Indian Army, air force and paramilitary forces such as the Border Security Force (BSF) and the Rapid Action Force. The earthquake was declared a national calamity and relief supplies were expedited to the disaster zone.[1] The Gujarat State Disaster Management Authority was swiftly established to coordinate the relief and reconstruction efforts and the Gujarat Disaster Management Act 2003 was passed to manage future disasters. The aftermath of the earthquake witnessed a flurry of relief actors ranging from international and local NGOs to corporations, government departments, neighbouring state governments, political parties and other civil society networks who engaged in rescue and relief operations, including providing medical aid, opening community kitchens and providing temporary shelter, food and other essential items. The relief situation was characterized by intense competition among donors who sought positive publicity and government bureaucrats played a crucial role in designing effective mechanisms for governance and coordination.

One solution deployed during the reconstruction phase was to allow private agencies and NGOs to 'adopt' villages as part of a public–private partnership. Reconstruction was then carried out by the private agency with the Gujarat government contributing around 50 per cent of the funds (Sud 2001). However, village adoption further exacerbated competition among donors over securing rights for rebuilding particular preferred sites. Villages with certain caste and religious configurations were more attractive to some agencies than others. Simpson (2004,

[1] In less than a week following the disaster, the government of Gujarat had received US$105 million, of which US$81 million was from the National Calamity Compensation Fund, US$18 million from the Prime Minister's Relief Fund and US$6 million from the Chief Minister's Relief Fund (Lahiri et al. 2001). The central government also made available about 95,000 metric tonnes of food and dispatched clothing, tents, medicines, fuel and communication equipment.

140) argues that organizations closely aligned with the BJP in Gujarat were allocated the most 'prestigious sites'. Yet, conversely, the presence of diverse and competing aid agencies enhanced the agency of some villagers who were able to play organizations off each other. Even so, donors of varying types sought to use their relief to impact the social, cultural, political and economic landscape of the Kutch region. Such was the case for the network of organizations associated with the RSS and the Sangh Parivar.

The RSS's Relief Work

A Sewa Bharati booklet *Punah Nirman Chunouti* (n.d.) states that on 26 January 2001, RSS *swayamsevaks* all over Gujarat were getting ready to prepare for *rashtra jagran abhiyan* (national awareness initiative) and *Bharat Mata Pujan* (worship of Mother India) in celebration of Republic Day. Soon after the tremors stopped, this 'ready army' of *swayamsevaks* was deployed in rescue operations. More than 20,000 *swayamsevaks* from all over Gujarat, many of whom had lost family and friends in the earthquake, jumped into action to assist in rescue, medical and cremation tasks. Accounts of *swayamsevaks* involved in relief reveal that the initial mobilization was carried out by local RSS *shakha* leaders who assumed the role of coordinators and mobilized village youth for relief. The most remarkable aspect about this phase however is the spontaneity with which the *swayamsevaks* jumped into relief action. As one *swayamsevak*, who had been an adolescent at the time of the earthquake relief work, mentioned:

> This (the act of doing service) comes to us very naturally. We are taught in *shakhas* from our childhood that serving the country is our foremost duty. Every single boy from my village plunged into rescuing people, nursing the wounded and later on feeding them and setting up tents for them. Nobody told us to do this ... Even now, we tell our children

these stories and inspire them to be ready for any calamity. (Bharat Ahir, Interview, 2012)

He further added that soon after the earthquake, messages were spread through word of mouth for *swayamsevaks* to assemble on a common ground. Many brought along friends and relatives who had no prior affiliation with the Sangh. Volunteers were then organized into groups and allocated different tasks. All groups re-assembled in the evening and reported back the status of their work to the chief coordinator. *Swayamsevaks* of all age groups including children were involved in performing various kinds of *seva*. As one *karyakarta* (Sangh worker) stated that many *bal* (child) *swayamsevaks* assisted doctors in dressing the injured patients, while the older *swayamsevaks* were entrusted with more difficult tasks such as removing debris, pulling out dead bodies and cremating them (Aakash Singh, Interview, October 2012). A month after the earthquake, volunteers from other parts of Gujarat started arriving. Only during the reconstruction phase were engineers, consultants and labourers emloyed on a paid basis.

A few days after the disaster, an RSS control room was set up at Hedgewar Bhavan (the Sewa Bharati head office in Ahmedabad) and nodal officers were appointed to coordinate relief activities. Ten other centres were also established for assessing requirements, dispatching material to relief centres and daily stock taking. Several senior RSS leaders such as Sheshadri and Sudarshan (ex-*sarsanghchalaks*) came down from Ahmedabad, Delhi and other parts of the country to visit the affected people of Kutch (Harish Bhai Patel, Sewa Bharati *karyakarta*, Interview, November 2012). The relief period lasted for about three months during which time Sewa Bharati functioned as the umbrella organization for the RSS, while trustees and Sangh office-bearers managed and monitored the operation. VHP on the other hand functioned partially as a parallel system and conducted its fundraising and operational activities separately from Sewa Bharati.

A prominent theme in the accounts of several *swayamse-vaks* was the active support of the government. Sewa Bharati claims that the district collector sought their help for the cremation of dead bodies a day after the catastrophe and that air force authorities cooperated with Sewa Bharati to transport injured people to Mumbai and Pune for treatment. As in the case of Odisha, here too, Sewa Bharati partnered closely with other Hindu organizations including the BAPS Swaminarayan Sanstha, VHP, Mata Amritanandamayi and the Ramakrishna Mission who also helped in fundraising.

The relief operation also provided an opportunity to the Sangh Parivar to undertake massive fundraising from various quarters. By the RSS's account, more than 22,000 donors, domestic and international, contributed to the earthquake relief and rehabilitation work by Sewa Bharati. Sangh Parivar's international fundraising bodies such as Sewa International UK, HSS in UK and IDRF in America effectively mobilized and facilitated this process. Similarly, VHP raised funds through the organization's counterparts in the UK and the USA. An important contribution was made by the Indian (mostly Gujarati) diaspora community settled in the UK, USA and Canada.[2] Fieldwork in Kutch revealed several stories of how several Kutchis living abroad had contributed generously towards the re-construction of their native villages. A majority of these donors channelled their funds through Hindu organizations such as the Sewa Bharati, VHP and Swaminarayan Sanstha.[3]

[2] Several studies in recent times have highlighted the strong support base of the Sangh Parivar among the Indian diaspora (see, e.g., Chaturvedi 2005; Katju 2005; Shukla 2001).
[3] Asghar Ali Engineer (2002) explains this phenomenon by arguing that Indian émigrés try to overcome their sense of rootlessness by being ultra-Hindu, contributing liberally to Hindutva organizations and providing many of the chief personnel to its overseas organizations. It is also necessary to take into account the fact that most Indians view the state as being corrupt and inefficient which motivates them to donate to private actors.

The public image of the Sangh Parivar received a tremendous boost after the earthquake relief. Sangh Parivar exploited
this opportunity to revamp its tainted image from being a
'communal' organization to an effective and efficient humanitarian actor. RSS publications highlight the secular nature
of relief offered by *swayamsevaks*. A 2001 publication titled
'Dharatikampanesarjano sad' (Responding to earthquake by
reconstruction) specifically highlights a 'group of Muslim volunteers' whose assistance was turned away by Muslim families
in Rampar village because the RSS had already provided relief
to them. Similarly, the RSS's weekly publication, *Organiser*, carried several stories of peoples' changed perceptions of the Sangh
after the earthquake. In one such story, an orthopaedic surgeon
who worked closely with the RSS is quoted as saying that his
prior impressions of the RSS and VHP were that they were only
concerned with 'temple construction' and that these views had
been changed as a consequence of witnessing their remarkable
relief work (Organiser, 18 February, 2001, 4). Even to this day,
while countering allegations relating to discrimination of relief,
Sewa Bharati activists frequently highlight that nine houses in
Chapredi village, which they had reconstructed after the earthquake, were allotted to Muslims.

The rescue and relief efforts of the RSS earned them accolades
from several quarters. All stakeholders who were interviewed
across Bhuj and Anjar unanimously extolled the work of the
swayamsevaks. A senior correspondent of Kutch Mitra, stated
in an interview,

> RSS people came from all over Gujarat and all over India
> during this phase. I have always seen them in action in times
> of calamity and disaster, they come and work very hard to
> retrieve the dead bodies and dispose them. They have very
> threadbare requirements and plunge themselves into action. I
> have seen their work also during the Morbi floods, the Cyclone
> in 1999. They come from nowhere and then they go back
> without claiming any credit or claim. (Manoj Chauhan 2012)

Several media reports and community accounts echoed these claims, emphasizing particularly the praise the RSS garnered vis-à-vis an ineffective state (Louis 2001, 909; Naqvi 2001). Like other grassroots community organizations, the RSS's familiarity with the terrain and their access to local networks enabled it to be better placed than the state to provide effective and immediate relief.

A local Congress leader from Anjar mentioned,

> Despite my reservations about the Sangh, I must admit that they did phenomenal work in providing rescue and relief post the earthquake. I remember how they had rescued people from under the rubble, taken out dead bodies from the debris and did their cremation as well. (Ajay Ahir, Interview, September 2012)

But this praise was not unqualified. The same media which painted the Sangh as a messiah after the earthquake also noted that the RSS had used the tragedy as a publicity exercise by positioning itself as a major donor of relief aid. With a BJP government in place, the relief actors backed by the Sangh were able to access a large chunk of the funds earmarked for relief and rehabilitation. More critical accounts have alleged that the RSS provided discriminatory relief and only catered to the Hindu population. In an article in the *Financial Express*, Kuldip Nayar (2001) alleged that Sangh activists had engaged in providing discriminatory relief by organizing relief camps in selective Hindu pockets and deliberately neglected 'lower'-caste Hindus and Muslims in some areas. He also alleged that the RSS and the VHP activists had 'hijacked' relief supplies in Kutch. The government, he alleged, appeared to have connived at such flagrant instances of bias and prejudice.

A Bhuj-based senior Muslim Congress party leader said that the relief process had been completely captured by the RSS–VHP cadres who concentrated their efforts only in Hindu dominated areas (Azam Khan, Interview, September 2012). This was corroborated by a news report published in the *Milli Gazette*:

> The RSS and VHP are almost running a parallel government. They have their own network and have quickly set up a good organizational structure. They have representatives at the airport to take charge of the government relief being brought by countless Indian Air Force sorties. In fact, they are working in tandem with the revenue officials of the district administration and the officials who have come in from Gandhinagar and Ahmedabad. It is apparent that the BJP's government ... has co-opted the Sangh Parivar and have, therefore, roped in its cadres in a big way for the relief operations ... the government relief camps have also been taken over by the RSS/VHP cadres. (Shashikumar and Varghese 2001)

The report goes on to say that the largest community kitchen in Bhuj was functioning in the Swaminarayan Temple where food was offered to anyone who stood in the queue. However, beneficiaries, many of who were also Muslims, were being asked to chant 'Jai Swami Narayan' (victory to Swami Narayan) or 'Jai Shri Ram' (victory to Lord Ram) by the RSS and VHP cadres. Similarly, in Jubilee Ground in Bhuj, where relief materials were being piled every day and where food was being prepared round the clock, the VHP cadres led the slogan-shouting and asked everyone to join in when they shouted 'Jai Shri Ram' (Shashikumar and Varghese 2001).

Sangh Parivar's Relief and Reconstruction in Three Villages

The following section provides a detailed overview of the Sangh Parivar's rehabilitation project in three villages of rural Kutch that were destroyed by the earthquake. It is also important to mention here that apart from village reconstruction projects, Sewa Bharati Gujarat engaged in several other rehabilitation activities in Kutch. Some of the important tasks include the construction of 220 *bhungas* (traditional houses made of mud and grass) across 10 villages in Bhuj, 31 *samaj mandirs* (community halls) and 62 schools (RSS-run Saraswati Shishu Mandirs).

With regard to village reconstruction, as part of the private–public partnerships and village 'adoption' scheme (discussed above) initiated by the state government, there were two broad approaches to reconstruction. The first was when private agencies only provided building materials to the local communities, who then constructed the houses with their own labour. The other approach involved contractors being employed by the private agency with the approval of the panchayat (local government) to carry out the work (Khera 2002). In the latter scheme, the donor agency rebuilt not only houses but panchayat ghars (meeting room for local government), schools, places of worship, health centres, etc. Sewa Bharati in partnership with Sewa International and VHP America embraced the second approach and reconstructed fourteen and eight villages across Gujarat respectively. In the remainder of this chapter, I address the impact of this work in three villages.[4] Chapredi, renamed as Atal Nagar, and Mitha Pasvaria were both adopted by Sewa Bharati. Lodai, renamed as Keshav Nagar, was adopted by VHP America.[5]

[4] In addition to these three villages, four other villages, namely, Raidhanpar, Juran (renamed as Jawahar Nagar), Jiyapar (renamed as Narayan Nagar) and Dudhai (renamed as Indraprastha), which were reconstructed by other agencies such as Caritas and Kutch Vikas Trust (KVT), the Congress party, BAPS Swaminarayan Sanstha and Rashtriya Swabhiman Trust, respectively, were also visited by the author to build a comparative perspective on how the process of reconstruction carried out here was different from those carried out by the RSS and VHP. Two out of these four donors, namely, BAPS Swaminarayan Sanstha and the Rashtriya Swabhiman Trust are close allies of the Parivar. Insights from these visits have not been included here due to space constraint.

[5] The data for this section is largely drawn from interviews conducted with several community members, swayamsevaks, VHP

Earthquake Memory

In Kutch, the memory of people is divided into two distinct timelines: pre- and post-earthquake. People in all the three primary villages under study remember the pre-earthquake days very fondly. Houses in the old village were kutcha or semi-*pucca* with very basic amenities and architecture such as a primary school, health centre, a *chabutra* (bird tower), a temple and shops. People remember the earthquake in many different and interesting ways. Several villagers in Keshav Nagar recounted that they were on the school grounds celebrating Republic Day in the morning when they experienced huge tremors. Since they had not experienced an earthquake before, many villagers thought that the neighbouring 'enemy' country Pakistan had bombed them. This narrative is an interesting fact given that several villages in Kutch are located near the border and live in an imminent threat from the 'enemy State'. Also, as discussed earlier, these threats had been fortified by the RSS in Gujarat since the 1965 war with Pakistan.

The earthquake had instilled such deep fears in the minds of the survivors that for almost a month after the disaster, many people slept in open grounds despite the provision of tents. Many community members reported that the tragedy had forced them to set aside their differences and cooperate with each other. This led to strengthening of community bonds in a way that was unprecedented. Although the earthquake had claimed more than 12,000 lives in Kutch, the number of casualties in the above-mentioned villages was relatively low. Only Lodai reported a high number of casualties as it is located very close to the epicentre of the earthquake.

Before the earthquake, all three villages consisted of semi-*pucca* (permanent) or *kutcha* (mud) houses, a primary

activists, village elders and leaders and personal observations in the three villages under study.

school, a *chabutra* (bird tower), a temple, and a few shops. The population ranged between 800–1200 people in each village. Hindus were the clear majority community in each with Ahirs,[6] an ethnic group classified as Other Backward Class by the Government of India, being the dominant caste group followed by Dalits (SCs), who were about 10 per cent of the population. Brahmins or the 'upper-castes' were only a small percentage. Muslims comprised less than 10 per cent of the total population in Chapredi and Lodai, while Mitha Pasvaria had no Muslim population. While more than 90 per cent of the community owned land and pursued agriculture as their chief occupation in all three villages, a small percentage of the community, particularly Dalits and Muslims, also worked as daily wage earners. Almost all Ahir families owned livestock such as goats, cows and buffaloes.

In all the three villages, local *swayamsevaks*/VHP activists were the first to initiate rescue and relief by mobilizing the community youth. RSS members reported in interviews that the discipline imbided in the *shakhas* helped them to organize efficiently after the earthquake. Sangh Parivar leaders took upon themselves the role of advocates and 'protectors' of the villagers. They galvanized support to drive away Christian NGOs, negotiated with the government officials on the amount of compensation to be paid for damages, and facilitated acquisition of land for reconstruction of new villages.

Although several agencies provided relief to these three villages, the choice for adoption for reconstructing the villages was made strategically from either side. These villages were 'natural' choices for the RSS and the VHP, as they already had a strong support base since before the earthquake. The RSS had carried

---

[6] The word 'Ahir' is a corrupted form of the Sanskrit word 'Abhira'. Ahir identify themselves as herdsmen (*gopas*) of Lord Krishna and claim Mathura and its neighbourhood as their original habitat. They believe that they came to Gujarat from Mathura with Lord Krishna.

out regular *shakhas* in Mitha Pasvaria and Chapredi since the early 1980s and VHP activists began actively organizing a Hindu *sangathan* in Lodai later the same decade.[7]

Community members in all three villages reported that re-building of their houses started within six months of the earthquake after meetings between the donor agency and the gram sabha (village assembly) of the respective village. Senior leaders of the Sangh and VHP visited these villages regularly during the planning process to discuss housing layout, design and mode of allocation. While other agencies had offered to rebuild their houses, community members stated that they were more comfortable with Sewa Bharati and VHP due to their familiarity with the organizations. While the processes followed for 'adoption' were perceived as being participatory in nature, certain decisions were perceived as 'imposed' by the donor agency. One such issue was the purchase of land for the new villages. Residents of Mitha Pasvaria mentioned that landowning farmers were forced by the government and donor agency to sell off their land at throwaway prices. Senior RSS leaders convinced the farmers to make available their land for the 'greater good'. Some members of Dalit and Muslim community in Mitha Pasvaria and Atal Nagar mentioned that their participation in meetings with the donor was minimal as all major decisions were taken by the sarpanch (village head) and his advisors, who were Ahirs.

[7] Similar dynamics were at work for those villages adopted by non-Sangh agencies. Jiyapar (renamed Narayan Nagar) in Nakhatrana block of Kutch was re-built by BAPS Swaminarayan Sanstha as it is dominated by Patels, a caste group who are devout followers of the Swaminarayan sect. Jawahar Nagar (originally called Juran and renamed after ex-Prime Minister Jawaharlal Nehru) was re-built by the Congress Party as the village has traditionally been a Congress stronghold. Organizations such as Caritas worked collaboratively with KVT (both Christian NGOs) in Raidhanpar, where the latter had been working for several years.

FIGURE 5.2 *Bhoomi Pujan Ceremony at Keshav Nagar*

Source: From a resident villager during fieldwork.

Reconstruction work was initiated with a *bhoomi pujan*[8] led by the donors. In Keshav Nagar, Praveen Togadia (VHP President) and Suresh Mehta (former chief minister of Gujarat) attended the *bhoomi pujan* with over 10,000 villagers (Figure 5.2). The ritual was followed by a large community feast. It was on this occasion that the village was renamed 'Keshav Nagar' after Keshav Baliram Hedgewar, the founder of the RSS, on the recommendation of Togadia. Similarly, Chapredi became 'Atal Nagar' after Atal Bihari Vajpayee, the then prime minister of the BJP-led national government. *Bhoomi pujans* were also attended by senior leaders from the Sangh Parivar such as Sudarshan (then *sarsanghchalak* of RSS) in Mitha Pasvaria and Atal Bihari

[8] A Hindu ritual conducted before initiating new construction projects to seek the blessings of Goddess Earth, to ward off possible obstacles and to increase positive vibrations which would enable a successful outcome.

Vajpayee (the then prime minister) and Keshubhai Patel (then chief minister of Gujarat) in Atal Nagar.

The inauguration ceremonies included speeches by the chief guests and other Sangh and BJP leaders who used these occasions to mobilize political support. Sometimes, these fora were also used by political leaders to assist in meaning making of the earthquake by taking recourse to Hindutva narratives. On the occasion of the laying of the foundation stone in Mitha Pasvaria village, *sarsanghchalak* Sudarshan called upon the community to make Mitha Pasvaria a self-reliant and model village. Sudarshan criticized the growing tendency of blindly following 'Western culture' and called for the need to recognize the interrelationship between humans, animals, birds and trees which had been earmarked by Hindu forefathers as 'vehicles to our deities'. Western culture, he stated, did not respect this relationship and as a consequence there had been massive deforestation and the massacre of cows, which led directly to natural disasters such as earthquakes.[9]

Post-Earthquake Housing Patterns

All the houses in the newly constructed villages were *pucca* in texture, had at least two rooms, a toilet and bathroom with drainage facilities within the courtyard and a gate. Residents of Atal Nagar said that Sewa Bharati decided to build three types of houses in consultation with the gram sabha, with house sizes depending on the extent of prior land ownership.[10]

---

[9] The reference to massacre of cows should be understood in the context of persistent efforts by the Hindu Right to ban cow slaughter in India. Sudarshan's speech was reported in RSS *sarsanghchalak* visit in Gujarat (RSS 2001).

[10] The classification was as follows: 100 sq. ft. plot for individuals possessing no land; 250 sq. ft. plot for individuals possessing 3–4 acres of land; and 400 sq. ft. plot for individuals possessing more than 5 acres of land.

On the basis of this differentiated classification, several families managed to get more than one house as the land was owned by different family members. Houses built on plot sizes of 250 yards and above have three rooms while the other houses have two rooms. Since most Ahirs in the village owned land, they were allotted larger houses while Muslims, Dalits and other 'lower' castes received smaller houses. A similar classification of house and land size was reported in interviews in Mitha Pasvaria. In Keshav Nagar, on the other hand, all villagers were allotted a standard house with two rooms, one kitchen and one bathroom built on a 200m plot. People in all the villages stated unanimously that they did not have to pay anything for construction of the houses.[11]

In keeping with patterns from the old villages, houses in the new villages except Mitha Pasvaria were segregated according to communities in which, for example, all houses of Ahirs were clustered together. According to interviews with some members of the Dalit community in Mitha Pasvaria, a system of ghettoized housing for the Dalits had originally been planned by Sewa Bharati too (Interview with residents of Mitha Pasvaria village, Anjar Block, September 2012). However, following a Dalit protest, a decision was made to allocate houses on the basis of a draw system. The design of the newly reconstructed colonies exacerbated religious ghettoization. While Mitha Pasvaria according to the locals had always been a Hindu village, Lodai and Chapredi had significant Muslim populations. When Keshav Nagar was reconstructed, none of the Muslims from the older village moved in, while in the case of Atal Nagar only eight families were allocated houses. In effect, this made the two new villages into Hindu hamlets. Moreover, while some villages built by non-Sangh Parivar donors have retained the earlier pattern of segregated housing based on caste and

[11] Some, however, later modified their houses to extend a room or increase veranda space.

religion, none of the village communities 'opted' to stay out-side the new colonies.[12] This reinforces the possibility that the villages built by the Sangh Parivar were conceptualized as Hindu villages, the actualization of which made the Muslim community reluctant to move in.

Yet it is difficult to say with certainty whether Muslim com-munities were left out on purpose by the donor. Residents inter-viewed in the old village did not suggest any deliberate attempt to keep them out of the new colonies. A few people from Lodai stated that they did not want to leave their old village as their houses were intact. One also cannot generalize any attempt at deliberate discrimination based on the community profile, except perhaps in Keshav Nagar where none of the Muslims moved from the older village of Lodai. But even there several Hindus also decided to stay back in Lodai and so this was not exclusive to the Muslim community. Some respondents also mentioned that they had rebuilt their houses with compensa-tion received from the government or with assistance from other donors.

The facilities in the new villages are unanimously regarded as an advance on the pre-earthquake situation with new roads, primary schools, bird towers, community halls, *panchayat ghars* (meeting room for local government), drainage systems and 24-hour electricity supply with very rare power cuts. Running water was also made available for at least 2–3 hours each day. Mitha Pasvaria and Keshav Nagar have a primary health centre within the bounds of the village which are frequented by a doctor twice a week. Keshav Nagar also has a veterinary clinic, a water hole for animals and a pond. Keshav Nagar and Atal Nagar particularly stand out in terms of their spacious com-plexes and amenities.

[12] Cases in point include Jawahar Nagar, adopted by the Congress party and Raidhanpar, adopted by KVT and Caritas.

In addition to the above, both Sewa Bharati and VHP also carefully manicured the physical landscape with a definitive 'Hindu' character. Grand *praveshdwars* (entrance gates) demarcate a clear boundary between the new settlements and the old village, along with those who stayed behind (Figure 5.3). They also serve to remind the villagers about the generosity of the donors. Since Ahirs are devotees of Lord Krishna, the donors installed a statue of the lord atop the *praveshdwars* (Figure 5.4). The names of donors have also been inscribed on water tanks (Figure 5.5) and memorial plaques (Figure 5.6). The construction of ostentatious *gaushalas* (cowsheds) has a symbolic significance as the cow is regarded as a sacred animal by the Hindus and the protection of cows is an important political agenda in the manifesto of the Hindu right. Similarly, Hinduism is inscribed in memorial plaques and the boundary walls of houses, which are imprinted with images of Hindu gods and goddesses. Hinduism

FIGURE 5.3 *Praveshdwar of Keshav Nagar*

Source: Author (field visit).

FIGURE 5.4 *Statue of Lord Krishna on Praveshdwar of Atal Nagar*

Source: Author (field visit).

FIGURE 5.5 *Water Tank in Atal Nagar Highlighting Sewa Bharti's Name*

Source: Author (field visit).

FIGURE 5.6 *List of Donors on Praveshdwar of Keshav Nagar*

Source: Author (field visit).

is also manifested in the celebration of Hindu festivals as community events and sounds and language (religious greetings, specific types of songs, etc.). Both Lodai and Chapredi, which are still inhabited, have a more cosmopolitan flavour and are devoid of the Hindu iconography which is difficult to miss in the new settlements.

All three villages also now have grandiose temples occupying prominent sites. Keshav Nagar has four temples, Atal Nagar has two, and Mitha Pasvaria has one. While the older villages also had temples, they were far more modest structures compared to the new structures.[13] Although a few Muslim families also

[13] For a detailed account of how modern environments are negotiated by Hindu organizations, see Reddy and Zavos (2009).

live in Atal Nagar, there is no mosque in the village. Muslims in Atal Nagar continue to visit the mosque in the old village (Chapredi). Local RSS activists claim that during the planning of reconstruction, Sewa Bharati had told the villagers that a mosque would be built if all Muslims from the older village Chapredi shifted to Atal Nagar. This, as already discussed, did not eventuate. Muslims in Atal Nagar, however, did not validate this information.

Although the new settlements are distinctly more 'modern' in terms of architecture and amenities, they continue to perpetuate societal inequalities based on caste and religion. This process of religious ghettoization was not a new feature instigated by the relief and reconstruction work but rather a further aggravation of a long-standing dynamic. The increasingly sharp demarcation between Hindu and Muslim communities is particularly apparent in Keshav Nagar and Atal Nagar. The earthquake relief presented an opportunity to the Sangh Parivar to insinuate itself more deeply into the affairs of village life and to perpetuate religious and caste-based hierarchies. Sangh Parivar activities did not intend to disrupt inequalities as this would be counter to its wider political goals inspired by a traditionalist vision of Hindu nationalism.

In a revealing account, a member of the Dalit community in Mitha Pasvaria mentioned that the 'upper caste' community would initially not allow Dalits to visit the village temple and even discouraged them from attending community feasts (Laxman, resident of Mitha Pasvaria, Interview, October 2012). When this issue was brought up before the RSS, they distanced themselves from it. This was reiterated by a native of Atal Nagar who stated that while the local community occasionally meets with the leaders of the Sangh to seek their advice on developmental issues of the village, the latter does not interfere in any of the community's social issues (Meera Ben, resident of Atal Nagar, Interview, September 2012). This strategy of 'non-interference' in selective issues helps maintain the status quo and its conservative ideology of Hindutva.

Current Activities of the Sangh Parivar

The rehabilitation work in the three villages opened up a continuous channel of engagement between the Sangh and the villagers. Members of the RSS and many villagers claim that even nearly 12 years after the earthquake, they have retained close connections with each other. This has been achieved through a series of mechanisms. RSS activists are active and visible participants in local Hindu festivals such as Janmashtami, Diwali and Holi. They also organize sports competitions, blood donation camps and other 'patriotic' programmes. VHP activists in Keshav Nagar said that they help organize the annual *trishul diksha* (self-defence training), including the use of tridents, for young Hindu men. Sewa Bharati and VHP have organized gram vikas (village development) programmes, including initiating the Kutch Kala Sewa Trust (See Figures 5.7 and 5.8), a women's

FIGURE 5.7 *Signpost outside Narayan Nagar for Sewa International's Kutch Kala Sewa Trust Project*

Source: Author (field visit).

FIGURE 5.8 *Memorial Plaque Showing Details of Inauguration of Kutch Kala Sewa Trust*

Source: Author (field visit).

self-help group which provides employment through training in traditional embroidery. Just as importantly, several villagers also stated that they often approached the donors whenever in need of advice or even money. A VHP activist of Keshav Nagar confirmed this and said that the 'party' tried its best to help the needy by arranging for assistance in cash and kind.

An important outcome of the RSS's relief effort was that it helped in the recruitment of new members. Interviews in Kutch revealed that many were inspired by the work of the 'men in khaki shorts' who had been the first to provide assistance after the disaster. According to a young man from Ratnal village, in Anjar block (Mukesh bhai, *swayamsevak*, Interview, September 2012):

> RSS has always had a strong presence in our village. Young boys of our village would often participate in the weekly *shakhas*. Somehow, I always stayed away from *shakha* activities.... On the day of the earthquake, the local RSS leader in our village organized us into groups of five; we together rescued about 50 people who were trapped under rubble, transported them to a nearby medical clinic and even cremated the bodies of those who were dead. Our village lost around 160 people that day. All the houses were damaged. Some 8–10 people died in my arms alone.... I was very impressed by the work of the Sangh that day. Since then, I have become an active member.

RSS relief efforts helped build a new cadre of *swayamsevaks* who, out of gratitude or respect, sought to be inducted into the organization. According to Sangh activists, this was an incidental outcome of their 'good work' and not a result of *a priori* planning. They however admitted that the *shakha* activities of the organization spiked immediately after the earthquake and that this momentum was sustained only in those villages which were reconstructed by the Sangh Parivar.

RSS members continue to organize regular *shakha* activities in the villages. This is also a primary mechanism of recruiting new members into the Sangh. According to an RSS activist, the process of strengthening a Hindu *sangathan* is a time-consuming exercise (Markandbhai, Sewa Bharati activist, Ratnal, Interview, October 2012). Boys as young as eight years old are encouraged to attend the *shakha*, which is usually conducted every Sunday on an open field. These boys are provided with physical training and introduced to discourses on nationalism through songs, prayers and games. Instead of any direct reference to religion, the emphasis is on protecting the Hindu Rashtra from the 'enemies'. They are advised to lead a moral life and abstain from alcohol, tobacco and womanizing. *Swayamsevaks* are also involved in *seva* activities such as organizing blood donation camps, cleaning *gaushalas* or organizing community feasts during Hindu festivals. These activities help build feelings of solidarity and fraternity among the group. Regular attendees are encouraged to bring in their friends and siblings. While attendance fluctuates depending on agricultural and educational activities, for many families attending the *shakha*, has become a part of their daily lives, and the *shakha* serves as a community space for people to meet and interact. Once a *shakha* stabilizes over a period of time, the RSS attempts to create a larger *sanghmandali* (Sangh group) which may cut across villages. These *mandalis* serve as discussion platforms where members organize meetings around topical issues which concern national security and patriotism. Members displaying dedicated interest and leadership qualities in *mandalis* and *shakhas* are groomed for further leadership in the Sangh through attending RSS camps. These members are intended to be the *margdarshak* (torchbearers) of Hindutva ideology.

Given its proximity to Pakistan—frequently described by the Hindu right as the 'enemy State'—one of the primary agendas of the Sangh in Kutch is 'border security'. The Seema Jankalyan Samiti (border welfare committee), which was started in Kutch after the earthquake by an RSS *swayamsevak* from Rajasthan, is a key actor in the mobilization and militarization of the border communities. This is done through a series of educational and cultural activities which effectively balkanize Hindu and Muslim communities in the region. A senior journalist from Bhuj, on condition of anonymity, revealed in an interview that since the pre-earthquake days, the Dalits who resided in border villages had served as informers to the police and BSF if they encountered suspicious activities. The Muslims residing in these villages allegedly did not favour this and would thus 'harass' the Hindus by 'forcing' them to adopt Islamic customs and culture. The interventions of some Muslim NGOs in this area post the earthquake apparently led to greater consolidation of the Muslims. Activists from Sewa Bharati therefore stepped in to 'salvage' the Hindus and started various *seva* projects in this region.

Apart from sporadic activities such as installing some water tanks, providing rations, installing tarpaulin as roof coverings during monsoons, buying utensils for young couples during their weddings, organizing medical camps, etc., the Sangh has also started more long-term projects for the Hindu Dalits in collaboration with the Seema Jankalyan Samiti. These include various ritual practices[14] and educational initiatives, with the latter involving attempts to inculcate patriotism in the hope that students will become part of a paramilitary reserve force that can be activated in a crisis. Through these initiatives, the Sangh seeks to heighten Hindu consciousness among the lower castes and also consolidate opposition to the 'enemy State'. Because this State is closely aligned in popular imaginations with Islam, 'border security' practices tend to readily conflate the identity of Muslims residing in the borders with opposition to Pakistan.

The Sangh's rhetorical attack on 'Muslim' Pakistan is part of a broader patriotic project aimed at restoring the glory of an idealized Vedic Golden Age of the Indian State. To help achieve this vision, the BJP political machine has fiercely contested state and parliamentary elections. Hindu residents of the reconstructed villages, with only a few exceptions in Lodai, stated that they consistently voted for the BJP even

[14] Seema Janakalyan Samiti has reinterpreted Raksha Bandhan by organizing a ceremony whereby women in the villages tie *rakhis* on BSF personnel as a mark of sisterly affection and gratitude for protecting the nation and to reassure BSF that 'they are not alone.'

before the earthquake rehabilitation. While the Sangh's active role in relief and reconstruction did not create this loyalty, it did help deepen it. An important reason for this is the non-distinction in their minds among the BJP and the Sangh Parivar. Appreciation for the reconstruction work thereby fed into the BJP's political project. As a young man of Atal Nagar said, 'The Party has built this village for us and has always helped us in need. We therefore unanimously vote for the BJP' (Mukul bhai, resident of Atal Nagar, Interview, September 2012).

An important political shift that occurred after the earth-quake was that the new villages voluntarily adopted the *samras* (absorbed, common interest) scheme. Introduced in 2001 by the state government, the *samras* scheme is a system of political representation whereby a sarpanch is chosen through mutual agreement without an election process.[15] The scheme has been fiercely criticized as a move to destroy grassroots level democracy. The ruling BJP government defends it on grounds of encouraging harmony. The system has obvious benefits for the majority community groups and similarly further margin-alizes minority groups. It should not be seen as coincidental that all three villages adopted this scheme soon after the earth-quake relief in which the BJP was prominent, both directly and through association.

Competing Mobilizations?

While the above-stated account may seem to suggest that the Hindu Right has successfully hegemonized their ideology, there are also signs of 'competing' mobilizations initiated through contact with other relief and reconstruction agencies as well as with ongoing commercial and industrial actors. A resident

[15] Under the scheme, the state government provides financial incentives for villages to appoint all-women *panchayats* (Bhan 2012).

of Mitha Pasvaria (Vignesh, Interview, October 2012) from the SC community said that his brief association with Action Aid (an NGO) as a volunteer for their Right to Food and Justice Programme during the earthquake relief phase inspired him to build awareness among his community and to negotiate with the village gram sabha for their rights. The efforts of this young man and a couple of his friends forced the gram sabha to take cognizance of the Dalit community's perspectives on village issues. This example provides a classic illustration of one of the biggest challenges to the RSS ideology: the assertion of the lower castes whose culture is far removed from the great tradition of Brahminical Hinduism which the RSS seeks to instil in them. Recent Dalit movements have defied the need for Sanskritization and argue instead that the untouchables should stand on their own and eradicate the caste system (Jaffrelot 2008). In Atal Nagar, which has only a small Muslim popu-lation, a newly arrived *maulana* (Islamic teacher; he arrived during the course of the field visit) has also sought to mobilize the Muslim community through evening lessons on the Quran. His presence stirred considerable local controversy, and when asked for an interview he was extremely circumspect, noting only that he was merely visiting a family friend and, in his spare time, helping provide guidance to young Muslims. The limited impact and precarious nature of these competing mobi-lizations should be seen as evidence of the increased power of the Sangh Parivar in the region since the 2001 disaster.

Conclusion

An analysis of the relief and rehabilitation process undertaken by the Sangh Parivar following the 2001 Bhuj earthquake reveals that the disaster provided an opportunity for the Sangh to establish and strengthen its contact with beneficiaries, civil society agencies, donors, Indian diaspora communities and the media. The Sangh Parivar strategically used this opportu-nity to position itself as a 'humanitarian' actor and downplay its image as a divisive communal agitator. The rendering of *seva* also facilitated intra group unity and instilled a feeling of pride and oneness among the *swayamsevaks* who participated in relief work.

Reconstruction projects were initiated in those villages where the RSS already had a base and the *seva* interventions only helped in strengthening this foundation. What is even more interesting to note is that despite a large-scale overhauling of existing village structures, the *seva* activities of the Parivar did not result in any radical rupturing of the pre-earthquake social and cultural patterns. In fact, in certain cases, caste and religious fault lines were reinforced.

But the case of the Sangh Parivar's deployment of *seva* is also deeply complex. Many community members regarded the work of the RSS as highly effective and efficient. Many of them even claim to be deeply inspired by the 'good work' of the Sangh so much so that they turned into lifelong volunteers of the movement. Finally, the case of Kutch forces reflection on the extent to which analysts can distinguish between grassroots-level civic organizations, national-level voluntary groups, diasporic networks, and State agencies in the case of contemporary India and the political, social, religious and humanitarian ramifications of these ambiguities. The use of public–private partnerships during the reconstruction blurred the distinction between the Sangh and the state, and demonstrated how the twin processes of secularization and sanctification pervaded the humanitarian space.

Conclusion

One of the most unique developments in the recent history of India has been the meteoric rise of Hindutva as a cultural and political ideology. Apart from the successful win of the BJP in the 2014 Lok Sabha elections, the party has also managed to form governments either individually or in partnership with a regional party in several states across the country. The initiative of writing this book has primarily been motivated by a deep sense of curiosity about this phenomenon and trying to make sense of what may be the possible reasons for its success. A specific focus on the *seva* activities of the Sangh Parivar in disaster situations has provided a useful entry point to contemplate on the same.

There are primarily three strands that this book delves into. Collectively, these three strands try to build a larger story that partly explains why the Sangh Parivar is so hugely popular today. The first builds an understanding of humanitarianism (especially in disaster contexts) as a complex and deeply political space. As the introductory chapter shows, the multitude of relief providers who inhabit this space have their own political agenda to fulfil and this is manifested not only in the ways in which relief agencies respond to disasters and engage in long-term rehabilitation projects but also in the meaning making of disasters themselves. An analysis of the disaster management scenario in India, since colonial times, makes it evident that both State and non-State, 'secular' and 'non-secular' actors partake in this politics. The analysis also reveals that it is an intensely dynamic space and is characterized by the contradictory processes of 'sanctification and secularization'. The intermeshing of these processes has made it all the more difficult to discern the differences between the 'secular' and the 'religious'. What is clear however is that the sacred dimensions of humanitarianism, which had been marginalized for long as a consequence of the association of development with secular–liberal ethics, are now being acknowledged again with renewed vigour. This is also the case in India as is evident from the growing role of religious and cultural organizations in humanitarianism.

The second strand that this book engages with is the category of *seva*. In examining the idea of *seva*, I tried to trace its genealogy from the concept of *dana* and analyse the ways in which the idea metamorphosed at different historical periods such as the Bhakti period, the colonial period, the early nationalist period and the post-Independence period. What becomes evident through this examination is that the concept and practice of *seva* has been constantly evolving and acquiring new characteristics in different time periods. *Seva* as a modern ethic, as a form of giving that imbibed several secular–rational characteristics evolved most distinctly during the colonial period as a consequence of the nationalist movement. This understanding of *seva*, which became an assertion of indigeneity and identity, has had the strongest impact on the contemporary imagination of *seva*, especially in the hands of Hindu nationalist organizations who claim to be deeply inspired by Vivekananda.

What remains constant throughout the evolution of *seva* though is the invocation of *seva* as a 'selfless act', a form of giving that is ideally devoid of any reciprocity. Now, it is evident that, in practice, *seva* is far from being a benign selfless act. The theoretical debates surrounding the idea of a 'free gift' have obvious relevance in this context. A careful exploration of the conceptualization and practice of *seva* in the RSS tradition makes it amply clear that it is essentially a stratagem to advance the project of building a strong 'Hindu Rashtra'. Despite its instrumental dimensions, however, the reason it continues to be so powerful is because people (both donors and recipients of *seva*) are instantly able to connect with its capacious meaning. Most *swayamsevaks*, who are the actual foot soldiers of the Sangh and who are working at the grassroots level, passionately believe that they are truly serving the nation by rendering a form of service that is not only unique but also superior to other forms of social welfare which may be either inspired by non-Hindu or Western religious traditions or secular–rational norms. This ontological shift in the understanding of *seva* has been facilitated by the discourses of the RSS leaders in their numerous writings and speeches. Given its indigenous moorings, *seva* thus is constructed as part of a larger idiom that help people make sense of their purpose for helping the needy and also help in identifying themselves with other practitioners. In turn, the recipients of *seva* enact their gratitude through a moral indebtedness that is often manifested in appropriating certain kinds of cultural behaviour. *Seva* thus becomes a process of identity performance. Paradoxically though, in practice, *seva* does not circumvent the secular–liberal ethos of the development space; in fact, it embraces it. All welfare programmes of the Sangh and its affiliates largely adhere to the modern principles of philanthropy which is evident in the processes of fundraising, bookkeeping, maintaining transparent records and encouraging volunteerism.

The third strand that this book tries to engage with is how the provision of aid in a disaster situation creates opportunities for political mobilization. In the following section, I provide a comparative analysis of how the *seva* activities of the Sangh Parivar, following two disasters (in Odisha and Gujarat) made way for a creative form of enlisting support. The underlying thread that cuts through this strand, stems from the conviction that the provision of aid in any form, necessarily entails reciprocation of some sort. This reciprocation may not always manifest in material terms. However, the very act of giving, especially to the poor, as Kidd (1996, 183) has argued, creates a fundamentally unequal relationship between the donor and the recipient and makes the recipient a 'material and moral debtor of the donor'. This psychological entrapment provides the beginning of any form of covert mobilization.

Converting Disasters into Opportunities

A central aim of this book has been to demonstrate how the RSS undertakes political mobilization through disaster relief and rehabilitation. This has been attempted through an exploration of the participation of the RSS and its affiliates in relief and rehabilitation processes in the aftermath of two disasters—the Odisha Super Cyclone of 1999 and the Gujarat earthquake of 2001. The nature and scale of disasters in both the states were similar in terms of the extensive damage caused to lives and property. In Odisha, the state administration remained paralyzed for almost a week after the cyclone struck and was unable to move any relief in the flood affected regions. In Gujarat, however, the state response was comparatively swifter and more efficient. The Bhuj earthquake of 2001 occurred barely 15 months after the Odisha Super Cyclone of 1999. During this period, the government at the Centre was led by the BJP, while the state governments of Odisha and Gujarat were led by the Congress and the BJP respectively. This political configuration had an important impact in the way the centre responded to the two disasters. In the case of Gujarat, the BJP-led NDA government at the centre declared the earthquake a national calamity and mobilized financial support from all quarters including international multilateral agencies. On the other hand, in Odisha, the Congress chief minister came under massive attack from the BJP–BJD combine at the state government for his inefficient handling of the disaster and received a lukewarm response from the centre. The central government even refused to declare it a national calamity. This alleged partisanship of the central government in the case of Gujarat came in for much criticism. Also, in the case of the Bhuj earthquake, enormous international media attention and the social capital of community networks in Kutch and diaspora networks abroad helped achieve a faster recovery.

The reconstruction phases in the two states however followed very different trajectories. In the case of Gujarat, the state government actively adopted a public–private partnership approach through which several private bodies including religious, cultural, corporate and secular 'non-governmental' organizations came forward to share the cost of reconstructing villages which had been damaged by the earthquake. In contrast to Gujarat, no comprehensive governmental reconstruction programme was organized by the Odisha state government. A majority of the houses, for those below poverty line, were reconstructed through the centrally sponsored Indira Awas Yojana while others were provided subsidized loans through HUDCO. Also, in contrast to Gujarat, the number of NGOs which took up whole scale reconstruction of villages or housing colonies were far fewer in number than in Gujarat. The relief and rehabilitation processes undertaken by the RSS and its affiliates in these two states were to a large extent influenced by the political dynamic of the government in power in the states and the centre during that time.

RSS Response: Relief Phase

Both Gujarat and Odisha had witnessed Hindutva mobilization and its expansion much before the Bhuj earthquake and the Super Cyclone had struck the respective states. The work of the RSS and various affiliates such as the VHP, VKA, Sewa Bharati (in Gujarat) and UBSS (in Odisha) and the ABVP had contributed towards establishing a foundation for Hindutva in Gujarat and Odisha by the 1990s. The capture of state power by BJP in Gujarat in 1995 had further entrenched the power of the Parivar while in Odisha its popularity had begun to grow soon after its alliance with the regional party BJD materialized in 1998.

The participation of the RSS in disaster relief in both the contexts was extensive and involved massive mobilization of its *swayamsevaks* not only in the states of Gujarat and Odisha but also from across the whole country. All relief activities were organized under the RSS's service wings in both the states—the Sewa Bharati in Gujarat and the UBSS in Odisha. The modus operandi of these affiliates was similar in terms of the manner of recruitment of volunteers, appeal for funds and distribution of relief and monitoring of aid.

During the course of the fieldwork, several *swayamsevaks*, who had participated in the relief work, claimed that soon after the disaster, they voluntarily sprang into action in their own local neighbourhoods without any directive from 'higher authorities' in the RSS. These volunteers, many of whom happened to be victims of the disaster themselves, were the first units of the RSS that actively mobilized youth from their own villages, formed them into groups and started rescuing people. Several community members of the affected villages, across the two states, reiterated that these *swayamsevaks* were the first to undertake rescue and relief work and that they actively engaged in cutting uprooted trees, clearing roads and debris and setting up community kitchens within a day of the disasters. Subsequently as the *prant*-level Sangh officials took charge, followed by several visits of senior Sangh members from Delhi, the entire relief operation came to be gradually consolidated and monitored from the state capitals. Thus, while in Gujarat, the control room was set up in Ahmedabad, in Odisha, relief was coordinated from Bhubaneswar. During this time, the national leadership of the Parivar also gave a clarion call to *swayamsevaks* all over the country to lend their services in the relief work.

In both the states, the RSS distributed relief material which consisted of food, water and other essential items. RSS affiliated organizations were also instrumental in coordination and distribution of relief materials that were coming in from other NGOs. Fieldwork in selected sites across both the states revealed that relief was primarily initiated in areas where the Sangh had some rudimentary base since the pre-disaster days. Local *swayamsevaks*, who had been active in building a Hindu *sangathan* since the pre-earthquake and pre-cyclone days, took the lead in consolidating relief in their villages. During the course of providing relief, *swayamsevaks* also started *shakhas* in all the villages where they worked. This rapidly increased *shakha* membership in the disaster affected areas across both the states, although it subsequently declined after the relief operation was over. The collective rendering of *seva* by swayamsevaks in the disaster affected regions of both these states, strengthened their bonds and heightened their sense of a common brotherhood that was dedicated to the nation's service. Several members reported that their participation in *seva* activities in a crisis situation had a profound influence in re-defining their world-views and their commitment towards the RSS was even more strengthened than before.

One aspect in particular which earned the *swayamsevaks* tremendous applause in both the states was their contribution in cremating dead bodies after the two disasters. This was especially relevant in Odisha, where other relief agencies hesitated to touch the putrefying dead bodies of humans and cattle which were found floating in the waters. Information collected from a range of stakeholders, including a few members of the minority community, did not point towards any discrimination on the basis of caste, class or religion by the RSS during the relief phase. In fact, in Odisha, *swayamsevaks* ran community kitchens for a couple of days in some select Muslim-dominated villages such as Chaulia, Erasama, Jagatsinghpur. As noted in Chapter 4, the UBSS also used this opportunity to project itself as a non-sectarian and secular humanitarian NGO by highlighting pictures of UBSS volunteers feeding Muslims. In Gujarat however several media reports (cited in Chapter 5) alleged that the RSS purposely neglected Muslim-dominated areas while providing relief and diverted all trucks carrying relief materials to Hindu villages.

The disasters led to greater bonding within the Sangh Parivar in both the states. Both Gujarat and Odisha witnessed a stream of visits by senior BJP members who supported the Sewa Bharati and the UBSS with funds and other resources. Other than the BJP, several other affiliates of the Parivar such as the VHP, Bajrang Dal, Friends of Tribal Society, NMO and ABVP joined hands with the RSS to facilitate and coordinate their relief efforts in the two states. Sewa International, the international fundraising wing of the Sewa Bharati, actively mobilized funds for the relief and rehabilitation efforts in both the states.

The disasters in the two states also helped the RSS strengthen its relationship with its partners. Members of Sewa Bharati in Gujarat and the UBSS in Odisha mentioned that the relief phase soon after the disasters provided them with an opportunity to work together with other 'like-minded' organizations such as Bharat Sevashram Sangha, Ramakrishna Mission Math, Mata Amritanandamayi, Chinmaya Mission, Swaminarayan Sanstha and Red Cross Society. In Odisha, some mathas in the Tirtol block of Jagatsinghpur district also joined hands with the RSS in coordinating relief work. Many of these organizations helped the RSS with finances for procurement of aid materials.

An important dimension of the relief work was that it brought the Sangh in contact with a large number of people in both the states. These people were not only the affected communities but also a range of stakeholders such as government functionaries, local notables, Hindu religious leaders and other cultural groups. Although the *swayamsevaks* mostly worked in those areas where they already had an existing support base, no matter how minimalistic it was, the relief operation definitely helped in projecting the Sangh as a conspicuous aid provider with a humanitarian agenda and strong organizational skills. Government functionaries such as district collectors sought the support of a 'disciplined cadre' of *swayamsevaks* on several occasions during this period.

Reconstruction and Rehabilitation Phase

While the modus operandi of the Sangh had much in common in Odisha and Gujarat during the relief phase, the rehabilitation phase differed in certain respects in the two states. These differences may be attributed to a number of reasons including the way in which the respective state governments handled the reconstruction activities after the disasters, the individual capabilities and commitment levels of the Sangh organizers and the relationship between the RSS and its political affiliate, the BJP.

As already mentioned, in Odisha, there was no systematic government-driven reconstruction programme after the cyclone and no structured mechanism to involve any private player in the reconstruction of villages. Barring a few organizations such as TATA Relief Committee, Action Aid, World Vision, BAPS Swaminarayan Sanstha and Ramakrishna Mission Math, which reconstructed houses and cyclone shelters in a few pockets, a majority of the houses were reconstructed under the centrally sponsored schemes or through subsided loans. In Gujarat, on the other hand, the state government laid down specific schemes by which private players were involved as important collaborators for reconstruction of villages. This facilitated organizations such as Sewa Bharati and VHP to play an active role in planning and implementing rehabilitation projects.

With the unflinching support of its political affiliate, the Sangh Parivar undertook large-scale reconstruction across several villages in rural Kutch which in turn opened up opportunities for a continued form of engagement with the victims of the Bhuj earthquake. Sewa Bharati 'adopted' 14 villages in Gujarat, in partnership with the government, and reconstructed them on the lines of a 'model' village (*prabhat* gram). It rebuilt not only houses but also community halls, temples, schools, health centres, roads and bird towers. Fieldwork conducted in two such villages, and one village reconstructed by the VHP, revealed that although the Hindus in these villages had always been ardent supporters of the RSS, a comprehensive effort was made by the Parivar through the post-earthquake reconstruction to further consolidate and reorganize this population into a stronger political community. This was achieved through a careful manicuring of the village landscape by constructing imposing *praveshdwars*, ostentatious temples, commemorative memorial plaques, retention of the existing ghettoization on the basis of caste and religion and in two cases renaming of the villages.

In the case of Odisha, on the contrary, the sociopolitical factors were not as favourable as in Gujarat, as the cyclone had had maximum impact on coastal Odisha, which has not been a traditional RSS hotbed. Perhaps therefore, instead of investing heavily in a region where they were not sure of high political returns, the RSS strategically diverted its resources into consolidating its organizational base and expanding its services in areas where it had conventionally enjoyed more support. Barring a few projects in the cyclone-affected areas, the UBSS mostly focused its attention towards tribal dominated districts which were not affected by the cyclone. It initiated a series of education- and health-related *seva* projects between 2000 and 2001 and also utilized its cyclone relief funds to considerably revamp the institutional infrastructure of the UBSS and establish units of yoga, naturopathy and physiotherapy within its campus. Even those projects which were particularly undertaken for the victims of the cyclone (such as cyclone shelters, orphanage and RSS schools) have been strategically utilized over the years to promote the Hindutva agenda.

A cursory glance of the rehabilitation projects across the two states reveals that the process was more planned and intensive in Gujarat than in Odisha. This may be partly attributed to the political configuration of the BJP in the two states. As already stated before, the Sewa Bharati received the support and patronage of the state government (i.e., the BJP) which facilitated them to intervene in villages where they undertook reconstruction. Moreover, there was an ideological convergence in this case as the ruling BJP party was the political affiliate of the Sangh Parivar. In Odisha, on the other hand, despite BJP's presence in the state government (in alliance with BJD) from 2000 onwards, it never assumed the kind of popularity and power it enjoyed in Gujarat due to other competing political forces.

In Gujarat, the RSS and the BJP are in a hand-in-glove situation. A majority of people in rural Kutch, who have a relationship with the Sangh, perceive it to be synonymous with the BJP, or at best the cultural wing of the BJP. This perception is hardly misplaced because the RSS and the BJP do have a strong symbiotic relationship that reinforces their common agenda. While the state government actively supports the *seva* projects of the Sewa Bharati at various levels and even legitimizes its 'cultural projects' under the garb of state intervention, the Sangh Parivar similarly engages in actively campaigning for BJP candidates before elections. Moreover, the brand image of Modi is exploited to the maximum by the Sangh activists who support and defend the political rhetoric of the ex-chief minister through their cultural and developmental activities. This difference in the relationship between the RSS and the BJP could be one possible explanation for the difference in the scales of mobilization in the two states after the two disasters.

Relief and rehabilitation during both the disasters provided an opportunity to the RSS in creating visibility for itself. In the case of Kutch, however, this also allowed for a deeper relationship with its beneficiaries. In Gujarat, several new projects and interventions, such as the Kutch Kala Sewa Kendra, were begun during the course of rehabilitation and pegged to the 'model' villages. Interventions of this nature, although seemingly benign, facilitated in maintaining a continuous channel of engagement with the beneficiaries. In Odisha, on the other hand, the relationship between the UBSS and the beneficiaries of cyclone relief is far more diluted. There could be several reasons for this. One possible explanation could be that the Super Cyclone had affected 12 districts of Odisha and RSS volunteers had spread themselves thinly across these districts. It was therefore not possible to make a deeper dent into any one community or cluster of communities during the limited period of relief operation. Moreover, the rehabilitation projects undertaken were very different from that of Gujarat: the UBSS did not 'adopt' any village. It needs to be noted here that a long-term association with the community becomes possible only when a group entrenches itself in the environment of the people and stays put for long. That did not happen in the case of the RSS in Odisha. Residents of several villages where the UBSS had provided relief seemed to remember little about the Sangh. Only those villagers that were active members of the RSS expressed that they occasionally met with *pracharaks* whenever they visited their village. Some of them also mentioned that the activities of the Sangh had completely declined as people in coastal villages were not enamoured by its ideology, given the popularity of BJD. Some members also mentioned that paucity of funds and the lack of a strong leadership within the state RSS faction were factors responsible for its decline. However, various health and educational projects undertaken after the cyclone made it possible for the UBSS to come in contact with a sizeable number of middle-class Odia people and be favourably looked upon by the population at large. They also helped the RSS to strengthen its base in certain parts of Odisha such as Cuttack, Bhubaneswar and the tribal districts of Odisha.

Both the UBSS and Sewa Bharti have evolved over the years in their respective states and have diversified their work from being purely a relief organization to one which implements other welfare activities. Therefore, while the UBSS continues to engage in relief work post natural disasters such as floods and cyclones, it also organizes awareness camps in coastal villages to prevent sun strokes, blood donation camps and free naturopathy, yoga treatment-cum-awareness camps and offering service during Hindu festivals.

In Gujarat, Sewa Bharati too undertakes a host of projects in different domains. Its projects range from providing educational scholarship to backward children to promoting women's self-help groups in villages. The organization also organizes *seva* through its 'Seema Jankalyan Samiti' which works in the villages bordering Pakistan to raise awareness about the imminent danger of infiltration from the 'enemy State'. The 'Seema Jankalyan Samiti' occasionally organizes medical camps, 'shishu raths' and urges village women to celebrate Raksha Bandhan with BSF.

The role of the Sangh Parivar in these two disasters points to an important feature of large 'religious/cultural' organizations in disasters situations: grassroots-level informal networks which operate through civil society are powerful actors in providing humanitarian aid. While the relief and rehabilitation work of the Sangh was characterized by a definite political agenda, one cannot overlook the caring or 'compassionate' (Davis and Robinson 2012) side of the movement, which was demonstrated through the organization's deep involvement with the local communities' immediate needs soon after the earthquake. By attending to this 'compassionate' side of the Sangh Parivar, and by acknowledging not only the effectiveness of their disaster relief work but also the ground swell of appreciation that this generated within Hindu communities in Kutch and coastal Odisha, the study does not aim to polish the image of the Hindu Right. Rather, it attempts to highlight under-analysed aspects of the moral complexity of evaluating the role of the RSS's humanitarian work in the aftermath of the two disasters. Despite the richness of his ethnographic description and the sophistication of his analysis, Simpson's (2014) recent 'political biography' of the Gujarat earthquake remains deeply sceptical of the possibility of any compassionate contributions amidst the diverse relief and humanitarian efforts of Hindutva activists. A greater openness to such possibilities and the appreciation of the humanitarian contributions of such actors, however politically distasteful, is nonetheless important for developing our understandings of the work of diverse cultural actors in disaster relief and reconstruction.

Humanitarian Response and the Role of the State

This book has thrown up several normative questions that deserve further investigation not only for the purpose of academic understanding but for improving processes in humanitarian response. What emerges as a contradiction from this research is that while on the one hand the RSS did commendable work in providing humanitarian assistance that benefitted several people; on the other hand, it encouraged a culture of political clientelism whereby only people with certain political lineages were able to access the benefits of rehabilitation. Through their village reconstruction project in Kutch, the organization also perpetuated pre-earthquake sociocultural patterns that polarized the affected communities on religious and caste lines by furthering the political ideology of Hindutva. In light of this, one may wonder whether organizations like the RSS are even desirable as service providers, particularly in crisis situations, when the disadvantaged and marginalized populations are doubly vulnerable. Should we then advocate for the State to be the sole proprietor of disaster management in all contexts? Surely that would be an erroneous judgment, since this research also demonstrates that in the whole scheme of things, the state vacillated from being a mute spectator in one context to being an active supporter of the RSS in the other.

As argued in Chapter 1 of this book, the history of disaster relief in India from colonial period onward demonstrates not only the enormity of power that the state exercises through the implementation of disaster relief but also its complicity in causing such disasters. During the colonial period, while enacting the role of a benevolent provider which engaged its citizens in food for work programmes, granted tax subsidies and opened up state granaries, the State also utilized the opportunity to strengthen its administrative control over the sub-continent. The Indian State after Independence has more often than not bungled in times of catastrophes and exploited the process of relief instead for fulfilling narrow political gains. Therefore, there is obviously no guarantee that a relief process solely carried out by the state would be benign or devoid of any political motive. This also ruptures the conventional belief that 'secular' aid providers like the State are more capable or efficient than their 'non-secular' counterparts.

Hindutva as a 'Sacred Form'?

In post-Independent India, the humanitarian field has been populated by a mix of religious, secular and politico-cultural groups. While I have acknowledged that such a typology is problematic due to multiple reasons, it is nevertheless useful in ascribing some pattern to an otherwise chaotic space. While some of these groups have largely enjoyed the support of the State due to their ideological affiliations, others have been more markedly 'non-governmental'. As in other parts of the world, from the mid-1980s onwards, there has been a proliferation in humanitarian activities of religious and cultural groups. This may be attributed to several factors such as the adoption of structural adjustment programmes which encouraged the rolling back of the State from social welfare delivery, growing recognition of the role of religious groups in development world over, the emergence of a strong Indian diaspora community and the invention of the Internet. With massive funding available at their end, religious and cultural groups have taken up large-scale social welfare projects, including rehabilitation after disasters, which have helped them in enlisting greater support for their ideologies. The growing visibility of Hindutva organizations in the humanitarian space is a manifestation of this process. In certain situations, as demonstrated in this book, they have also been assisted in their endeavour by an empathetic State, thus leading to a situation whereby a symbiotic public–private partnership has endowed these groups with more access to political power. Why are cultural groups like the RSS becoming more popular now, in the realm of humanitarianism, and even otherwise?

I would like to end by spending some time reflecting upon the nature of the Hindu nationalist movement in India and understanding the possible reasons for the upsurge in its popularity in recent times. Studies on the expansion of the Sangh Parivar in different regions of India[1] have thrown up interesting insights on the reasons for its rise as a political power. However, none of these studies attempt to undertake a more generic analysis for the phenomenal rise of Hindutva as a political ideology in the pan-Indian context. The book begins with the proposition that the theory of secularization seems to have failed in India, as elsewhere, as religion has made a convincing comeback in the public sphere. This is evident in the installation of yogis[2] as chief ministers, the prolonged continuation of discourses surrounding the construction of a Ram Temple in Ayodhya, mass protests against the imposition of 'secular' values such as opening up of temples to all genders and in the constant invocation of expressions such as *seva, dana, runa* and 'dharma' (moral code of conduct) in everyday public discourse. Here, I expand on this idea a little further by trying to

---

[1] See, for instance, Heeger (1972), Jayaprasad (1991), Hansen (1999), Jaffrelot (1996), Kanungo (2003), Sud (2011), Thachil (2011), Bhattacharjee (2016) for an account of the rise of Hindutva in Punjab, Kerala, Maharashtra, Odisha, Gujarat, Chhattisgarh and Assam, respectively.

[2] A yogi is one who has mastered the philosophy of yoga and who is considered to be at an advanced spiritual stage.

examine if the phenomenon of Hindutva is symptomatic of a resurgence of 'religion' or something else? The inadequacy of religion as a universal and essentialized category has already been established by several scholars such as Peter Van der Veer (1995), Talal Asad (1993, 2003) and Timothy Fitzgerald (2003). These scholars have argued that the idea of 'religion' as a realm separate from the 'secular' has a distinct Western European legacy that can be located in the rise of modernity which was accompanied by the emergence of the nation state. John Milibank (2006) has further argued that the category of religion is ideologically loaded and it serves the purpose of privatizing and 'managing' the non-secular institutions so that they can be discarded as 'myths' and 'unscientific' ideas. The idea of the 'secular' on the other hand acquires a natural ascendancy as it is considered to be in direct opposition to the 'religious' and thus legitimately becomes the space for politics, economics, science, etc. Here, I use these broad set of ideas to start thinking about what could be an alternative and a more appropriate category to describe phenomena that may draw upon certain elements of religiosity but is not 'religious'?

Drawing from the theoretical framework offered by Gordon Lynch (2012), I find it more appropriate to use the term 'sacred form' to understand contemporary Hindutva. Building on the works of Durkheim, Edward Shils, Robert Bellah and Jeffrey C. Alexander, Lynch defines the 'sacred' as follows:

> The sacred is defined by what people collectively experience as absolute, non-contingent realities which present normative claims over the meanings and conduct of social life. Sacred forms are specific, historically contingent, instances of the sacred. Sacred forms are constituted by constellations of specific symbols, thought/discourse, emotions and actions grounded in the body. The normative reality represented by a sacred form simultaneously constructs the evils which profane it, and the pollution of this sacred reality is experienced

by its adherents as a painful wound for which some form of restitution is necessary. (Lynch 2012, 29)

Lynch further adds that the sacred is a 'communicative structure', imbued with power, that 'constructs the idea of human society as a meaningful, moral collective' (Lynch 2012, 133). What is of particular relevance to the contemporary Indian context is Lynch's discussion on the concept of the sacred in modern societies. Lynch says that although the form and significance of sacred forms are contingent and contextual, there are some general traits about the nature of the sacred in late modern societies. Contrary to more homogenous societies, he argues, which are organized in relation to an omnibus sacred form, 'late modern societies are characterized by the simultaneous presence of multiple sacred forms that exert complementary and conflicting fields of influence' (Lynch 2012, 135). In this scenario, therefore, which is far more complex than Durkheim's integrative model of the sacred, conventional ideas of religion are not helpful in understanding the operative category of the sacred in the modern world (Lynch 2012, 37).

If one were to analyse the Hindu nationalist movement through the above framework, it would become evident that Hindutva today indeed operates like a 'sacred form' that although connected to Hinduism is also different from it. The communicative structure of this sacred system is built with the help of symbols and discourses relating to issues of building the Ayodhya Temple, prohibition of cow slaughter, promotion of yoga, protection of Hindu culture from the onslaught of the 'others' and the rejuvenation of Hindu institutions such as *seva*. In this regard, it is important to note that even though the RSS's goal of protecting Hindu dharma, ideology of building a robust Hindu Rashtra and the use of specific symbols of worship imparts to it a 'Hindu character' (Nair 2009), it has always maintained that it is a 'cultural' group. The concept of the Hindu Rashtra is constructed around the idea of

Hindu culture which is identified as the national culture. This recourse to culture, which is a seemingly apolitical category, when compared to religion, is advantageous as it encompasses practically everything ranging from customs, rituals and festivals to political behaviour. The political project, which lies at the heart of Hindutva makes a back door entry through culture. In this scheme of things, the religious dimension, to the extent that it exists, is only instrumental and is appropriated from certain outward forms of the Hindu religion.

Since Independence, Indian public life has been characterized by a liberal political tradition that was actively promoted by the existing political regime led by the charismatic leadership of Nehru. Given the secular leanings of Nehru and Ambedkar, they were largely convinced that ascriptive identities such as religion and caste are regressive institutions which needed to be controlled and regulated. The partition of the country on religious lines in the backdrop of Independence further reiterated the idea that religion was a divisive category. In this political milieu, religion as an institution was kept at bay and never acknowledged as a legitimate participant in the political realm. The political leadership also undertook important initiatives such as abolishing untouchability (provided in Article 17 of the Indian Constitution), codifying and partially reforming the Hindu Personal Law, regulating Hindu religious institutions through opening up of Hindu religious places to all sections of Hindus and enacting temple regulation laws.[3] Even though the Indian State undertook the regulation of institutions of other religions, such as the regulation of the Central Wakf Council, the extent of these interventions was much more limited than

---

[3] Here, the State primarily drew upon the provision contained in Article 25(2) of the Indian Constitution which allows the State to regulate or restrict any economic, financial, political or other secular activity which may be associated with religious practice and provide for social welfare and reform or the throwing open of Hindu religious institutions of a public character to all classes and sections of Hindus.

in the case of Hindu institutions (Thiruvengadam 2017, 199). This obviously did not go down well with the conservative sections of the Hindu population who perceived this as a direct attack not only on their religion but also on their culture and larger way of life.

The Hindu conservative ideology, to the extent that it existed since the freedom movement, was effectively marginalized in public life. The success of the Hindu nationalists may be partially attributed to their attempts at partially reversing this political culture and re-introducing Hindutva as a legitimate sacred form since the early 1980s. The Ram Janmabhoomi Movement that eventually led to the demolition of the Babri Masjid is perhaps the most spectacular feat that they achieved in this regard. What is more important to acknowledge here however is that this facilitated a distinct change in the larger political culture of the country by introducing (for the first time) an unmistakable religious idiom that resonated with large sections of the Hindus.[4] It is this context that one needs to situate the popularity of Hindu expressions such as *seva*, *dana* and *dharma*. Frequent deployment of such 'indigenous' categories form part of a larger strategy therefore to resurrect religion in a largely secular space as an assertion of one's identity. As scholars such as T. N. Madan (1987) and Ashish Nandy (1998) have persuasively argued, it seems 'secularism' paradoxically did actually make way for more extremist Hindu movements to flourish in modern India.

Lynch (2012, 122) mentions that the power of sacred forms lies in that they offer a means for those burdened with the

---

[4] Sunil Khilnani (2003) has argued that Indira Gandhi often 'flirted with religious sentiments and appeals' for electoral purposes and that it was the 'secular modernist Indian elite' who first introduced the idea of religious affiliations in national politics. While I do acknowledge this, I wish to emphasize that the Sangh Parivar played a key role in popularizing this aspect.

'anomie of modern life', as the sacred helps an 'ongoing re-moralization of society'. This does not however mean that the political culture preceding the ascendance of Hindutva was devoid of any moral ethic. A strong sense of civic nationalism which constantly celebrated a national unity cutting across religious and linguistic diversities had been the predominant normative force in Indian politics since Independence. The attractiveness of religion however needs to be situated in the larger context of a certain apathy or dissociation with modernity at large. As Kaustuv Roy (2017, 207) eloquently puts it,

In the wake of the unprecedented success of scientific and technological thinking in relating to the outer world, all other modes of relating to the cosmos other than the positivist appeared as superstition and destined to be superseded by so-called mature forms; these enlightened forms were secular, meaning shorn of any reference to the divine or the transcendental. Between transformation and material flourishing, the world, especially of European man, chose the latter, to be imposed on the rest of the world through colonialism and imperialism. Shorn of enchantment (imbued with spirit), the world increasingly appeared as a consumable, a resource to be exploited, and human beings as discrete, monadic entities.

While the advancement of Hinduism is one important sacred form that dominates Hindutva, there are other seemingly contradictory sacred forms like that of 'secularism' that also influence the shaping of Hindutva. As Partha Chatterjee (1994) has pointed out, the Hindu Right 'is perfectly at peace' with the structures and procedures of the modern state such as secularism. In fact, the common refrain that the Hindu nationalists have often come up with is that they are the 'true secularists' while the Congress is a 'pseudo-secular' party. Thus, issues of neoliberal 'development' that are typically associated with the secular realm are unapologetically invoked by Hindutva leaders, especially the present Prime Minister Narendra Modi.

Finally, one last aspect about the 'sacred' that is worthy of mention here is its trait of being a double-edged sword. Lynch warns us that while sacred forms 'provide symbolic and emotional resources' to people, the irony is that they also make us less able to live without conflict in heterogeneous societies (Lynch 2012, 123). Identification with sacred forms therefore can also legitimize violence, polarize societies and more importantly, when adopted by political elites, becomes a basis for repressive social orders (Lynch 2012, 136). The more virulent forms of Hindu nationalism in the contemporary India make this characteristic evident.

I see this book as the first step towards developing an intellectual project that helps us understand better the reasons for the popularity of Hindutva in contemporary India. Electoral victories aside, it is important to recognize that there is overwhelming support in society at large for the ideology of Hindu nationalism today. The reasons for the Sangh Parivar's popularity need to be interrogated beyond the influence of caste, class factors in localized contexts. These factors can be located only by attempting to understand the moral and religious life worlds and the cultural anxieties of common people who support this movement. I hope this book incites curiosity among those researching on the RSS and propels them to adopt alternative methodologies and philosophical orientations while studying Hindutva.

Bibliography

Primary Sources

Reports

Asian Development Bank. *Asian Development Bank Civil Society Brief 'Overview of Civil Society Organizations'*. ADB Nongovernment Organization and Civil Society Center, Publication Stock No. ARM090269, June 2009.

Awaaz (South Asia Watch). *In Bad Faith? British Charity and Hindu Extremism*. London, 2004. Available at http://www.awaazsaw.org (Accessed on 2 April 2008).

Behera, Aurobindo, and H. S. Sarkar, eds. *Rising to the Occasion: Civil Society Response to the Orissa Super Cyclone, 1999*. Bhubaneswar: OSDMA and CARE India, Orissa Office, 2003.

Bhuj Earthquake of January 26, 2001. Available at http://www.imd.gov.in/section/seismo/static/bhuj_equake.html (Accessed on 24 April 2012).

CAG. *Comptroller and Auditor General Audit Report (Civil)*. CAG, Gujarat, 31 March 2002.

CAG. *Performance Audit of Civil Disaster Preparedness in India of Union Government, Ministry of Home Affairs*. CAG, report no. 5, 2013.

Census of India. *Census of India Reports*. 2001, 2011.

Chatterji, Angana, and Mihir Desai, eds. *Communalism in Orissa: Report of the Indian People's Tribunal on Environment and Human Rights.* Indian People's Tribunal Secretariat, September 2006.

Chiroiu, L., and G. André. *Damage Assessment Using High Resolution Satellite Imagery: Application to 2001 Bhuj, India, Earthquake.* Available at http://www.unisdr.org/files/2966_BhujIndiaearthquake2001.pdf (Accessed on 12 February 2019).

Citizen's Inquiry Committee. *Untold Story of Hindukaran (Proselytism of Adivasi (Tribal) in Dangs (Gujarat, India).* People's Union for Civil Liberties (PUCL) Report, 4 January 2006.

Das, Subrat. *Public Policy towards Natural Disasters in India: Disconnect between Resolutions and Reality.* New Delhi: Centre for Budget and Governance Accountability, 2005.

Earthquake Engineering Research Institute (EERI) Special Earthquake Report, *EERI Newsletter* 35, no. 4 (April 2001).

Foreign Contribution Regulation Act (FCRA) Annual Reports 2000–2012.

Government of India Report. *Non-Profit Institutions in India, A Profile and Satellite Accounts in the Framework of System of National Accounts.* New Delhi: Ministry of Statistics and Programme Implementation, March 2012.

Human Rights Watch World Report 2000—India. 1 December 1999.

India: Orissa Cyclone, Appeal No. 28/1999. International Federation of Red Cross and Red Crescent Societies, 13 November 2002.

Indian Red Cross Society. *Operations Update: India/Gujarat Earthquake—Recovery and Rehabilitation* (Appeal No. 20/01). New Delhi: Indian Red Cross Society, 30 October 2001.

Kutch Nav Nirman Abhiyan. *Coming Together.* June 2001, September 2001, January 2002, August 2002, and March 2003, Kutch Nav Nirman Abhiyan.

Kutch Navnirman Abhiyan. *Abhiyan's Journey Post the 2001 Earthquake.* n.d.

Lahiri, A. K., T. K. Sen, R. K. Rao, and P. R. Jena. *Economic Consequences of the Gujarat Earthquake.* Earthquake Assessment Mission of the Asian Development Bank and the World Bank, 2001. Available at http://www.nipfp.org.in/media/medialibrary/2013/04/dp01_nipfp_001.pdf (Accessed on 15 October 2011).

Lawry White Simon. *Evaluation of the India Earthquake Response, Gujarat Earthquake Operation—Inception Report.* International Federation of Red Cross and Red Crescent Societies, September 2001.

Ministry of Home Affairs. *Together, Towards a Safer India.* Newsletter of the Ministry of Home Affairs. Disaster Management Division, Ministry of Home Affairs, Government of India, August 2005.

———. *Report No. 5 of 2013 – Performance Audit of Disaster Preparedness in India of Union Government, Ministry of Home Affairs.* New Delhi: CAG, 2013.

Narayan, Deepa, Robert Chambers, Meera K. Shah, and Patti Petesch. *Voices of the Poor Crying Out for Change* (World Bank Report). Washington: Oxford University Press, 2000.

Narula, Smita. *Politics by Other Means: Attacks against Christians in India*, vol. 11, no. 6 (C). Human Rights Watch, 1999.

Patel, Aakar, Dileep Padgaonkar, and B. G. Verghese. *Rights and Wrongs: Ordeal by Fire in the Killing Fields of Gujarat.* New Delhi: Editors Guild of India, May 2002.

People's Union for Democratic Rights. *'Maaro! Kaapo! Baalo!' State, Society and Communalism in Gujarat.* Delhi: People's Union for Democratic Rights, 2002.

Planning Commission. *India Human Development Report 2011: Towards Social Inclusion.* New Delhi: Institute of Applied Manpower Research, Planning Commission. Available at http://www.iamrindia.gov.in/media_coverage_compilation/IHDR_Summary.pdf (Accessed on 20 January 2013).

———. *State: Gujarat Report, 2012.* Available at http://planningcommission.nic.in/plans/finres/fr_2013_14/fr_gujrat.pdf (Accessed on 10 September 2013).

Ramakrishna Mission, Belur Math. *Orissa Super Cyclone Relief and Rehabilitation Project Report.* July 2000.

Rao, Ramesh, Narayan Komerath, Beloo Mehra, Chitra Raman, Sugrutha Ramaswamy, and Nagendra Rao. *A Factual Response to the Hate Attack on the India Development and Relief Fund (IDRF).* 2003. Available at http://www.letindiadevelop.org/thereport/ (Accessed on 14 January 2012).

Rashtriya Sewa Bharati Annual Bulletin 2016–17. Available at http://rashtriyasewabharati.org/about-us/annual-reports/ (Accessed on 8 November 2018).

Sewa Bharati. *Sewa Sadhana Report, year 8, vol. 8.* Chaitra Shukla Pratipada, Vikrami Samvat 2070 (11 April 2013).

Sinha, Anil Kumar. *Report on Recovery and Reconstruction Following the Orissa Super Cyclone in October 1999.* Asian Disaster Reduction Center, 2002, 2 Available at http://www.adrc.asia/

publications/recovery_reports/pdf/Orissa.pdf (Accessed on 27 November 2012).

———. *The Gujarat Earthquake 2001*. Asian Disaster Reduction Center, Available at http://www.adrc.asia/publications/recovery_reports/pdf/Gujarat.pdf (Accessed on 3 January 2012).

UNISDR. *Learning from Disaster Recovery: Guidance for Decision Makers*. Asian Disaster Reduction Center, International Strategy for Disaster Reduction Secretariat and United Nations Development Programme, 2007.

United Nations Disaster Management Team. *Orissa Super Cyclone Situation Report 9*. 2 December 1999. Available at http://img.static.reliefweb.int/report/india/orissa-super-cyclone-situation-report-9 (Accessed on 3 July 2011).

United Nations Disaster Management. 1999. *United Nations Disaster Management Team Report*, 2 December 1999.

Web, South Asian Citizens. *Foreign Exchange of Hate: IDRF and the American Funding of Hindutva*. Mumbai, India, and the South Asia Citizens Web, France: Sabrang Communications & Publishing Pvt. Ltd, 2002.

World Bank and Asian Development Bank. *India: Gujarat Earthquake Recovery Program Assessment Report*. Submitted to the Government of Gujarat and the Government of India, Ministry of Human Resource Development, Department of Higher Education, 14 March 2001.

World Bank. *India—Gujarat Emergency Earthquake Reconstruction Project (English)*. Washington, DC: World Bank, 29 April 2009.

Publications of RSS and Its Affiliates

'3 Years of Achievements (April 2009 to March 2012)'. Sewa International Kutch, n.d.

'Samaj Mandir'. Sewa Bharati, Gujarat, Sewa Bhavan, Karnavati, 2002.

'VHP of America Announces Gujarat Earthquake Volunteer Program', *Vishwa Hindu Parishad Newsletter*, 9 April 2001.

Bharata Bharati. 2014. 'Re-conversion to Hinduism Was Approved by Acharyas in Udupi in 1964–65'. 24 December 2014. Available at https://bharatabharati.wordpress.com/2014/12/24/re-conversion-to-hinduism-was-approved-by-acharyas-in-udupi-in-1964-65-daijiworld-media/ (Accessed on 12 February 2019).

Chauthaiwale, Arvind. 'More than 35,000 Service Projects Across the Country. Another Face of Vishwa Hindu Parishad'. *Sewa Sadhana*, year 3, vol. 3, Varsh Pratipada (April 2008).

Deoras, Balasaheb. 'Problems Will Be Solved through Constructive Works, Not through Agitations'. *Sewa Sadhana*, year 3, vol. 3, Varsh Pratipada (7 April 2008), 12.

HSS (n.d.). Blog Post published on the website of the Hindu Swayamsevak Sangh, USA (HSS), https://www.hssus.org/blog/new-jersey-vijaya-dasami-utsav (Accessed on 20 April 2013).

Organiser. 'Mass Funeral or Cyclone Victims'. *Organiser* 51, no. 21 (December 1999): 20.

———. 'Massive Rehabilitation Work by UBSS'. *Organiser* 51, no. 23 (2 January 2000).

———. 'Only Swayamsevaks Cremated Corpses'. *Organiser* 51, no. 21 (19 December 1999): 18.

———. 'RSS in Charkhi Dadri: Ready Selfless Service'. *Organiser* 48, no. 19 (8 December 1996): 11.

———. Massive Relief Operation by RSS'. *Organiser* 51, no. 19 (5 December 1999).

Parande, Shyam. 'Sewa Is the Manifestation of Divine Energy'. Sewa Sadhna, Chaitra Shukla Pratipada, Vikrami Samvat 2069 (23 March 2012), 19.

Rai, Champat. 'VHP at a Glance'. Hindu Vivek Kendra. Available at http://www.hvk.org/2014/0914/39.html (Accessed on 12 March 2018).

Report of the Visit to Earthquake Struck Gujarat by Sewa Team Comprising of Dr. Yashwantji Pathak, Sah-Sanyojak Vishwa Vibhag, Shri Arjun Lalji Sharma. Sewa International UK and Shri Shyam Parande, 5–7 February 2001. Available at http://www.hssworld.org/homepage/html/seva/Gujarat/sewa_report.html (Accessed on 17 July 2012).

RSS. *RSS Sar Sanghchalak Visit in Gujarat*. Press Note, 17 April 2001. Available at http://hvk.org/archive/2001/0401/105.html (Accessed on 21 January 2016)

Sadhvi Ritambhara. 'Salute to the Herculean efforts of Sewa Bharati'. *Sewa Sadhana*, year 3, vol. 3, Varsh Pratipada (7 April 2008), 35.

Seshadri H. V. *RSS: A Vision in Action*. Bangalore: Sahitya Sindhu Prakashana, 2012.

Sewa Bharati. 'Dhartikamp ane Sarjano sad' (Gujarati) [Earthquake and the Call for Reconstruction]. Sewa Bharati, 2001.

————. 'Punah Nirman Chunouti'. Sewa Bharati, Gujarat, n.d.

Sewa International. *Earthquake in Gujarat.* New Delhi: Sewa International, 9 March 2001.

Sewa Kunj: An Insight into Seva Activities. New Delhi: Aravali Printers and Publishers, 2015.

Sewa Sadhana I. Rashtriya Sewa Trust, Chaitra Shukla Pratipada, Vikrami Samvat 2069, 23 March 2012.

Sewa Sadhana. 'Amera Vanvasi Village: Scaling New Heights'. *Sewa Sadhana*, Varsh Pratipada, Vikrami Samvat 2066 (27 March 2009), 73.

————. 'Interview with Sitaram Kedilaya (former Akhil Bharatiya Sewa Pramukh, RSS)'. *Sewa Sadhana I*, Chaitra Shukla Pratipada, Vikrami Samvat 2069 (23 March 2012), 13.

————. 'Nettancode Shakha of Kanyakumari District: A Pledge for All Round Development'. Sewa Sadhana, Chaitra Shukla Pratipada, Vikrami Samvat 2070 (11 April 2013), 27.

Sewa Sadhana. March 2007, year 1, vol. 1, Varsh Pratipada (19 March 2007).

UBSS. 'Kandhamal Speaks'. UBSS, Odisha, n.d.

Seva (UBSS newsletter) 3, no. 4 (January–March 2012)

Seva (UBSS newsletter) 3, no. 2 (July–September 2011).

Seva (UBSS newsletter) 3, no. 4 (July–September 2010).

Seva (UBSS newsletter) 3, no. 3 (October–December 2011).

UBSS. *Super Cyclone in Orissa: UBSS in the Forefront of Relief and Rehabilitation.* n.d.

————. *The Nation Responds: UBSS in Action to Bring Relief, Solace and Self Reliance to the Victims of Super Cyclone.* Vijaywada: Kala Kendra Printing Press, 2000.

VHP. 'Hope in Gujarat Rekindled by VHP of America World Hindu Council'. *VHP Brochure*, n.d. Available at http://www.movingpixels.in/print/pdfs/VHPAbrochure.pdf (Accessed on 9 November 2012).

Newspapers

Aron, Sunita. Interview with Vijay Bahuguna, titled, 'I am answerable to my conscience: Vijay Bahuguna', *Hindustan Times*, 24 June 2013. Available at www.hindustantimes.com/india/i-am-answerable-to-my-conscience-vijay-bahuguna/story-aqUqE2NQzxH502cEBDQApM.html (Accessed on 12 August 2013).

Bhan, Swati. '"Samras" Making Headway in Gujarat'. *The Deccan Herald,* 2012. Available at http://www.deccanherald.com/content/217280/content/217419/F (Accessed on 16 December 2012).

Bhattacharya, Amit. 'Geologist Explains Why Uttarakhand Tragedy was Man-made'. *Times of India,* 26 June 2013. Available at https://timesofindia.indiatimes.com/india/Geologist-explains-why-Uttarakhand-tragedy-was-man-made/articleshow/20780742.cms (Accessed on 8 August 2013).

Biswas, Soutik. 'Tales of the Living Dead'. *Outlook,* 22 November 1999.

Burke, Jason. 'Religious Aid Groups Try to Convert Victims'. *The Observer,* 16 January 2005.

Chatterjee, Angana. 'Learning in Saffron: RSS Schools Orissa'. *Asian Age,* New Delhi, 11 November 2003. Available at http://www.sacw.net/DC/CommunalismCollection/ArticlesArchive/anganaNov2003.html (Accessed on 5 July 2011).

Gusain, Raju. 'Superstition or Co-incidence? Locals Believe Kali Avatar Dhari Devi Unleashed the Floods for Revenge'. *India Today,* Dehradun, 26 June 2013. Available at https://www.indiatoday.in/mail-today/story/dhari-devi-unleashed-the-floods-for-revenge-168152-2013-06-26 (Accessed on 8 August 2013).

Mohanty, Debabrata 'Memories etched on sand', *The Telegraph,* Calcutta, January 13, 2005. Available at https://www.telegraphindia.com/opinion/memories-etched-on-sand/cid/1021285 (Accessed on July 20, 2011).

Naseem, S. M. 'The Unfinished Story'. *Dawn,* 8 October 2007.

Nayar, Kuldip. 'Discriminating against the Distressed in a Democracy'. *Indian Express,* 2001.

New Indian Express (Bhubaneswar)

New York Express

Organiser. 'Mass Funeral for Cyclone Victims'. *Organiser* 51, no. 21 (1999): 20.

———. 'Appeal for Hindu Sufferers'. *Organiser* 8 (1947): 10.

———. 'Delhi Medicos Land Relief Work by RSS, VHP'. *Organiser* 31 (2001): 8.

———. 'Massive Rehabilitation Work by UBSS'. *Organiser* 51, no. 23 (2000): 10.

————. 'Massive Relief Operation by RSS'. *Organiser* 51, no. 19 (1999): 9.

————. 'RSS in Charkhi Dadri: Ready Selfless Service'. *Organiser* 48, no. 19 (1996): 11.

————. 'Sarsanghchalak for Orissa Relief'. *Organiser* 51, no. 18 (1999): 5.

Phillips, Tom. 'Haiti Earthquake: Religion Fills the Void Left by Aid Agencies'. *The Guardian,* 24 January 2010.

Rath, Shrikant. 'Mahatma Gandhi, K. R. Narayanan and Plague'. *The Hindu,* 12 March 2002. Available at https://www.thehindu. com/thehindu/op/2002/03/12/stories/2002031200180100.htm (Accessed on 3 December 2013).

Shashikumar, V. K., and George K. Varghese. 'Relief Work Takes Communal Color'. *The Milli Gazette,* 2001. Available at http://www.milligazette.com/Archives/15022001/Art01.htm (Accessed on 26 September 2012).

Singh, Mahendra. 'Odisha, Bihar Show Biggest Drop in Percentage of Poor'. *The Times of India,* 24 July 2013. Available at https:// timesofindia.indiatimes.com/india/Odisha-Bihar-show-biggest-drop-in-percentage-of-poor/articleshow/21286897.cms (Accessed on 17 September 2013).

The Hindu (Chennai)

The Telegraph (Kolkata)

The Times of India (New Delhi)

Times News Network. 'Kedarnath: Idols, Nandi Survive Cloudburst, Flood'. *Times of India,* 21 June 2013. Available at http:// timesofindia.indiatimes.com/india/Kedarnath-Idols-Nandi-survive-cloudburst-flood/articleshow/20690485.cms (Accessed on 8 August 2013).

Tomlinson, Chris. 'Hindu Nationalists Mobilize for Quake Relief'. *Associated Press,* 2 February 2001.

Electronic Media

BBC
CNN-IBN
Fox News
NDTV

Websites

For the research purposes, websites of the following institutions/organization were visited:
Akhil Bhartiya Vanvasi Kalyan Ashram
Catholic Relief Services, India
Hindu Books Universe
Hindu Swayamsevak Sangh
Indian Red Cross
National Disaster Management Authority
National Disaster Management, India
Odisha State Disaster Management Authority (OSDMA)
Organiser
Rashtriya Sewa Bharati
Rashtriya Swayamsevak Sangh
Save the Children, India
Sewa International
Vidya Bharati Akhil Bhartiya Shiksha Sansthan
Vishva Hindu Parishad

Secondary Sources

Books

Andersen, Walter K., and Shridhar Damle. *The RSS: A View to the Inside*. New Delhi: Penguin Viking, 2018.
————. *Brotherhood in Saffron: The RSS and Hindu Revivalism*. Boulder and London: Westview Press, 1987.
Asad, Talal. *Formations of the Secular: Christianity, Islam, Modernity*. Stanford, CA: Stanford University Press, 2003.
————. *Genealogies of Religion: Discipline and Reasons of Power in Christianity and Islam*. Baltimore, MD: Johns Hopkins University Press, 1993.
Banerjee, S. C. *A Brief History of Dharmasastra*. New Delhi: Abhinav Publications, 1999.
Barnett, M., and J. Stein, eds. *Sacred Aid: Faith and Humanitarianism*. New York: Oxford University Press, 2012.
Barnett, Michael. *Empire of Humanity: A History of Humanitarianism*. Ithaca, NY: Cornell University Press, 2011.
Basu, Tapan, Pradip Datta, Sumit Sarkar, Tanika Sarkar, and Sambuddha Sen. *Khaki Shorts and Saffron Flags: A Critique of Hindu Right*. Delhi: Orient Longman, 1993.

Bayly, C. A. *Origins of Nationality in South Asia. Patriotism and Ethical Government in the Making of Modern India.* Delhi: Oxford University Press, 1998.

Beckerlegge, Gwilym. *Swami Vivekananda's Legacy of Service: A Study of the Ramakrishna Math and Mission.* New Delhi: Oxford University Press, 2006.

Berti, Daniela, Nicolas Jaoul, and Pralay Kanungo, eds. *Cultural Entrenchment of Hindutva: Local Mediations and Forms of Convergence.* Delhi: Routledge, 2011.

Bradley, Penuel K., and Matt Statler, eds. *Encyclopedia of Disaster Relief.* Vols 1 and 2. New York, NY: SAGE Publications, 2011.

Cammett, Melani. *Compassionate Communalism: Welfare and Sectarianism in Lebanon.* Ithaca, New York: Cornell University Press, 2014.

Cavanaugh, W. *The Myth of Religious Violence: Secular Ideology and the Roots of Modern Conflict.* Oxford: Oxford University Press, 2009.

Chatterjee, Angana. *Violent Gods: Hindu Nationalism in India's Present: Narratives from Orissa.* New Delhi: Three Essays Collective, 2009.

Chatterjee, P., and G. Pandey, eds. *Subaltern Studies VII. Writings on South Asian History and Society.* Delhi: Oxford University Press, 1992.

Clarke, Gerard, and Michael Jennings, eds. *Development, Civil society and Faith-based Organisations: Bridging the Sacred and the Secular.* London: Palgrave Macmillan, 2008.

Cohn, Bernard S. *Colonialism and Its Forms of Knowledge: The British in India.* Princeton, NJ: Princeton University Press, 1996.

Copley, Antony, ed. *Hinduism in Public and Private: Hindutva, Gender and Sampradaya.* New Delhi: Oxford University Press, 2003.

Dasgupta, Surendranath. *A History of Indian Philosophy.* Vol. 4. Delhi: Motilal Banarasidass, [1922] 1976.

Davis, N. J., and R. V. Robinson. *Claiming Society for God: Religious Movements and Social Welfare.* Bloomington and Indianapolis, IN: Indiana University Press, 2012.

Deneulin, Séverine, and Masooda Bano. *Religion in Development: Rewriting the Secular Script.* London: Zed Publishers, 2009.

Derrida, Jacques. *Given Time: I. Counterfeit Money.* Translated by Peggy Kamuf. Chicago, IL: University of Chicago Press, 1992.

Desphande, B. V., and S. R. Ramaswamy. *Dr. Hedgewar, the Epoch-Maker: A Biography* (online). Available at http://samvada.org/files/Dr-HEDGEWAR-THE-EPOCH-MAKER (Accessed on 17 May 2012).

————. *Dr. Hedgewar, the Epoch-Maker: A Biography*. Bangalore: Sahitya Sindhu Parakashana [1981] 2015.

Engineer, Asghar Ali, ed. *The Gujarat Carnage*. New Delhi: Orient Longman, 2003.

Farquhar, J. N. *Modern Religious Movements in India*. New Delhi: Munshiram Manoharlal Publishers, [1915] 1998.

Fassin, Didier. *Humanitarian Reason: A Moral History of the Present*. California Scholarship Online, May 2012. DOI:10.1525/california/9780520271166.001.0001

Feener, Michael. *Sharia and Social Engineering: The Implementation of Islamic Law in Contemporary Aceh, Indonesia*. Oxford: Oxford University Press, 2013.

Fitzgerald, Timothy. *The Ideology of Religious Studies*. New York, NY: Oxford University Press, 2003.

Gandhi, Rajmohan. *Mohandas: A True Story of a Man, His People, and an Empire*. New Delhi: Penguin, 2007.

Golwalkar, M. S. *Bunch of Thoughts*. Bangalore: Jagarana Prakashana, [1966] 1980.

Goyal, D. R. *Rashtriya Swayamsevak Sangh*. New Delhi: Radha Krishna Prakashan, 1979.

Guha, Ramachandra. *India after Gandhi: The History of the World's Largest Democracy*. London: Pan Macmillan, 2017.

Hansen, Thomas Blom. *The Saffron Wave: Democracy and Hindu Nationalism in Modern India*. New Delhi: Princeton University Press, 1999.

Haynes, Jeffrey. *Religion and Development: Conflict or Cooperation?* London: Palgrave Macmillan, 2007.

Heim, Maria. *Theories of the Gift in South Asia: Hindu, Buddhist, and Jain Reflections on Dana, Religion in History, Society, and Culture*. New York, NY: Routledge, 2004.

Jaffrelot, Christophe. *The Hindu Nationalist Movement and Indian Politics: 1925 to 1990s*. Delhi: Columbia University Press, 1996.

————. *The Sangh Parivar: A Reader*. New Delhi: Oxford University Press, 2005.

Jaffrelot, Christophe, and Thomas Blom Hansen, eds. *The BJP and the Compulsions of Politics in India*. New Delhi: Oxford University Press, 1998.

Jayal, Niraja Gopal. *Citizenship and Its Discontents: An Indian History*. Cambridge and London: Harvard University Press, 2013.

Jayaprasad, K. *RSS and Hindu Nationalism: Inroads in a Leftist Stronghold*. New Delhi: Deep & Deep Publications, 1991.

Jones, Kenneth W. *Socio-Religious Reform Movements in British India*. New Delhi: Cambridge University Press, 1994.

Juergensmeyer, M. *Radhasoami Reality: The Logic of a Modern Faith*. Princeton, NJ: Princeton University Press, 1991.

Kane, P. V. *History of Dharmasastra*. Vol. II, part II. Poona: Bhandarkar Oriental Research Institute, 1974.

Kanungo, Pralay. *RSS's Tryst with Politics: From Hedegwar to Sudarshan*. New Delhi: Manohar, 2003.

Kapoor, Ilan. *The Postcolonial politics of Development*. London and New York, NY: Routledge, 2008.

Katju, Manjari. *Vishva Hindu Parishad and Indian Politics*. New Delhi: Orient Longman Publications, 2003.

Kent, Randolph C. *Anatomy of Disaster Relief: The International Network in Action*. London and New York, NY: Pinter Publications, 1987.

Khilnani, Sunil. *The Idea of India*. New Delhi: Penguin Books, 2003.

Knut A. Jacobsen. 'Sevā'. In *Brill's Encyclopedia of Hinduism*, edited by Knut A. Jacobsen, Helene Basu, Angelika Malinar, Vasudha Narayanan (online), 2012. Available at http://dx.doi.org.lib-proxy1.nus.edu.sg/10.1163/2212-5019_beh_COM_2050280 (Accessed on 21 June 2018).

Kochanek, Stanley, and Robert Hardgrave. *India: Government and Politics in a Developing Nation*. Boston, MA: Thomson/ Wadsworth, 2008.

Ludden, David, ed. *Making India Hindu: Religion, Community and Politics of Democracy in India*. New Delhi: Oxford University Press, 1996.

Lynch, Gordon. *The Sacred in the Modern World: A Cultural Sociological Approach*. Oxford: Oxford University Press, 2012.

MacKean, Lise. *Divine Enterprises. Gurus and the Hindu Nationalist Movement*. Chicago, IL: University of Chicago Press, 1996.

Mahajan, Gurpreet, and Surinder Jodhka, eds. *Religion, Community & Development: Changing Contours of Politics and Policy in India*. New Delhi: Routledge, 2010.

Mahmood, Saba. *Politics of Piety: The Islamic Revival and the Feminist Subject*. Princeton, NJ: Princeton University Press, 2004.

Mauss, Marcel. *The Gift: Forms and Functions of Exchange in Archaic Societies*. New York, NY: W.W. Norton and Company Inc, 1925.

Milibank, John. *Theology and Social Theory: Beyond Secular Reason*. 2nd ed. Malden, MA: Wiley Blackwell, 2006.

Misra, Girish K., and G. C. Mathur, eds. *Natural Disaster Reduction.* New Delhi: Reliance Publishing House and Institute of Public Administration, 1993.

Nandy, Ashish, Shikha Trivedy, Shail Mayaram, and Achyut Yagnik. *Creating a Nationality: The Ramjanmbhoomi Movement and the Fear of the Self.* New Delhi: Oxford University Press, 1995.

Nath, Vijay. *Dana: Gift System in Ancient India a Socio-economic Perspective.* Delhi: Munshiram Manoharlal Publishers, 1987.

Parvathy, A. A. *Hindutva, Ideology and Politics.* New Delhi: Deep & Deep Publications, 2003.

Radice, William, ed. *Swami Vivekananda and the Modernisation of Hinduism.* New Delhi: Oxford University Press, 1999.

Rajgopal, Arvind. *Politics after Television: Hindu Nationalism and the Reshaping of the Public.* New Delhi: Cambridge University Press, 2001.

Ranade, Eknath. *Seva Vrat: Sadhya aur Sadhana.* Noida: Jagriti Prakashan, 2011.

Rist, Gilbert. *The History of Development: From Western Origins to Global Faith,* 4th ed. London: Zed Books, 2014.

Roth, G., and C. Wittich, eds. *Economy and Society.* New York, NY: Bedminster Press, 1968.

Roy, Kaustuv. *Limits of the Secular: Social Experience and Cultural Memory.* Springer, 2017.

Saberwal, Satish, and Mushirul Hasan, eds. *Assertive Religious Identities India and Europe.* New Delhi: Manohar, 2006.

Samal, K. C., S. Meher, N. Panigrahi, and S. Mohanty. *State, NGOs and Disaster Management.* New Delhi: Rawat Publications, 2005.

Sen, Amartya. *Poverty and Famines: An Essay on Entitlement and Deprivation.* New York, NY: Oxford University Press, 1981.

Shani, Ornit. *Communalism Caste and Hindu Nationalism: The Violence in Gujarat.* New Delhi: Cambridge University Press, 2007.

Sharma, Sanjay. *Famine, Philanthropy and the Colonial State: North India in the Early Nineteenth Century.* New Delhi: Oxford University Press, 2001.

Sharma, Sriram, and Lajpat Rai. *A History of the Arya Samaj.* New Delhi: Munshiram Manoharlal, 1992.

Skocpol, Theda. *Diminished Democracy: From Membership to Management in American Civic Life.* Norman: University of Oklahoma Press, 2003.

Smith, A. O., and S. M. Hoffman, eds. *The Angry Earth: Disaster in Anthropological Perspective*. London and New York, NY: Routledge, 1999.

Srivastava, S. *History of Indian Famines and Development of Famine Policy 1858–1918*. Agra: Sri Ram Mehra and Company, 1968.

Srivatsan, R. *Seva, Saviour and State: Caste Politics, Tribal Welfare and Capitalist Development*. New Delhi: Routledge, 2015.

Sud, Nikita. *Liberalization, Hindu Nationalism and the State*. New Delhi: Oxford University Press, 2005.

———. *Liberalization, Hindu Nationalism and the State: A Biography of Gujarat*. New Delhi: Oxford University Press, 2012.

Swahananda, Swami. *Swami Vivekananda's Concept of Service*. Chennai: Adhyaksha Ramakrishna Math, 2015.

Thapar, Romila. *Somnath: The Many Voices of a History*. New Delhi: Verso, 2004.

Thiruvengadam, Arun. *The Constitution of India: A Contextual Analysis*. Oxford and Portland, OR: Hart Publishing, 2017.

Tvedt, Terje. *Angels of Mercy or Development Diplomats? NGOs and Foreign Aid*. Oxford: Africa Press, 1998.

Varadarajan, Siddharth, ed. *Gujarat: The Making of a Tragedy*. New Delhi: Penguin Books, 2002.

Vivekananda, Swami. *The Complete Works of Swami Vivekananda*. Vols 1–5. Calcutta: Advaita Ashram, 2013.

Warrier, Maya. *Hindu Selves in a Modern World: Guru Faith in the Mata Amritanandamayi Mission*. London and New York, NY: Routledge, 2005.

Watt, Carey. *Serving the Nation: Culture of Service, Association, and Citizenship in Colonial India*. New Delhi: Oxford University Press, 2005.

Williams, R. *Jaina Yoga: A Survey of the Medieval Sravacaras*. London: Oxford University, 1963.

Williams, Raymond Brady. *An Introduction to Swaminarayan Hinduism*. Cambridge: Cambridge University Press, 2001.

Yagnik, Achyut, and Suchitra Sheth. *The Shaping of Modern Gujarat: Plurality, Hindutva and Beyond*. New Delhi: Penguin Books, 2005.

Zavos, John. *The Emergence of Hindu Nationalism in India*. New Delhi: Oxford University Press, 2000.

Zavos, John, Andrew Wyatt, and Vernon Hewitt, eds. *The Politics of Cultural Mobilization in India*. New Delhi: Oxford University Press, 2004.

Book Chapters

Anderson, Leona. 'Contextualizing Philanthropy in South Asia: A Textual Analysis of Sanskrit Sources'. In *Philanthropy in the World's Traditions*, edited by Warren F. Ilchman, Stanley N. Katz, and Edward L. Queen II, 57–78. Bloomington and Indianapolis, IN: Indiana University Press, 1998.

Beckerlegge, G. 'Swami Vivekananda and Seva: Taking "Social Service" Seriously'. In *Swami Vivekananda and the Modernisation of Hinduism*, edited by William Radice, 158–193. New Delhi: Oxford University Press, 1999.

———. 'RSS's Tradition of Selfless Service'. In *The Politics of Cultural Mobilization*, edited by John Zavos, Andrew Wyatt, and Vernon Hewitt, 105–135. New Delhi: Oxford University Press, 2004.

———. 'Saffron and *Seva*: The Rashtriya Swayamsevak Sangh's Appropriation of Swami Vivekananda'. In *Hinduism in Public and Private: Hindutva, Gender and Sampradaya*, edited by Antony Copley, 31–65. New Delhi: Oxford University Press, 2003.

Brady Williams, Raymond. 'Representations of Swaminarayan Hinduism'. In *Public Hinduisms*, edited by John Zavos, Pralay Kanungo, Deepa S. Reddy, Maya Warrier, and Raymond Brady Williams, 176–189. New Delhi: SAGE Publications, 2012).

Chatterjee, Partha. 'Secularism and Tolerance'. In *Secularism and Its Critics*, edited by Rajeev Bhargava. New Delhi: Oxford University Press, 1998.

Clarke, Gerard. 'Religion and Development: Challenges for Donors and for Faith Groups'. In *Faith in Civil Society: Religious Actors as Drivers of Change*, edited by Heidi Moksnes and Mia Melin, 13–30. Uppsala: Uppsala University, 2013.

Collier, David. 'The Comparative Method'. In *Political Science: The State of the Discipline II*, edited by Ada W. Finifter, 105–119. Washington, DC: American Political Science Association, 1993.

Daly, Patrick, and Yenny Rahmayati. 'Cultural Heritage and Community Recovery in Post-Tsunami Aceh'. In *From the Ground Up: Perspectives on Post Tsunami and Post Conflict Aceh*, edited by Patrick Daly, R. Michael Feener, and Anthony Reid, 57–78. Singapore: Institute of Southeast Asian Studies Press, 2012.

Davis, Richard H. 'The Iconography of Rama's Chariot'. In *Making India Hindu: Religion Community, and the Politics of Democracy in India*, edited by David Ludden, 27–54. New Delhi: Oxford University Press, 2005.

Fountain, Philip. 'Blurring Mission and Development in the Mennonite Central Committee'. In *Mission and Development: God's Work or Good Works?*, edited by Mathew Clarke, 143–166. London and New York: Continuum, 2012.

Gold, Daniel. 'Organized Hinduisms: From Vedic Truths to Hindu Nation'. In *Fundamentalisms Observed the Fundamentalism Project*, vol. 4, edited by M. E. Marty, and R. S. Appleby, 531–593. Chicago, IL, and London: University of Chicago Press, 1992.

Hoffman, S. M., and A. O. Smith. 'Anthropology and the Angry Earth: An Overview'. In *The Angry Earth: Disaster in Anthropological Perspective*, edited by A. Oliver-Smith and S. M. Hoffman, 1–16. London and New York, NY: Routledge, 1999.

Hoffman, Susanna M. 'After Atlas Shrugs: Cultural Change or Persistence after a Disaster'. In *The Angry Earth: Disaster in Anthropological Perspective*, edited by A. Oliver-Smith and S. M. Hoffman, 302–326. London and New York, NY: Routledge, 1999.

Hoyez, Anne-Cecile. 'Health Yoga and the Nation: Dr. Karandikar and the Yoga Therapy Centre, Pune, Maharashtra'. In *Cultural Entrenchment of Hindutva, Local Mediations and Forms of Convergence*, edited by Daniela Berti, Nicolas Jaoul and Pralay Kanungo, 145–160. Delhi: Routledge, 2011.

Jaffrelot, Christophe. 'Hindu Nationalism and the Social Welfare Strategy'. In *Development, Civil Society and Faith-based Organisations: Bridging the Sacred and the Secular*, edited by Gerard Clarke and Michael Jennings, 240–259. London: Palgrave Macmillan, 2008.

Juergensmeyer, M., and Darrin McMahon. 'Hindu Philanthropy and Civil Society'. In *Philanthropy in the World's Traditions*, edited by W. F. Ilchman, S. N. Katz, and E. L. Queen II, 263–278. Bloomington and Indianapolis, IN: Indiana University Press, 1998.

Kanungo, Pralay. 'Diasporic Politics of Hindu Nationalism in the United States'. In *International and Transnational Political Actors: Case Studies from the Indian Diaspora*, edited by Eric Leclerc. Delhi: Manohar, 2011.

Katju, Manjari. 'The Vishva Hindu Parishad Abroad'. In The *Sangh Parivar: A Reader*, edited by Christophe Jaffrelot, 429–435. New Delhi: Oxford University Press, 2005.

Kroessin, M., and A. S. Mohamed. 'Saudi Arabian NGOs in Somalia: "Wahabi" Da'wah or Humanitarian Aid?' In *Development, Civil Society and Faith-based Organisations: Bridging the Sacred and the*

Secular, edited by Gerard Clarke and M. Jennings, 187–213. London: Palgrave Macmillan, 2008.

Lobo, Lancy. 'Christianization, Hinduization and Indigenous Revivalism among the Tribals of Gujarat'. In *Margins of Faith: Dalit and Tribal Christianity in India*, edited by Rowena Robinson and Joseph Marianns Kujur, 211–232. New Delhi: SAGE Publications, 2010.

Nandy, Ashish. 'The Politics of Secularism and the Recovery of Religious Toleration'. In *Secularism and Its Critics*, edited by Rajeev Bhargava. New Delhi: Oxford University Press, 1998.

Patel, Sujata. 'Seva, Sangathanas and Gurus: Service and the Making of the Hindu Nation'. In *Religion, Community & Development: Changing Contours of Politics and Policy in India*, edited by Gurpreet Mahajan and Surinder Jodhka, 102–128. New Delhi: Routledge, 2010.

Sarkar, Tanika. 'Educating the Children of the Hindu Rashtra'. In *The Sangh Parivar: A Reader*, edited by Christophe Jaffrelot, 197–206. New Delhi: Oxford University Press, 2005.

———. 'Hindutva's Hinduism'. In *Public Hinduisms*, edited by John Zavos, Pralay Kanungo, Deepa S. Reddy, Maya Warrier, and Raymond Brady Williams, 264–282. New Delhi: SAGE Publications, 2012.

Shah, Ghanshyam. 'Caste, Hindutva and the Making of Mob Culture'. In *Gujarat: The Making of a Tragedy*, edited by Siddharth Varadarajan, 416–425. New Delhi: Penguin India, 2002.

Simpson, Edward. 'Hindutva as a Rural Planning Paradigm'. In *The Politics of Cultural Mobilization in India*, edited by John Zavos, Andrew Wyatt, and Vernon Hewitt, 136–165. New Delhi: Oxford University Press, 2004.

Sundar, Nandini. 'Adivasis vs. Vanavasi'. In *Assertive Religious Identities: India and Europe*, edited by Satish Sabherwal and Mushirul Hasan, 357–390. Delhi: Manohar, 2006.

Thapar, Romila. '*Dana* and Dakshina as Forms of Exchange'. In *Cultural Pasts: Essays in Early Indian History*, edited by Romila Thapar, 521–535. New Delhi: Oxford University Press, 2000.

Van der Veer, Peter. 'Hindu Nationalism and the Discourse of Modernity: The Vishva Hindu Parishad'. In *Accounting for Fundamentalisms: The Dynamic Character of Movements*, edited by M. E. Marty and R. S. Appleby, 653–668. Chicago, IL, and London: The University of Chicago Press, 2004.

Voix, Raphael. 'Social Services, Muscular Hinduism and Implicit Militancy'. In *Cultural Entrenchment of Hindutva Local Mediations and Forms of Convergence*, edited by Daniela Berti, Nicolas Jaoul, and Pralay Kanungo, 209–238. New Delhi: Routledge, 2011.

Warrier, Maya. 'The Seva Ethic and the Spirit of Institution Building in the Mata Amritanandamayi Mission'. In *Hinduism in Public and Private: Hindutva, Gender and Sampradaya*, Antony Copley. New Delhi: Oxford University Press, 2003.

Journal Articles

Aguirre, Ben, Russell R. Dynes, Kendra James, and Rory Connell. 'Institutional Resilience and Disaster Planning for New Hazards: Insights from Hospitals'. *Journal of Homeland Security and Emergency Management* 2, no. 2 (2005): 1–17.

Alesina, A., and D. Dollar. 'Who Gives Foreign Aid to Whom and Why?' *Journal of Economic Growth* 5, no. 1 (2000): 33–63.

Amenta, E., N. Caren, E. Chiarello, and Y. Su. 'The Political Consequences of Social Movements'. *Annual Review of Sociology* 36 (2010): 287–307.

Auvinen, Juha, and E. Wayne Nafziger. 'The Sources of Humanitarian Emergencies'. *The Journal of Conflict Resolution* 43, no. 3 (1999): 267–290.

Bassnett, Susan. 'Faith, Doubt, Aid and Prayer: The Lisbon Earthquake of 1755 Revisited'. *European Review* 14 (2006): 321–328.

Bhattacharjee, Malini. 'Seva, Hindutva and the Politics of Post-Earthquake Reconstruction in Rural Kutch'. *Asian Ethnology* 75, no. 1 (2016): 7.

Benthall, Jonathan. 'The Red Cross and Red Crescent Movement and Islamic Societies, with Special Reference to Jordan'. *British Journal of Middle Eastern Studies* 24, no. 2 (1997): 157–177.

Berenschot, Ward. 'Everyday Mediation: The Politics of Public Service Delivery in Gujarat, India'. *Development and Change* 41, no. 5 (2010): 883–905.

Berger, J. 'Religious Non-governmental Organizations: An Exploratory Analysis'. *Voluntas: International Journal of Voluntary and Nonprofit Organizations* 14, no. 1 (2003): 15–39.

Bordia, Devika. 'The Ethics of Des Seva: Hindu Nationalism, Tribal Leadership and Modes of Sociality in Rajasthan'. *Contributions to Indian Sociology* 49, no. 1 (2015): 52–76.

Bornstein, Erica. 'The Impulse of Philanthropy'. *Cultural Anthropology* 24, no. 4 (2009): 622–651.

Brewis, Georgina. '"Fill Full the Mouth of Famine": Voluntary Action in Famine Relief in India 1896–1901'. *Modern Asian Studies* 44, no. 4 (2010): 887–918.

Bunker, Ellsworth. 'The Voluntary Effort in Disaster Relief'. *The ANNALS of the American Academy of Political and Social Science* 309, no. 1 (1957): 107–117.

Burlet, Stacey. 'Gender Relations: "Hindu" Nationalism, and NGO Responses in India'. *Gender and Development* 7, no. 1 (1999): 40–47.

Burton, I., and R. W. Kates. 'Perception of Natural Hazards in Resource Management'. *Natural Resources Journal* 3 (1964): 412–441.

Bush, Robin, Philip Fountain, and Michael Feener. 'Religious Actors in Disaster Relief: An Introduction'. *International Journal of Mass Emergencies and Disasters* 33, no. 1 (2015): 1–16.

Chakraborty, Dipesh. 'The Power of Superstition in Public Life in India'. *Economic & Political Weekly* (2008): 16–19.

Chandler, David. 'The Road to Military Humanitarianism: How the Human Rights NGOs Shaped a New Humanitarian Agenda'. *Human Rights Quarterly* 23 (2001): 678–700.

Chandran, D. Suba, N. Manoharan, Vibhanshu Shekhar, Jabin T. Jacob, Raghav Sharma, and Sandeep Bharadwaj 'Disaster Relief Diplomacy'. *Indian Foreign Affairs Journal* Vol. 4, no. 2 (2009): 63–80.

Chatterjee, Partha. 'Secularism and Toleration'. *Economic & Political Weekly* 29, no. 28 (1994): 1768–1777.

Chaturvedi, Sanjay. 'Diaspora in India's Geopolitical Visions: Linkages, Categories, and Contestations'. *Asian Affairs* 32, no. 3 (2005): 141–168.

Chester, D. K., and A. M. Duncan. 'Responding to Disasters within the Christian Tradition, with Reference to Volcanic Eruptions and Earthquakes'. *Religion* 40 (2010): 85–95.

Clarke, Gerard. 'Faith Matters: Faith-Based Organisations, Civil Society and International Development'. *Journal of International Development* 18 (2006): 835–848.

Cooper, Drury A., Richard Olson Stuart, and Van Belle A. Douglas. 'The Politics of Humanitarian Aid: U.S. Foreign Disaster Assistance 1964–1995'. *The Journal of Politics* 67, no. 2 (2005): 454–473.

Copeman, Jacob. 'The Gift and Its Forms of Life in Contemporary India'. *Modern Asian Studies* 45, no. 5 (2011): 1051–1094.

Das, Kumar. 'Social Mobilisation for Rehabilitation: Relief Work in Cyclone-affected Orissa'. *Economic & Political Weekly* 37, no. 48 (30 November–6 December 2002): 4784–4788.

De Haan, Arjan, and Amaresh Dubey. 'Poverty, Disparities, or the Development of Underdevelopment in Orissa'. *Economic & Political Weekly* 40, no. 22–23 (28 May 2005): 2321–2329.

Dyahadroy, Swati. 'Exploring Gender, Hindutva and Seva'. *Economic and Political Weekly* 44, no. 17 (2009): 65–73.

Editorial. 'Earthquake Politics of Relief', *Economic & Political Weekly* 20, no. 45 (6 November 1993): 2424.

Editorial. 'Political Uses of Cyclone'. *Economic & Political Weekly* 12, no. 52 (24 December 1977): 2118–2119.

Editorial. 'Politics of Earthquake Relief'. *Economic & Political Weekly* 3, no. 3 (20 January 1968): 188–189.

Editorial. 'Politics of Relief'. *Economic & Political Weekly* 28, no. 45 (6 November 1993): 2424.

Editorial. 'The Inundation of Morvi'. *Economic & Political Weekly* 14, no. 34 (25 August 1979): 1454.

Editorial. 'The Other Tragedy'. *Economic & Political Weekly* 37, no. 17 (27 April–3 May 2002): 1564.

Editorial. "'Natural' Calamity?" *Economic & Political Weekly* 6, no. 45 (6 November 1971): 2258.

Engineer, Ashgar Ali. 'Gujarat Riots in the Light of the History of Communal Violence'. *Economic & Political Weekly* 37, no. 50 (14 December 2002): 5052–5053.

Fara, Katiuscia. 'How Natural Are "Natural Disasters"? Vulnerability to Drought of Communal farmers in Namibia'. *Risk Management* 3 (2001): 47–63.

Ferris, E. 'Faith-based and Secular Humanitarian Organizations'. *International Review of the Red Cross* 87, no. 858 (2005): 311–325.

Fischer, Henry W. 'The Sociology of Disaster: Definitions, Research Questions, and Measurements Continuation of the Discussion in a Post-September 11 Environment'. *International Journal of Mass Emergencies and Disasters* 21, no. 1 (March 2003): 91–107.

Fountain, Philip M., Sara Louise Kindon, and Warwick E. Murray. 'Christianity, Calamity, and Culture: The Involvement of Christian Churches in the 1998 Aitape Tsunami Disaster Relief'. *The Contemporary Pacific* 16, no. 2 (2004): 321–355.

Fuller, Christopher. 'Vinayaka Chaturthi Festival and Hindutva in Tamil Nadu'. *Economic & Political Weekly* 36, no. 19 (2001): 1607–1616.

Gandhi, K. R. Krishna. 'Politics of Flood Relief vs Flood Control'. *Economic & Political Weekly* 16, no. 47 (21 November 1981): 1889–1891.

Garrett, Thomas, and Sobel Russell. 'The Political Economy of FEMA Disaster Payments'. *Economic Inquiry* 41, no. 3 (2003): 496–509.

Hasan, Mushirul. 'Adjustment and Accommodation: Indian Muslims after Partition'. *Social Scientist* 18, no. 8/9 (1990): 48–65.

Hardiman, David. 'Purifying the Nation: The Arya Samaj in Gujarat 1895–1930'. *The Indian Economic and Social History Review* 44, no. 1 (2007): 41–65.

Hattori, Tomohisa. 'Reconceptualizing Foreign Aid'. *Review of International Political Economy* 8, no. 4 (2001, Winter): 633–660.

Haynes, Douglas E. 'From Tribute to Philanthropy: The Politics of Gift Giving in a Western Indian City'. *The Journal of Asian Studies* 46, no. 2 (May 1987): 339–360.

Heeger, A. Gerald. 'Discipline Versus Mobilization: Party Building and the Punjab Jana Sangh'. *Asian Survey* 12, no. 10 (October 1972): 864–878.

Helland, Christopher. 'Diaspora on the Electronic Frontier: Developing Virtual Connections with Sacred Homelands'. *Journal of Computer-mediated Communication* 12 (2007): 956–976.

Henry, Jacques. 'Continuity, Social Change and Katrina'. *Disasters* 35, no. 1 (2011): 220–242.

Hensman, Rohini. 'The Gujarat Model of Development: What Would It Do to the Indian Economy?' *Economic & Political Weekly* 49, no. 11 (15 March 2014). Available at https://www.epw.in/node/129173/pdf (Accessed on 12 February 2019).

Hertzberg, Michael. 'Waves of Conversion? The Tsunami, "Unethical Conversions" and Political Buddhism in Sri Lanka'. *International Journal for Mass Emergencies and Disasters* 33, no. 1 (2015).

Jalali, Rita. 'Civil Society and the State: Turkey after the Earthquake'. *Disasters* 26, no. 2 (2002): 120–139.

———. 'International Funding of NGOs in India: Bringing the State Back In'. *Voluntas: International Journal of Voluntary and Nonprofit Organizations* 19, no. 2 (June 2008): 161–188.

Jesse, D. Lecy. 'Aid Effectiveness after the Gujarat Earthquake: A Case Study of Disaster Relief'. *Journal of Development and Social Transformation* 4 (November 2007): 5–12.

Kanungo, Pralay. 'Hindutva's Entry into a Hindu Province: Early Years of RSS in Orissa'. *Economic & Political Weekly* 48, no. 31 (2 August 2003): 3293–3303.

———. 'Hindutva's Fury against Christians in Orissa'. *Economic & Political Weekly* (13 September 2008): 16–19.

———. 'Shift from Syncretism to Communalism'. *Economic & Political Weekly* 49, no. 14 (5 April 2014): 48–55.

Kanungo Pralay, and Satyakam Joshi. 'Carving Out a White Marble Deity from a Rugged Black Stone? Hindutva Rehabilitates Ramayana's Shabari in a Temple'. *International Journal of Hindu Studies* 13, no. 3 (Special Issue: Temple Publics—Religious Institutions and the Construction of Contemporary Hindu Communities; 2009): 279–299.

Kapur, Anu. 'Insensitive India: Attitudes Towards Disaster Prevention and Management'. *Economic & Political Weekly* 40, no. 42 (15–21 October 2005): 4551–4560.

Kaviraj, Sudipta. 'Religion and Identity in India'. *Ethnic and Racial Studies* 2, no. 2 (1997): 325–344.

Khera, P. D. 'Ethnography of an Earthquake'. *Economic & Political Weekly* 37, no. 11 (16 March 2002): 1021–1023.

Kidd, Alan J. 'Philanthropy and the 'Social History Paradigm'. *Social History* 21, no. 2 (May 1996): 180–192.

King, Richard. 'Orientalism and the Modern Myth of "Hinduism"'. *Numen* 46, no. 2 (1999): 146–185.

Klein, Ira. 'Death in India, 1871–1921'. *The Journal of Asian Studies* 32, no. 4 (August 1973): 639–659.

Kondapalli, Srikanth. 'Tsunami and China: Relief with Chinese Characteristics'. *Asian Affairs* 17 (January 2005): 130–133. Available at https://core.ac.uk/download/pdf/12515109.pdf Appendix Number 37, pp. 130-33. (Accessed on 19 May, 2016).

Kreps, G. A. 'Sociological Inquiry and Disaster Research'. *Annual Review of Sociology*, Vol. 10. (1984), pp. 309–330.

Laidlaw, James. 'A Free Gift Makes No Friends'. *The Journal of the Royal Anthropological Institute* 6, no. 4 (December 2000): 617–634.

Lochtfeld, James G. 'The Construction of the Kumbh Mela'. *South Asian Popular Culture* 2, no. 2 (2004): 103–126.

Louis, Prakash. 'Gujarat: Earthquake and After'. *Economic & Political Weekly* 36, no. 11 (17–23 March 2001): 908–910.

Lucia, Amanda J., '"Give Me Sevā Overtime": Selfless Service and Humanitarianism in Mata Amritanandamayi's Transnational Guru Movement'. *History of Religions* 54, no. 2 (2014): 188–207.

Ludborg, P. 'Foreign Aid and International Support as a Gift Exchange'. *Economics and Politics* 10 (July 1998): 127–141.

Madan, T. N. 'Secularism in Its Place'. *Journal of Asian Studies* 46, no. 4 (1987): 747–759.

Mahadevia, Darshini. 'Privatising Earthquake Rehabilitation'. *Economic & Political Weekly* 36, no. 39 (29 September–5 October 2001): 3670–3673.

Mehta, Lyla. 'Reflections on the Kutch Earthquake'. *Economic & Political Weekly* 36, no. 31 (4–10 August 2001): 2931–2936.

Mehta, Makrand. 'Gandhi and Ahmedabad, 1915–20'. *Economic & Political Weekly* 40, no. 4 (22–28 January 2005): 291–299.

Merli, Claudia. 'Context-bound Islamic Theodices: The Tsunami as Supernatural Retribution vs Natural Catastrophe in Southern Thailand'. *Religion* 40 (2010): 104–111.

Mishra, Dinesh Kumar. 'The Bihar Flood Story'. *Economic & Political Weekly* 32, no. 35 (30 August–5 September 1997): 2206–2217.

Mishra, Surya Narayan. 'Naveen Patnaik Authors a New Chapter for Orissa'. *Economic & Political Weekly* 44, no. 39 (26 September 2009): 148–150.

Mohanty, Manoranjan. 'Orissa Elections and Kalahandi's Tularam'. *Economic & Political Weekly* 33, no. 5 (31 January 1998): 204–206.

Mohapatra, Bishnu N. 'Politics in Post-Cyclone Orissa'. *Economic & Political Weekly* 35, no. 16 (15–21 April 2000): 1353–1355.

Morgenthau, Hans. 'A Political Theory of Foreign Aid'. *The American Political Science Review* 56, no. 2 (June 1962): 301–309.

Morris, Davis, and Seitz Steven Thomas. 'Disasters and Governments'. *Journal of Conflict Resolution* 26, no. 3 (1982): 547–558.

Nelson, Travis. 'Determinants of Disaster Aid: Donor Interest or Recipient Need?' *Global Change, Peace and Security* 24, no. 1 (February 2012): 109–126.

———. 'Rejecting the Gift Horse: International Politics of Disaster Aid Refusal'. *Conflict, Security & Development* 10, no. 3 (2010): 379–402.

Oliver-Smith, Anthony. 'Anthropological Research on Hazards and Disasters'. *Annual Review of Anthropology* 25 (1996): 303–304.

Parry, Jonathan. 'The Gift, the Indian Gift and the "Indian Gift"'. *Man, New Series* 21, no. 3 (September 1986): 453–473.

Pati, Biswamoy. 'Between Then and Now-Popular Memory in Orissa'. *Economic & Political Weekly* 32, no. 24 (15 February 1997): 1393–1394.

———. 'Biju Janata Dal: Signal for Change'. *Economic & Political Weekly* 44, no. 9 (9 February 2009): 12–13.

Peterson, Marie Juul. 'Islamizing Aid: Transnational Muslim NGOs after 9.11'. *Voluntas: International Journal of Voluntary and Nonprofit Organizations* 23, no. 1 (March 2012): 126–155.

Pushpanath, K. 'Disaster without Memory: Oxfam's Drought Program in Zambia'. *Development in Practice* 4, no. 2 (June 1994): 81–91.

Quarantelli, E. L., and Russell R. Dynes. 'Response to Social Crisis and Disaster'. *Annual Review of Sociology* 3 (1977): 23–49.

Ramanna, Mridula. 'Local Initiatives in Health Care: Bombay Presidency, 1900–1920'. *Economic & Political Weekly* 39, no. 41 (9–15 October 2004): 4560–4567.

Rangaswami, Amrita. 'A Generation Being Wiped Out'. *Economic & Political Weekly* 9, no. 48 (30 November 1974): 1973–1976.

Ray, C. N. 'A Note on the Disaster Management Bill, 2005'. *Economic & Political Weekly* 40, no. 47 (19 November 2005): 4877–4879, 4881.

Ray-Bennett, Nibedita S. 'The Influence of Caste, Class and Gender in Surviving Multiple Disasters: A Case Study from Orissa, India'. *Environmental Hazards Human and Policy Dimensions* 8 (2009): 5–22.

Reddy, D., and J. Zavos. 'Temple Publics: Religious Institutions and the Construction of Contemporary Hindu Communities'. *International Journal of Hindu Studies* 13, no. 3 (2009): 241–260.

Reddy, Deepa. 'Hindutva as Praxis'. *Religion Compass* 5, no. 8 (2011): 412–426.

Roy, Ramashray. 'General Elections, 1996—BJP's Emergence as Third Force in Orissa'. *Economic & Political Weekly* 32, no. 44–45 (8 November 1997): 2893–2899.

Samal, Kishor C. 'Facing Sudden Impact: Experience of Orissa Super Cyclone 1999'. *Man & Development* (March 2006): 91–106.

Sarkar, Subhradipta, and Archana Sarma. 'Disaster Management Act, 2005: A Disaster in Waiting?' *Economic & Political Weekly* 41, no. 35 (2–8 September 2006): 3760–3763.

Sen, Siddhartha. 'Some Aspects of State–NGO Relationships in India in the Post-Independence Era'. *Development and Change* 30 (1999): 327–355.

Shaw, Rajib, and Ravi Sinha. 'Towards Sustainable Recovery: Future Challenges after the Gujarat Earthquake, India'. *Risk Management* 5, no. 3 (2003): 35–51.

Shukla, Sandhya. 'Locations for South Asian Diasporas'. *Annual Review of Anthropology* 30, no. 1 (2001): 551–72.

Simpson, Edward. 'State of Play Six Years after Gujarat Earthquake'. *Economic & Political Weekly* 42, no. 11 (17 March 2007): 932–937.

———. 'The "Gujarat" Earthquake and the Political Economy of Nostalgia'. *Contributions to Indian Sociology* (December 2005): 219–249.

Skaria, Ajay. 'Gandhi's Politics: Liberalism and the Question of the Ashram'. *The South Atlantic Quarterly* 101, no. 4 (2002, Fall): 955–986.

Skocpol, T., M. Ganz, and Z. Munson. 'A Nation of Organizers: The Institutional Origins of Civic Voluntarism in the United States'. *American Political Science Review* 94, no. 3 (2000): 527–546.

Spivak, Gayatri Chakravorty. 'Religion, Politics, Theology: A Conversation with Achille Mbembe'. *Boundary 2* 34, no. 2 (2007): 149–170.

Srivastava, S. S., and Rajesh Tandon. 'How Large Is India's Non-Profit Sector?' *Economic & Political Weekly* 40, no. 19 (7–13 May 2005): 1948–1952.

Stallings, Robert A. 'Weberian Political Sociology and Sociological Disaster Studies'. *Sociological Forum* 17, no. 2 (June 2002): 281–305.

Sud, Nikita. 'Earthquake Response: Beyond Bricks and Mortar'. *Economic & Political Weekly* (1 September 2001): 3353–3354.

———. 'From Land to the Tiller to Land Liberalisation: The Political Economy of Gujarat's Shifting Land Policy'. *Modern Asian Studies* 41, no. 3 (May 2007): 603–637.

Suhrud, Tridip. 'Modi and Gujarati "Asmita"'. *Economic & Political Weekly* 43, no. 1 (5–11 January 2008): 11–13.

Sukma, Rizal. 'Indonesia and the Tsunami: Responses and Foreign Policy Implications'. *Australian Journal of International Affairs* 60, no. 2 (2006): 213–228.

Sundar, Nandini. 'Teaching to Hate: The R.S.S.'s Pedagogical Programme'. *Economic & Political Weekly* 39, no. 16 (2004): 1605–1612.

Thachil, Tariq. 'Embedded Mobilization: Nonstate Service Provision as Electoral Strategy in India'. *World Politics* 63 (2011): 434–469.

Tvedt, Terje. 'The International Aid System and the Non-Governmental Organisations: A New Research Agenda'. *Journal of International Development* 18 (2006): 677–690.

Van der veer, Peter. 'The Secular Production of Religion'. *Etnofoor* 8, no. 2 (1995): 5–15.

Weiss, Holger. 'Reorganising Social welfare among Muslims: Islamic Voluntarism and other Forms of Communal Support in Northern Ghana'. *Journal of Religion in Africa* 32 (February 2002): 83–109.

Widgery, Alban G. 'Ethical Aspects of the Religion of the Sikhs'. *The Journal of Religion* 9, no. 2 (1929): 281–290.

Yamini, Aiyar, and Meeto Malik. 'Minority Rights, Secularism and Civil Society Author'. *Economic & Political Weekly* 39, no. 43 (23–29 October 2004): 4707–4771.

Zahir-ud-din. 'South Asia Earthquake: Civilian and Government Responses'. *Economic & Political Weekly* 40, no. 44/45 (29 October–4 November 2005): 4666–4667.

Zavos, John. 'Small Acts, Big Society: Sewa and Hindu (Nationalist) Identity in Britain'. *Ethnic and Racial Studies* 'Small Acts, Big Society: Sewa and Hindu (Nationalist) Identity in Britain.' Ethnic and Racial Studies 38 (2), 2015, pp. 243–58: 1–15.

Zmolek, Mike. 'Aid Agencies, NGOs and Institutionalization of Famine'. *Economic & Political Weekly* 25, no. 1 (6 January 1990): 37–48.

Other Articles

Allen, Henry Moe. 'Notes on the Origin of Philanthropy in Christendom'. *Proceedings of the American Philosophical Society* 105, no. 2 (21 April 1961): 141–144.

Anand, Priya. 'Hindu Diaspora and Religious Philanthropy in the United States'. Paper Presented at the 6th International Society for Third Sector Research, Toronto, July 2004. Available at https://c.ymcdn.com/sites/www.istr.org/resource/resmgr/working_papers_toronto/anand.priya.pdf (Accessed on 12 September 2012).

Anglin, Roland V. 'Building the Organizations that Build Communities: Strengthening the Capacity of Faith and Community-based Development Organizations'. *U.S.*

Department of Housing and Urban Development Office of Policy Development and Research (2004): 1–301.

Barenstein, J. D. 'Housing Reconstruction in Post-earthquake Gujarat: A Comparative Analysis'. *The Humanitarian Practice Network at the Overseas Development Institute*, network paper 54, April 2006.

Claudia, Meier, and C. S. R. Murthy. 'India's Growing Involvement in Humanitarian Assistance'. *Global Public Policy Institute*, research paper no. 13, March 2011.

Dreze, Jean. 'Famine Prevention in India'. Working paper no. 45, World Institute for Development Economics Research of the United Nations University, 1988, 12.

Dynes, Russell R. 'Noah and Disaster Planning: The Cultural Significance of the Flood Story'. Preliminary paper no. 265, University of Delaware, Disaster Research Centre, Newark, DE, 1998.

Eidinger, John M. ed. *Gujarat (Kutch) India M7.7 Earthquake of January 26, 2001 and Napa M5.2 Earthquake of September 3, 2000.* Monograph no. 19, Technical Council on Lifeline Earthquake Engineering, American Society of Civil Engineers, 144–145. June 2001.

Fountain, Philip. 'The Myth of Religious NGOs: Development Studies and the Return of Religion'. In *International Development Policy: Religion and Development*, 9–30. London: Palgrave Macmillan, 2013.

Holmgaard, Sanne Bech. 'Forget Who We are and Let the People Free: Changing Christianities and Tradition in Post-tsunami Samoa'. Master's thesis, Department of Archaeology and Social Anthropology, Faculty of Humanities, Social Sciences and Education University of Tromsø, 2011.

Jose, Vinod K. 'The Emperor of Uncrowned: The Rise of Narendra Modi'. *Caravan Magazine* (1 March 2012).

Lahiri, Ashok K. et al. 'Economic Consequences of the Gujarat Earthquake'. Discussion paper no. 2001/1, National Institute of Public Finance and Policy, India, 2001.

Mariz, Tadros. 'Faith-Based Organizations and Service Delivery Some Gender Conundrums'. Gender and Development Programme Paper Number 11, *United* Nations Research Institute for Social Development, September 2010.

Mondal, Sudipto. 'In Coastal Karnataka, History of Communalism Is Yet to be Written'. *Hindustan Times*, 9 September 2015.

Nair, Padmaja. 'Religious Political Parties and their Welfare Work: Relations between the RSS, the Bharatiya Janata Party and the Vidya Bharati Schools in India'. Religions and Development Research Program, Working Paper 37, 2009.

Nanda, Meera. 'Postmodernism, Hindu Nationalism and "Vedic science"'. *Frontline* 21, no. 1 (3–16 January 2004). Avaliable at https://frontline.thehindu.com/static/html/fl2026/stories/20040102000607800.htm (Accessed on 7 September, 2018)

Nurdin, Muhammad Riza. 'Caliphization through Rehabilitation: Huzbut Tahrir Indonesia in Response to Aceh Post-Tsunami'. Paper presented at Salvage and Salvation: Religion, Disaster Relief, and Reconstruction in Asia Conference, Asia Research Institute, National University of Singapore, 22–23 November 2012.

Price, Gareth, and Mihir Bhatt. 'The Role of the Affected State in Humanitarian Action: A Case Study on India'. Humanitarian Policy Group Working Paper, Overseas Development Institute, 7. April 2009.

Reghunath, Leena Gita. 'The Believer: Swami Aseemanand's Radical Service to the Sangh'. *Caravan* (1 February 2014).

Simpson, Edward. *Was There Discrimination in the Distribution of Resources after the Earthquake in Gujarat? Imagination, Epistemology, and the State in Western India* (Research monograph). London: London School of Economics and Political Science, 2008.

Smith, G. 'Holistic Disaster Recovery: Creating a More Sustainable Future'. Federal Emergency Management Agency, Emergency Management Institute Higher Education Project, 2004.

Thapar, Romila. 'Syndicated Moksha'. In *Seminar*, vol. 313, 14–224. Imagined Religious Communities, September 1985.

Yagnik, Achyut. 'The Pathology of Gujarat'. *Seminar*, 19–22, May 2002.

Electronic Sources

'India Says 5,748 Missing in Floods Now Presumed Dead'. *Fox News*, 15 July 2013. Available at http://www.foxnews.com/world/2013/07/15/india-says-5748-missing-in-floods-now-presumed-dead/ (Accessed on 8 August 2013).

'Tata Steel Dedicates 435 Houses for Orissa's Cyclone-affected'. Press release, Tata Steel, 11 June 2002. Available at https://www. tatasteel.com/media/newsroom/press-releases/india/2002/ tata-steel-dedicates-435-houses-for-orissas-cyclone-affected/ (Accessed on 9 February 2012).

Akhil Bharatiya Vanavasi Kalyan Ashram. 'Service Project at a Glance (Organisation Info/All India)'. Available at http:// kalyanashram.org/organisational-information-as-on-oct-2018/ (Accessed on 18 March 2019).

Ambros, Barbara. 'My Take: Japanese New Religions' Big Role in Disaster Response'. 2011. Available at http://religion.blogs.cnn. com/2011/03/22/my-take-japanese-new-religions-big-role-in-disaster-response/ (Accessed on 10 May 2013).

Bajeli-Datt, Kavita. 'Muslim Cleric Says Quake Caused by Govt. Oppression'. India Abroad News Service, 2 February 2001. Available at http://www.hindunet.org/hvk/articles/0201/4.html (Accessed on 7 June 2012).

Bhattacharjee, Malini. 'Beware the Politics of Seeing Religious "Meaning" in Disasters'. *The Wire*, 21 May 2015. Available at http://thewire.in/2015/05/21/beware-the-politics-of-seeing-religious-meaning-in-disasters/ (Accessed on 15 February 2016)

Gandhi, M. K. 'Forward'. In *Constructive Programme (Its Meaning & Place)*, 2. Ahmedabad: Navajivan Mudranalaya, 1941. Available at http://mkgandhi.org/cnstrct/cnstrct.htm (Accessed on 14 July 2013).

Inaba, Keishin. 'Religion's Response to the Earthquake and Tsunami in Northeastern Japan'. Available at http://www. rk-world.org/dharmaworld/dw_2011octdecreligionsresponse (Accessed on 30 August 2012).

McGirk, Jan. 'Kashmir: The Politics of an Earthquake'. *Opendemocracy.net*, 19 October 2005. Available at http://www. opendemocracy.net/debates/article.jsp?id=2&debateId=43&ar ticleId=2941 (Accessed on 24 August 2008).

McLaughlin, Levi. 'Assessing the Place of Religion in Recent Japanese Disaster Responses'. Sophia University Institute of Comparative Culture Lecture Series on Cultural Responses to Disasters, Organized by the ICC Project Unit '3/11 as Crisis and Opportunity', 5 June 2012. Available at http://icc.fla. sophia.ac.jp/html/events/2012-2013/120605_Post311Talk3. pdf (Accessed on 9 June 2012).

Ministry of Home Affairs. *Disaster Risk Management and the Role of Corporate Sector: The Indian Perspective*. National Disaster Management Division and Confederation of Indian Industry, n.d. Available at http://www.ndmindia.nic.in/WCDRDOCS/DRM%20&%20The%20role%20of%20Corporate%20Sector.pdf (Accessed on 22 March 2013).

Organiser. 'Remembering RSS Founder Dr. KB Hedgewar on His 123th Birthday on Yugadi'. 22 March 2012, *Organiser*. Available at http://samvada.org/2012/news/remembering-rss-founder-dr-kb-hedgewar-on-his-123th-birthday-on-yugadi/ (Accessed on 31 August 2012).

Pattnaik, Sudhir. 'Orissa, Who Cares?' Available at http://www.sabrang.com/cc/archive/2001/feb01/cobox3.htm (Accessed on 10 November 2012).

Pratt, Larry. 'The Politics of Disaster'. Available at http://www.newswithviews.com/Pratt/larry68.htm (Accessed on 7 August 2008).

Shashi Kumar, V. K. 'The Truth about World Vision'. 25 March 2009. Available at http://www.crusadewatch.org/index.php?option=com_content&task=view&id=1051&Itemid=28 (Accessed on 9 November 2013).

Thengadi, D. B. *What Sustains Sangh* (online). Available at http://hindubooks.org/dbthengadi/what_sustains_sangh/page1.htm (Accessed on 20 May 2012).

Therwath, Ingrid. 'Cyber-Hindutva: Hindu Nationalism, the Diaspora and the Web'. April 2012. Available at http://www.e-diasporas.fr/working-papers/Therwath-Hindutva-EN.pdf (Accessed on 26 September 2013).

VHP. 'All India Activity'. Available at https://vhp.org/vhp-glance/seva/all-india-activity/ (Accessed on 18 March 2019).

Vidya Bharati. Akhil Bharatiya Shiksha Sansthan. Available at http://vidyabharti.net/ (Accessed on 18 March, 2019).

Vishnu, G. 'Sangh Owns One of the Fastest Growing Education Projects'. Tehelka, 26 April 2011. Available at http://www.tehelka.com/story_main49.asp?filename=Ws200411HINDUTVA.asp (Accessed on 25 August 2013).

Wisner, Ben, Piers Blaikie, T. Cannon, and I. Davis. *At Risk: Natural Hazards, People's Vulnerability and Disasters*. 2nd ed. Available at http://www.preventionweb.net/files/670_72351.pdf (Accessed on 27 June 2012).

Magazines

Banerjee, Ruben. 'Beyond Public Gaze, Sangh Parivar Outfits in Orissa are Making Political Hay'. *India Today,* 27 January 2003.

Chattopadhyay, Suhrid Shankar. 'Killer Cyclone'. *Frontline* 16, no. 24 (1999). Available at https://frontline.thehindu.com/static/html/fl1624/16240220.htm (Accessed on 22 July 2011).

Kanungo, Pralay. 'Attempts at Appropriation'. *Frontline,* 8 February 2013.

Nanda, Meera. 'Postmodernism, Hindu Nationalism and "Vedic science"'. *Frontline* 21, no. 1 (3–16 January 2004). Avaliable at https://frontline.thehindu.com/static/html/fl2026/stories/20040102000607800.htm (Accessed on 7 September 2018).

Naqvi, Saba. 'The Long and the Shorts of It'. *Outlook India,* 12 February 2001. Available at http://www.outlookindia.com/article.aspx?210847 (Accessed on February 26, 2008).

Venkatesan, V. 'A Hate Campaign in Gujarat'. *Frontline* 16, no. 2 (1999).

Index

Lisbon earthquake of 1755, 31
Lord Jagannath, 113

Madhok, Balraj, 89
Malviya, Madan Mohan, 44
marginalization of religious,
55
Marwari Relief Society of
Calcutta, 88
Mata Amritanandamayi Math,
7, 12, 50, 125, 150, 181
Matru Runa, 81
Medhe, Pramila, 122
Mehta, Suresh, 158
Ministry of Agriculture, 40
Modi, Narendra, 5, 194
Mohapatra, Ajit Prasad, 121
Montague-Chelmsford reforms
in 1919, 51
Moonjee, Mukund Rao, 74,
113
moral economy, 14
Morbi Floods of 1979, 145
Morley-Minto reforms of 1909,
73

N.W.F. Province, 1
Nanda, Meera, 82
Nandy, Ashish, 82
Narayan, Jayaprakash (JP), 47,
88, 92
National Disaster Management
Act (NDMA), 15, 40, 43
National Disaster Management
Division, 40
National Emergency from
1975–1977, 2, 5
National Medicos Organisation
(NMO), 103
natural disasters, 19, 31, 34,
67, 105, 159, 186

natural hazards, 20, 33
Navnirman movement of
1974, 145
Nehru Yuva Kendra Sangathan
(NYKS), 43
Nehru, Motilal, 85
Non-Cooperation Movement,
73
non-reciprocity, notion of, 81
non-state
agencies role in humanitarian relief, 41–43

Odisha State Disaster
Mitigation Authority
(OSDMA), 117
Odisha Super Cyclone in 1999,
8, 10, 22, 40, 109, 177
appeal to central govern-
ment for assistance, 117
creation of cyclone shelters,
130
expansion of *seva* activities
in non-cyclone affected
areas, 134–139
impact and relief opera-
tions, 116–118
land tilling and orphanage
construction, 129
rehabilitation efforts of RSS
and UBSS, 127–128
relief efforts provided by
RSS, 118–127
Saraswati Shishu Mandir,
130–134
Odisha
geographical location of,
111
Hindu nationalism emer-
gence in, 113

religion
  contribution to humanitari-
    anism, 55
  and development, relation-
    ship between, 55
  entanglement, 56
  role in development after
    Independence, 54
religious aid agencies, role in
    disaster management,
    14–19
Rishi Runa, 81

sacred, 7
  definition of, 190
  forms, 21–22, 25, 190, 193,
    194, 195
Saha Prant pracharak of
    Odisha, 121
Samaj Runa, 81
sanctification of humanitari-
    anism, 29
sangathans (creation of a
    devoted and efficient
    organization of patriotic
    men), 62
Sangh Parivar, 2, 4, 5, 27, 142,
    145, 146, 148, 150, 168,
    171, 173, 174, 176, 186,
    195
  communal mobilization
    undertaken by, 26
  deployment of *seva*, 173
  humanitarian activities of, 8
  in Odisha, emergence and
    growth, 113–116
  popularity of, reasons for,
    174–177
sannyas (asceticism), 68
Saraswati Bal Vidyalaya, 92

Saraswati Shishu Mandir, 89
Saraswati Shishu Mandir, 92,
    114, 122
Saraswati, Lakshmanananda,
    109, 115
Sarvodaya Samaj, 45
sat-chit-aanand, 82
Satya Shodhak Samaj, 44
Satyagraha movement, 87
Savarkar, V. D., 73
Save the Children, 41, 46, 47
secular, 5, 7
secular liberalism, 27
secularism, 5, 25
secularization process, 28
  political project of, 54
Seema Jankalyan Samiti
    (border welfare commit-
    tee), 169, 186
selflessnes, notion of, 14
Sen, Amartya, 35
Servants of India Society, 44
Seshadri, Sarkaryavah H. V.,
    121
Sethi, Raghunath, 113
seva activities by Sangh
    Parivar, 4, 7, 27, 50, 56,
    57, 76, 78, 85–86, 110,
    175, 193
  activities in Arya Samaj,
    63–64
  beneficiaries of, 96–99
  conceptualization in RSS,
    79–85
  during Bhakti period, 59–61
  during colonial period,
    61–63
  fortification of, 86–88
  and gift, 12–14
  and India diaspora, 103–106

About the Author

Malini Bhattacharjee is an Assistant Professor at Azim Premji University in Bengaluru. She has earned her doctorate, MPhil and MA degrees in political science from Jawaharlal Nehru University, New Delhi. She started her career at the International Federation of Red Cross and Red Crescent Societies, South Asia Regional Delegation in New Delhi and subsequently worked in a conflict resolution firm named Metaculture in Bengaluru. She joined Azim Premji Foundation in 2010 and is a part of Azim Premji University since 2012.

Her research interests revolve around the issues of religious identity, ethnicity and political conflict, politics of humanitarianism and the intersections emerging between religion and development. She is particularly interested in the politics of Hindu nationalism and the political dimension of its *seva* (service) activities.

She also has an interest in elementary educational policy in India and has spent a fair amount of time in researching on the implementation of the Right of Children to Free and Compulsory Education Act (aka RTE Act) in Karnataka.

In her current role at Azim Premji University, she teaches courses on politics and democracy, Indian politics, governance, religion and development, and religion, state and democracy.

During her free time, Malini loves playing with her daughter and watching movies.